Rhodes in the Hellenistic Age

Rhodes in the Hellenistic Age

By

RICHARD M. BERTHOLD

Cornell University Press

ITHACA AND LONDON

CORNELL UNIVERSITY PRESS GRATEFULLY ACKNOWLEDGES
A GRANT FROM THE ANDREW W. MELLON FOUNDATION
THAT AIDED IN BRINGING THIS BOOK TO PUBLICATION.

Copyright © 1984 by Cornell University

First published 1984 by Cornell University Press.
Published in the United Kingdom by
Cornell University Press Ltd., London.

International Standard Book Number 0–8014–1640–X
Library of Congress Catalog Card Number 83–23127

Printed in the United States of America

*Librarians: Library of Congress cataloging information
appears on the last page of the book.*

*The paper in this book is acid-free, and meets the guidelines
for permanence and durability of the Committee on Production
Guidelines for Book Longevity of the Council on Library Resources*

For Denise, Mary Rose, Juniper,
and of course the Earl

Contents

Maps

Preface

> Out of the swirling sea came forth
> an island, held by the father of the sharp rays,
> ruler of the fire-breathing horses; lying there with the nymph Rhodes
>   he got
> seven sons, who showed the wisest minds among men of old,
> and of these one got Camirus,
> Ialysus, the eldest, and Lindus; apart from one another they held,
> with the land of their father divided in three,
> their share of cities, their abodes being named after themselves.
> —Pindar, *Olympian Odes* VII, 69–71

TO the average person the name Rhodes means little more than the title of an impressive scholarship and a place connected with one of the Seven Wonders. The more cosmopolitan might recall that Rhodes is one of those sunny Aegean isles so favored by Teutonic tourists, and some, especially those who have visited the island, will remember it as the home of the bloody Knights of St. John during their struggles with the Turks. But few, it seems, are at all aware of Rhodes' real significance in Western history and the vital role it played in the age following Alexander the Great.

Classical scholars have of course long recognized the importance of the island republic in the Hellenistic period and especially in the Roman conquest of the East; yet for all that awareness, Rhodian affairs have been surprisingly neglected by recent historians. Since the turn of the century only two books have been devoted to ancient Rhodes, Hendrik van Gelder's *Geschichte der alten Rhodier* (The Hague 1900), a general history of the island, and Hatto Schmitt's *Rom und Rhodos* (Munich 1957), a specific treatment of the period of Roman involvement in Greek affairs. These works, together with Friedrich Hiller von Gaertringen's article "Rhodos" in Pauly-Wissowa (Supp. V, 1931), form the entire corpus of major literature on ancient Rhodes for the last eighty years.

This paucity of modern scholarship alone suggests that a reexamination of Rhodian history is warranted, and a consideration of the works mentioned above confirms this suggestion. Van Gelder's book, though still the only major treatment of Rhodian history and society and thus very useful, is eighty years out of date, while Hiller von Gaertrigen's article, now a half century old, is naturally too brief to cover the subject in depth. Schmitt's work is more recent, but examines only one act of the Rhodian drama and does so unevenly, fully half the work being devoted to the Rhodian-Roman contact at the end of the fourth century and the settlement at Apamea.

This work attempts to remedy these deficiencies and provide a full picture of Rhodes' actions and policies from the political union of the island and the stormy years of the fourth century to the conclusion of an alliance with Rome and the extinction of Rhodes' freedom in the second. This is a political history, and its primary goal is to present a detailed narration and analysis of Rhodian foreign affairs. The social structure of the republic is consequently given only cursory treatment, and cultural activities are all but ignored. Economic matters receive more attention, but only insofar as they relate to the politics of the Rhodian state. Otherwise, however, I have attempted to gather together every bit of evidence that bears on the history of the Rhodian republic.

In detailing the course of the island's history, I have also sought to provide some understanding of the principles and reasoning behind the foreign-policy decisions of the Rhodians. It is my contention, and hardly a radical one, that throughout the third century Rhodes maintained its independence and prosperity by pursuing a course of studied neutrality, tempered by a constant concern for the preservation of a balance of power among the great monarchies. I further believe that

Rhodes did not willfully abandon its successful policies during the second century, but rather was forced by events to support the ultimately disruptive cause of Rome, and that only during the Third Macedonian War was there a momentary slip in the strict rationality of Rhodes' strategic thinking.

This work is intended for classical scholars, though the text should be generally comprehensible to the general reader. It should be noted, however, that the economics of academic publishing in these troubled times has necessitated a curtailment of the notes. Only the most important secondary references are given, and older or general works, such as van Gelder's book, are cited only on specific points. More important, little space is devoted to the citation and expression of opposing (and thus in my opinion incorrect) views.

With regard to the inevitable problem of transliterating Greek names, I follow in this book a policy of enlightened inconsistency: the Latinized version is generally used, except in those cases where the Greek form appears more natural (for example, Delos). All translations from the Greek and Latin are mine, and unless otherwise noted all dates are B.C.

In the course of writing this history I received help on a couple of very specialized questions, and this aid is acknowledged in the notes. I also thank Tony Raubitschek for reading this work in manuscript. Beyond these debts of gratitude, I have only Klio to thank; it was her inspiration that carried me through this labor.

RICHARD M. BERTHOLD

Albuquerque, New Mexico

Abbreviations

The following abbreviations have been used for frequently cited works; other abbreviations used are either standard or self-explanatory.

Briscoe
: John Briscoe, *A Commentary on Livy, Books XXXI–XXXIII* (Oxford 1973).

Casson
: Lionel Casson, "Grain Trade in the Hellenistic World," *TAPA* 85 (1954) 168–87.

F&B
: Peter M. Fraser and George E. Bean, *The Rhodian Peraea and Islands* (Oxford 1954).

Hansen
: Esther V. Hansen, *The Attalids of Pergamon*, 2d ed. (Ithaca 1971).

Head
: Barclay V. Head, *Historia Numorum*, 2d ed. (Oxford 1911).

Holleaux
: Maurice Holleaux, *Etudes d'épigraphie et d'histoire grecques* (Paris 1938).

Magie
: David Magie, *Roman Rule in Asia Minor* (Princeton 1950).

Maiuri
: Amadeo Maiuri, *Nuova Silloge epigrafica di Rodi e Cos* (Florence 1925).

Olshausen
: Eckart Olshausen, *Prosopographie der hellenistischen Königsgesandten* I (Louvain 1974).

Ormerod
: Henry Ormerod, *Piracy in the Ancient World* (London 1924).

Rostovtzeff   Michael Rostovtzeff, *The Social and Economic History of the Hellenistic World* (Oxford 1941).

Schmitt   Hatto Schmitt, *Rom und Rhodos* (Munich 1957).

Staats.   Hermann Bengtson and Hatto Schmitt, *Die Staatsverträge des Altertums,* vols. 2 and 3 (Munich 1962–69).

Thiel   Johannes Thiel, *Studies on the History of Roman Seapower in Republican Times* (Amsterdam 1946).

van Gelder   Hendrik van Gelder, *Geschichte der alten Rhodier* (The Hague 1900).

Walbank   Frank W. Walbank, *A Historical Commentary on Polybius,* 3 vols. (Oxford 1957–79).

Rhodes in the Hellenistic Age

CHAPTER I

The Fourth Century

WHEN Alexander died of fever in Babylon in June 323 and the Rhodians expelled their Macedonian garrison and embarked upon a century and a half of independence and power, the young republic passed a turning point in its history. For most of the previous two hundred years the island had suffered, to varying degrees, the chronic Greek ailments of foreign intervention and internal instability. From the time of Darius I to the defeat of Xerxes, the Rhodian poleis had paid tribute to the Great King;[1] thereafter, having enrolled in the Delian League, they paid it to the Athenian demos, under whose tutelage the Rhodian democrats were able to overturn the traditional oligarchies.[2] In 411, with Spartan support, the oligarchs overthrew the democratic governments in turn and brought the island over to the Peloponnesians and the financial exactions of the Spartan leadership. The revolt from Athens of course did nothing to secure Rhodes' autonomy, but in its wake came an event that would lay the foundation of Rhodes' later greatness: the synoecism of the island and establishment of the Rhodian republic.

1. Aesch. *Pers.* 852–95. There was possibly a siege of Lindus in 494 or 490 (*Lind. Temp. Chron.* C65–74, D1–59) and Rhodes contributed ships to Xerxes' fleet (Diod. 11.3.8). For more detailed notes on the fourth century, see R. M. Berthold, "Fourth Century Rhodes," *Hist.* 29 (1980) 32–49. For the early history of Rhodes, which is poorly known, see van Gelder 63–72.

2. It is not clear when Rhodes revolted and joined the Delian League; see Herod. 9.106.4; R. Meiggs, *The Athenian Empire* (Oxford 1973) 55–56, 414–15.

Of this political union and the events that led up to it the sources say unfortunately very little. The exile Dorieus appears to have played an instrumental role in the revolt of 411, but it is almost impossible to assess his part in subsequent events. Dorieus was a Diagorid, a member of the powerful old aristocratic family of Ialysus, and in 412 he had joined the Spartan fleet with a squadron of warships brought from Thurii, the place of his family's exile.[3] By the end of the year the Peloponnesian fleet, now grown to ninety-four vessels stationed at Cnidus, had driven the Athenians out of Rhodian waters,[4] and this deliverance, together with the presence of their countryman among the Spartan command, apparently decided the Rhodian oligarchs that their time had come. An appeal for intervention was made, perhaps through Dorieus, and the Spartan nauarch Astyochus, convinced of the value of Rhodian resources, moved the fleet to Camirus in January 411. Without Athenian support and without city walls, the democrats could offer no resistance, and the oligarchs were back in business.[5]

One of the most immediate concerns of the new rulers was the inevitable reaction of the democrats and of the Athenians, who could not be expected to remain passive in the face of Rhodes' defection. The Athenian fleet at Samos had in fact also sailed to Rhodes at the news of the oligarchic coup, but had arrived too late to prevent the revolt, and the Athenians had now to content themselves with raiding the island from their bases at Chalce and Cos. These raids were not hindered in the least by the presence of the enemy fleet, inasmuch as the Peloponnesians kept their vessels beached for the eighty days that they remained on the island.[6] When at the end of the winter the Spartan fleet did finally take action, it left for Miletus, and in its absence the oligarchs' position apparently began to weaken. By midsummer it was necessary for Dorieus to return with a squadron in order to quell a democratic uprising, but when he departed for the

3. On the fame and exile of the Diagorids, see Paus. 4.24.2–3, 6.7.1–4; Pin. *Ol.* 7; Thuc. 8.35.1; Xen. *Hell.* 1.5.19.

4. Thuc. 8.39.1–43.2.

5. Thuc. 8.44.1–2. Of the Dorian Pentapolis, Camirus, Cnidus, and Cos were unwalled (Thuc. 8.35.3, 41.2), so it is probable that Lindus and Ialysus were also.

6. Thuc. 8.44.3–4, 55.1.

Hellespont several months later, the oligarchs, under the leadership of the Diagorids, were firmly in control.[7] This time the Rhodians were left on their own, since Spartan naval power was temporarily destroyed the following year at Cyzicus.[8]

With the departure of Dorieus, nothing more is heard of Rhodes until the island was ravaged by Alcibiades in 408,[9] but presumably during these years the oligarchs were taking the first steps toward the political union of the island. On the basis of a proxenia decree found at Lindus and dated to this time, it is possible to postulate a transitional phase of some sort of sympolity during the period between the oligarchic revolution and the synoecism, and this hypothesis is supported by the survival of elements of sympolity in the final republican constitution.[10] Given the Greek attitude regarding autonomy, such an intermediate step of a more limited association of the cities is very plausible, and it may be seen as the first Rhodian response to the Athenian threat. In the ensuing three years, however, Athenian raids, especially that of Alcibiades, convinced the oligarchs of the need for the greater strength and protection that complete union would bring, and synoecism was decided upon.[11] This appears to be a reasonable

---

7. Thuc. 8.60.2–3; Diod. 13.38.5, 45.1; Xen. *Hell.* 1.1.2. It was the Diagorids that were overthrown in 395; see below.

8. Xen. *Hell.* 1.1.1–23; Diod. 13.49.2, 51.8.

9. Diod. 13.69.5.

10. C. Blinkenberg and K. F. Kinch, "Exploration archéologique de Rhodes (Fondation Carlsberg). Troisième Rapport," *Bull. de l'Acad. Roy. des sciences et des lettres de Dan.* 1905, no. 2, 34–48. This important inscription (= *Syll.*³ 110) is worth quoting in full: Ἔδοξε τᾶι β]ολᾶι ἐπὶ π[ρ/υτανίων τ]ῶν ἀμφὶ Δει[ν?/........ αν Πυθέω Αἴ[γ or ν/..... τ]ὸν ἐγ Ναυκράτ/ιος] ἑρμανέα πρόξενον/ ἦμ]εν Ῥοδίων πάντων κα/ὶ αὐτὸν καὶ ἐκγόνους, κ/αὶ ἦμεν αὐτῶι καὶ ἔσπλ/ο]ν καὶ ἔκπλον καὶ αὐτῶ/ι κα]ὶ ἐκγόνοις ἀσύλι κ/αὶ ἀσ]πονδὶ καὶ πολέμο/καὶ εἰρ]ήνης. The island is already unified, since there is a central authority, βολά and πρυτάνεις, and since the Rhodians are referred to collectively, Ῥοδίων πάντων, but this last expression shows also that the synoecism had not been completed, as the normal designation in all later inscriptions is simply Ῥόδιοι. (I have examined all relevant inscriptions available to me without finding a similar use of Ῥόδιοι πάντες.) Further, this inscription was found at Lindus rather than at Rhodes, where one would expect it to be displayed if that city had already been built. On sympolity and signs of earlier unity at Rhodes, see E. Szanto, *Das griechische Bürgerrecht* (Freiburg 1892) 140–42; A. Momigliano, "Note sulla storia di Rodi," *Riv. Fil.* 14 (1936) 49–51.

11. See, e.g., E. Kuhn, *Über die Entstehung der Städte der Alten* (Leipzig 1878) 210; G. Busolt, *Griechische Geschichte* (Gotha 1904) III.2, 1586.

reconstruction of events, but it must be remembered that the whole notion of a transitional sympolity rests on the very slender evidence of a single inscription and must therefore be considered conjectural.

In any case, in the course of 408/7 the three poleis of Ialysus, Camirus, and Lindus surrendered their autonomy to form a Rhodian republic, and shortly thereafter work was begun on a new capital city—Rhodes.[12] Although the synoecism probably allowed the oligarchs to consolidate better their own position in the state, it was nevertheless in the best interests of all Rhodians. The whole ought to prove greater than the sum of the parts, and union would, it was hoped, bring Rhodes increased economic and military power and subsequent independence from foreign intervention. At the same time construction of a large new city with excellent harbors at the northeast extremity of the island would allow the Rhodians to make the best use of their commercially strategic position in the eastern Mediterranean. Eighty-five years of internal troubles and outside interference still remained before the young republic could come of age, but with the synoecism the Rhodians had laid the foundation of their later greatness. All that Rhodes would become economically, politically, and militarily in the Hellenistic age depended ultimately on the union of the island, on the willingness of the three Rhodian cities to abandon the autonomy so jealously guarded by the Greek polis. This was the cardinal event in Rhodes' history.

In the autumn of 408, probably before the synoecism had been initiated, Spartan naval power finally reappeared at Rhodes, in the form of the nauarch Lysander, who collected ships from the Rhodians and sailed off north to find the Athenians. The Peloponnesian fleet was again at Rhodes in 406 and in 405, an indication of Rhodes' importance in the Ionian War, but there is then no word of the island for almost a decade.[13] Since, however, the Spartan fleet is found operating out of Rhodes from 398 to 396,[14] it is reasonable to surmise

12. Diod. 13.75.1; Strabo 14.2.9–11 (654–55); Psd.-Arist. 43 (816–17 D); Eust. *ad Il.* 2.656 (315); Conon 47. On the city, see below, chap. 2.

13. 408: Xen. *Hell.* 1.5.1; Diod. 13.70.2; 406: Xen. *Hell.* 1.6.3; 405: Xen. *Hell.* 2.1.15, 17. Rhodians are found in the army of the younger Cyrus (Xen. *Anab.* 3.3.16–17, 4.15, 5.8; Arr. *Anab.* 2.7.8).

14. Diod. 14.79.4–5; Isoc. 4.142.

that during this period the island served as the main Spartan naval station in the east. If it did, the already harsh nature of postwar Spartan rule could only have been aggravated for the Rhodians by the continued presence of the nauarch and fleet. Whatever the case, the Rhodians certainly found Spartan hegemony an oppressive burden; when heard of again in 396, they are found in revolt.

As might be expected, the revolt was accomplished with the aid of foreign intervention, in this case the Persian fleet under the command of the Athenian exile Conon. In late 398 or early 397 Conon arrived in Caria with the first forty vessels of the new fleet and in the course of the year was blockaded in Caunus by 120 ships under the Spartan nauarch Pharax. Pharax could not, however, face the supporting army bought up by Artaphernes and Pharnabazus; compelled to retire, he returned to his base at Rhodes. Then, according to Diodorus, "Conon, having collected eighty triremes, sailed to the Chersonese, while the Rhodians, having thrown out the Peloponnesian fleet, revolted from the Lacedaemonians and received Conon with his entire fleet into the city." What this seems to mean is that in late 397 or early 396 Conon, acting in conjunction with the Rhodians, feinted toward the west and drew the enemy fleet out of the harbor at Rhodes. Then, while the Rhodians perhaps took some measures to close the port to the Spartans, Conon moved his own fleet to the island.[15]

Contrary to what was almost a traditional practice in the Greek world, the defection from Sparta was not immediately accompanied by an internal revolution. The Rhodian oligarchs must therefore have been a party to the plot, since the interval of a year between the revolt and the overthrow of the oligarchy otherwise makes no sense. That the Diagorids and their supporters were thus willing to abandon the political security guaranteed by the alliance with Sparta is a strong indication of just how oppressive that alliance was. Preferring inde-

15. Diod. 14.79.4–5; Isoc. 4.142. The chronology is unsure, but the longer the time between the revolt and the revolution, the more time to build up feeling against the Diagorids (I. Bruce, *An Historical Commentary on the "Hellenica Oxyrhynchia"* (Cambridge 1967) 74). The chronology of Spartan nauarchs found in R. Sealey, "Die spartanische Nauarchie," *Klio* 58 (1976) 349–52, seems best. The "Chersonese" referred to by Diodorus must be the Rhodian, i.e., the Loryma peninsula; see F&B 65–68.

pendence or even Persian suzerainty (which could still be expected to lead to an easing of the financial burden), the oligarchs presumably calculated that alliance with the Great King would not threaten their rule and that leading the people in a national revolt might even strengthen it. If so, they were sadly mistaken, for in the summer of 395 the oligarchic government was toppled by a democratic revolution led by Dorimachus. The Diagorids and eleven supporters were killed in the insurrection, and others were driven into exile.[16]

In this revolution Conon appears to have been a silent partner, for the fleet made no move to defend the oligarchs and he himself found it convenient to sail for Caunus with twenty ships just before the insurrection broke out. As an Athenian he probably had democratic leanings, but the most compelling motive for his cooperation was undoubtedly the simple calculation that in a war against Sparta an oligarchic government could never be as completely reliable as a democratic one. On the other hand, keeping Rhodes out of Spartan hands was the admiral's prime objective, and he was not so completely sure of the success of the democrats as to be willing to be identified with their cause before the revolution was accomplished. Consequently, in order to avoid any allegations of complicity should the insurrection fail, he was careful to be absent in Caunus when it broke out. The bulk of the fleet remained at Rhodes, however, providing the conspirators with psychological support and possibly also a means of escape in the event of failure.[17]

With the success of the revolution Conon returned to Rhodes, where soon after his arrival he and the Rhodians captured a convoy of Egyptian supply ships that unwittingly put into the island on their way to Sparta.[18] The admiral was then forced by the growing problem of pay for his sailors to travel to Babylon to discuss financial matters and the conduct of the war. The Rhodian Timocrates' subversive mission to Greece later in the year was probably one result of

16. *Hell. Oxy.* 10.1–3; see also I. Bruce, "The Democratic Revolution at Rhodes," *CQ* 55 (1961) 169–70, *Comm. Hell. Oxy.* 97–98. The Hellenica Oxyrhynchia shows clearly that the revolution came after Conon was in the harbor.

17. *Hell. Oxy.* 10.1; Paus. 6.7.6. Conon possibly also felt some regard and gratitude toward the Diagorids and did not wish to be present at their fall (Bruce, *Comm. Hell. Oxy.* 99).

18. *Hell. Oxy.* 10.3; Diod. 14.79.7; Just. 6.2.1–3.

these discussions.[19] The Spartan reaction to the Rhodian defection, meanwhile, was immediate and vindictive: Dorieus, who happened to be in the Peloponnesus at the time and probably had nothing to do with the revolt, was arrested and executed.[20] And although there is no direct evidence, the appointment of Agesilaus as supreme commander over both land and sea operations in Asia was probably in part also a response to the loss of Rhodes. But the days of Spartan naval power were numbered, and in the summer of 394 Conon and his cocommander, Pharnabazus, virtually destroyed the Spartan fleet in a battle off Cnidus.[21]

In the wake of Cnidus, Sparta's Aegean hegemony began rapidly to crumble. The news of Cnidus was enough to cause many states to expel their garrisons and break with Sparta, while others were persuaded by a visit from Conon's fleet, which was making a parade through the Aegean.[22] For the moment, at least, Rhodes was now secure from any return of Spartan domination, but there were other potentially dangerous powers. Athens was at present no threat, although Conon's victory could pave the way for a resurgence of its naval power, but there remained Rhodes' recent benefactor, Persia. There was not the slightest sign that the Great King had any designs for more direct control of Rhodes, but the strategically important island had once been part of the empire, and in the general sweep of Persian success the king might attempt to make it so again. Further, even if the central government was not interested, there was the more immediate danger of the western satraps, who in their increasingly independent and competitive roles might view the island as a tempting addition to their own power.[23] Probably in response to such concerns, and possibly with the prompting of Conon, Rhodes thus joined with other maritime states in the Aegean in forming a league. This league is known only through its federal coinage, which displays

19. Conon: *Hell. Oyx.* 14.2–3; Diod. 14.81.4–6; Nep. *Conon* 3.2–4.2; Just. 6.2.11–16; Timocrates: Xen. *Hell.* 3.5.1; Paus. 3.9.8; Plut. *Arta.* 20.3–4, *Mor.* 211b.
20. Paus. 6.7.6.
21. E.g., Xen. *Hell.* 3.4.27–29, 4.3.10–12; Diod. 14.83.4–7; Plut. *Ages.* 10.5–6; Paus. 3.9.6; Nep. *Conon* 4.3–4. On Cnidus and its aftermath, see C. D. Hamilton, *Sparta's Bitter Victories* (Ithaca 1979) 227–30.
22. Diod. 14.84.3–4; Xen. *Hell.* 4.8.1–2; Dem. 20.68.
23. As would Mausolus of Halicarnassus forty years later; see below.

on the reverse the device of the allied city and on the obverse the uniform type of the young Heracles strangling the serpents and the legend ΣΥΝ.[24] Inasmuch as the device of Heracles and the serpents is also found on the coinage of Thebes during this period, the league may be associated with the anti-Spartan coalition raised in 395 under the leadership of Thebes and its formation dated probably to 393.[25] The alliance was friendly toward Athens, and Rhodes, Samos, Ephesus, Cnidus, Iasus, and later Byzantium were certainly members, but otherwise nothing is known.[26] By 390 Samos, Ephesus, and Cindus had been retaken by the Spartans, and it is likely that if any remnant of the league survived until 387/6, it was broken up by the Peace of Antalcidas.[27]

Whatever the exact purpose of the league, the one thing it certainly failed to achieve for the Rhodians was peace; within five years of the democratic revolution the island was prey to civil war and renewed foreign intervention. In late 391 or early 390 a group of exiled Rhodian oligarchs appeared at Sparta seeking help for their cause, and the Spartans, eager to bring the island back under their influence, responded by dispatching in 390 eight ships under the command of Ecdicus.[28] Sailing to Cnidus, Ecdicus learned that the Rhodian dem-

24. See W. H. Waddington, "Confédération de quelques villes de l'Asia Mineure et des îles après la bataille de Cnide (A.C. 394)," *Rev. Num.* 7 (1863) 223–24; E. Schönert-Geiss, *Die Münzprägung von Byzantion* (Berlin-Amsterdam 1970) I, 31–35, 126–28. The four known Rhodian examples all lack the ΣΥΝ inscription; it is not at all clear what, if anything, this lack means. E. Babelon, *Traité des monnaies grecques et romaines* (Paris 1901–32) II.2, 1017–20, believes that a rare Rhodian gold stater (#1695) celebrates the battle of Cnidus.

25. P. Gardner, *A History of Greek Coinage, 700–300 B.C.* (Oxford 1918) 358; Diod. 14.82.1–4. See also G. L. Cawkwell, "The ΣΥΝ Coins Again," *JHS* 83 (1963) 152–54.

26. Lampsacus, Cyzicus, Croton, and Zacynthus adopted the type, but not the weight or the legend ΣΥΝ; Croton and Zacynthus were certainly not members. An Athenian decree dated to this period, *IG* xii.1 977 (= *Syll.*³ 129 = Tod 110), describes as allies of Athens two members of the league, Rhodes and Cnidus (Κνι]δίους and not Λιν]δίους, as Lindus was no longer an independent state).

27. Xen. *Hell.* 4.8.17, 22–23. The league probably lasted at least until 389, when Byzantium joined.

28. Xen. *Hell.* 4.8.20–21, 25. Diod. 14.97.1–4, 99.5 has a different version, in which the oligarchs appeal to Sparta after successfully ousting the democrats from the city and the positions of the two factions during the strife are reversed. Xenophon seems preferable for three reasons: (1) he presumably had better sources of informa-

ocrats still had the upper hand and possessed twice as many ships as himself, and he consequently made no movement against the island. In a very short time he was replaced in command by Teleutias, who arrived at Cnidus with an additional nineteen sail, and the entire fleet then departed for Rhodes, being further augmented on the way by the capture of ten Athenian vessels.[29] To counter this renewed Spartan naval activity, the Athenians sent out forty ships under Thrasybulus, who decided, however, that the democrats could temporarily maintain their position unaided, while he capitalized on opportunities in the Hellespont. Very possibly the fleet sailed back to Rhodes in 389/8, after Thrasybulus' death at Aspendus, but in any case nothing more is heard of the situation on the island, and the outcome of the civil war is not clear.[30]

When Thrasybulus sailed north, the democrats appeared to have the upper hand, controlling all the cities and having already inflicted one defeat on their enemies, while the oligarchs, supported by the Spartan fleet, were in control of a single fortress.[31] On the other hand, Thrasybulus' judgment that he could not do much harm to the oligarchs is an indication of the strength of their position and suggests that while the democrats essentially controlled the island, they could not quickly bring the war to an end. At least they could not do so while the Spartans remained, and the question of the outcome of the

---

tion via the Spartans; (2) he must have been very interested in the activities of Teleutias, inasmuch as he was Agesilaus' brother; (3) four years seems a short time for the oligarchs to regroup and succeed in ejecting the democrats from the city. For the opposing view, see G. Busolt, *Der zweite athenische Bund* (1875) 671–73. Arist. *Pol.* 5.2 (1302b.21–23) and 5.5. (1304b.27–31) probably refer to the oligarchic revolution instigated later by Mausolus.

29. Xen. *Hell.* 4.8.22–24. According to Diod. 14.97.3, Eudocimus (Ecdicus?) put in at Rhodes.

30. Xen. *Hell.* 4.8.25–31; Diod. 14.94.1–4, 99.4–5. Diodorus says that the fleet, under the leadership of the captains, sailed to Rhodes and joined the democrats; Xenophon says only that Agyrrius was sent out to replace Thrasybulus. It would be reasonable for the fleet to move on to Rhodes, as this was the original destination, and the presence of the ships at Rhodes would explain why they were seemingly not heard of again, despite pressing needs in the Hellespont and the Saronic Gulf. This hypothesis fits also with Antalcidas' apparent abandonment of the oligarchs in 388.

31. Xen. *Hell.* 4.8.25. Diod. 14.97.1–2, 99.5 has the situation reversed, but it is very reasonable that Teleutias would and could establish a fortress on the island for the exiled oligarchs (G. Grote, *A History of Greece*² [London 1888] VII, 528).

war hinges on the whereabouts of the Spartan fleet. That fleet did in fact sail west, probably sometime in the course of 389, while Thrasybulus was in the northeast, and although twenty-five vessels under the command of Hierax were sent back to the island, Hierax was presently replaced by Antalcidas, who concentrated Spartan naval strength in the east in the struggle for the Hellespont.[32] By the time of the King's Peace in 387/6, then, the Rhodian democrats, possibly with Athenian aid, had had at least a year in which to overpower the vastly outnumbered oligarchs while the Spartan navy was busy elsewhere, and it is very difficult to believe that they did not do so. After 387/6 Rhodian autonomy was then guaranteed by the Peace, and although Sparta was somewhat cavalier in its interpretation of the terms of the Peace, it appears extremely unlikely that the Rhodians were subject to any overt Spartan pressures in the years following 387/6. With the failure of its Asian imperialist adventure, Sparta's interest in the eastern Aegean waned; it was enough that Athens should be prevented from reestablishing its old naval power base. Besides, there were problems closer to home, especially after 382, and operations in the east not only would be a distraction, but also would risk the renewal of Persian aid to Sparta's enemies.[33]

After the Peace of Antalcidas there is no word of Rhodes until 378/7, when it is found enrolling as a charter member in the Second Athenian League. Inasmuch as five of the other founding states— Thebes, Chios, Methymna, Mitylene, and Byzantium—already had alliances with Athens, it is likely that Rhodes did also, but substantial evidence is lacking.[34] Rhodes' reason for accepting Athens' invitation was certainly security, the security provided by an anti-Spartan, pro-

32. Xen. *Hell.* 5.1.2–6.

33. On Sparta's activities with regard to the peace, see T. Ryder, *Koine Eirene* (London 1965) 39–57; for the sources and terms of the peace, see *Staats.* II, no. 242. Diod. 15.28.2–3 speaks of the Rhodian "secession" (ἀπόστασιν) from the Spartans in 378/7, but he says the same about Chios, Byzantium, and Mytilene, which certainly already had alliances with Athens; see below, n. 34. Isoc. 4.163 indicates that Rhodes was not under Spartan control around 380; the island was certainly democratic after 378/7 (Dem. 13.8–9, 15.17–21), and there is no word of any change of government before then.

34. Diod. 15.28.2–4; *IG* ii² 43 (= *Syll.*³ 147 = Tod 123). Thebes: *IG* ii² 40; Chios: *IG* ii² 34 (= *Syll.*³ 142 = Tod 118); Methymna: *IG* ii² 42 (= *Syll.*³ 149 = Tod 122);

democratic alliance of maritime states. The league would offer the
island protection also from the agents of the Great King, especially
from the growing power of the Carian dynast Hecatomnus, but this
would have been a secondary consideration. In 378/7 the first bloom
of Carian power was still in the future, while the present threat and
bitter memory of Spartan domination in the early 390s must have
loomed very large in the minds of the Rhodian democrats.

Having joined the Athenian League, Rhodes once more disappears
from view, and during its twenty years as an Athenian ally only one
brief glimpse of the island is allowed. That glimpse comes in 363,
when a Theban armada led by Epaminondas appeared in Aegean
waters, seeking to cause disaffection among Athens' allies, especially
the strong naval powers of Byzantium, Chios, and Rhodes. The
hundred Theban warships scared off any Athenian opposition and
reached Byzantium, which seems to have revolted from Athens,
along with Chalcedon and Ceos, but although these operations
aroused pro-Theban sentiments at Chios and Rhodes, it does not
appear that either of these states actually revolted.[35] The warm reception accorded the Theban incursion, however, does indicate a change
of attitude on the part of Rhodes and the other allies. When the league
was formed, allied fear of a resurgence of Athenian imperialism was
pushed into the background by greater fear of Sparta and by Athenian
assurances and safeguards written into the league charter, but by 363
the alliance appeared to some of the members to be heading the way
of its fifth-century predecessor. After the defeats of Naxos and Leuc-
tra, Sparta had ceased to be any threat to the islanders, and many of

---

Mytilene; *IG* ii² 40; Byzantium: *IG* ii² 41 (= *Syll.*³ 146 = Tod 121); also *Staats.* II, nos.
248, 254–58. On Rhodes, see S. Accame, *La lega ateniese del secolo IV a.C.* (Rome
1941) 15–16, 32–33, whose argument is far from convincing.

35. Diod. 15.79.1; Isoc. 5.53; Plut. *Philop.* 14.2; Ceos: *IG* xii.5 594 (= *Syll.*³ 172 =
Tod 141); see also *IG* ii² 111 (= *Syll.*³ 173 = Tod 142). Byzantium and Chalcedon
were raiding grain ships in 362 (Dem. 50.6, 17); operations were undertaken to regain
the Chersonese (Dem. 23.149–59); and Timotheus "conquered Byzantium" (Nep.
Tim. 1.2) (but see Busolt, *Bund* 810). Diodorus' statement "ἰδίας τὰς πόλεις [Rhodes,
Chios, and Byzantium] τοῖς Θηβαίοις ἐποίησεν" cannot be understood literally, and
J. Cargill, *The Second Athenian League* (Berkeley 1981) 169, feels it may be a doublet
from the Social War, but if so, why is Cos not mentioned and why "ἰδίας . . . τοῖς
Θηβαίοις"? It is easier to believe the passage reflects some sort of favorable response
from the cities.

them increasingly felt that the financial burdens and constant danger of resurgent Athenian domination were no longer justified.[36] In the minds of many members the alliance had more than outlived its usefulness, and Epaminondas' heralds consequently found many willing listeners. Rhodes' receptivity to the Theban cause in the Aegean is thus understandable; it offered the possibility of liberation from Athens. Why, on the other hand, the island did not actually revolt when Epaminondas appeared is not clear. Possibly, mindful of Thebes' complete lack of any naval tradition and its hitherto purely continental interests, the Rhodians decided that the better position was to wait upon events, while cautiously expressing their pro-Theban sympathies. If this was the case, the Rhodians decided wisely, for the following year the new naval policy of Thebes died with Epaminondas on the field of Mantinea.[37]

But the decisive break between Rhodes and Athens was not long in coming. In 357 the smoldering discontent of the allies exploded into warfare as Rhodes, Cos, and Chios joined Byzantium in open revolt.[38] The time seemed ripe; not only did it appear that Athens would soon be embroiled with Philip II over Amphipolis, but the islands had been promised support by Mausolus, the new dynast of Caria.[39] The Athenians responded to the news of the revolt by quickly sending to Chios a force of sixty ships under Chabrias, but in the course of besieging the city the fleet was defeated by the rebels and withdrew northward to operate against Byzantium. The following year an allied fleet of 100 sail ravaged islands loyal to Athens and laid siege to Samos, while the Athenians dispatched another 60 vessels to the fleet in the Hellespont. The rebels lifted the siege of Samos and

36. On the structure of the league, see Accame 107–42; Cargill 115–45. On the failures of the league, see esp. Busolt, *Bund* 821–53, for the traditional view; Cargill passim and esp. 146–88 makes a reasonable if not absolutely compelling case that this league was not simply a rerun of the first.

37. Diod. 15.79.2 postulates Theban mastery of the sea had Epaminondas lived. On the Theban naval adventure, see J. Buckler, *The Theban Hegemony, 371–362 B.C.* (Cambridge 1980) 169–75.

38. On the revolt, see Busolt, *Bund* 853–59. Cargill 178–86 explains the defections in terms of the rebels' pursuing their own ambitions, rather than simply revolting against Athenian oppression.

39. Mausolus was generally seen, at least by the Athenians, as the instigator of the revolt (Dem. 15.3); he certainly could and did profit from it.

sailed north to cover Byzantium, and after some maneuvering, part of the Athenian fleet was defeated in an abortive attack in the straights of Chios. In order to raise money to pay his troops, the Athenian commander Chares then employed his force in the service of Artabazus, the rebellious satrap of Hellespontine Phrygia, and this action promptly earned Athens the hostility of Artaxerxes Ochus. When word reached Athens that the king was ready to support Mausolus and the rebels with the Phoenician fleet unless Asia were evacuated, the Athenians decided not only to bow to the Persian ultimatum but also to give up the war against their erstwhile allies. In 355 peace was made, and Athens recognized the independence of the four rebel states.[40]

No sooner had Rhodes freed itself from Athens, however, than it discovered that it had fallen under the power of Mausolus. Given the proximity and growing power, particularly naval, of its Carian neighbor, the revolt from Athens and cooperation with the ambitious dynast had entailed a certain gamble for the island, and now the Rhodian democrats found themselves the losers. Once the war was ended, Mausolus had no problem engineering an antidemocratic coup, and a narrow oligarchic clique led by Agesilochus became the ruling power and instrument of Carian domination on the island.[41] Mausolus himself died soon afterward, in 353/2,[42] but his sister/wife

40. Diod. 16.7.3–4, 21.1–22.2, 34.1; Nep. *Chab.* 4.1–3, *Tim.* 3.1–4; Plut. *Phoc.* 6.1; Isoc. 7.8–10, 81, 8.16, 15.63; Dem. 15.3; Schol. Dem. 3.28; Trog. *Prol.* 6; Polyaen. 3.9.15, 29; see further *Staats.* II, no. 313. Rhodes' role in the war may have been given particular stress by the Athenians (Schol. Dem. 15.1; Ribbeck *Com. Rom. Frag.* 96). Timotheus and Iphicrates were accused and tried for accepting bribes from Chios and Rhodes (e.g., Dinar. 1.14, 3.17; Nep. *Tim.* 3.4–5, *Iphic.* 3.3; Isoc. 15.129); perhaps Timotheus in reality attempted negotiations because of the friendship of his father, Conon, with Rhodes and Chios (P. Cloché, *La politique étrangére d'Athènes de 404 à 338 avant Jésus-Christ* [Paris 1934] 161).

41. Dem. 5.25 (referring to Idrieus?), 13.8, 15.3, 14–15, 19, 27–28; Athen. 10.444e–45a; Arist. *Pol.* 5.2 (1302b.21–23), 5.5 (1304b.27–31); Lucian *Dial. Nekr.* 29.1 (429). A Carian garrison supported the oligarchs (Dem. 15.14–15). On Mausolus' rule: Polyaen. 7.23.1; Arist. *Oec.* 2.13–15 (1348a–b). Cos and Chios were also taken: Dem. 5.25, 15.27; G. F. Hill, "Some Coins of Southern Asia Minor," *Anatolian Studies Presented to Sir Wm. Ramsay* (Manchester 1923) 207–9. See S. Hornblower, *Mausolus* (Oxford 1982) 123–34.

42. Diod. 16.36.2; Pliny *HN* 36.4.30, 6.47 (wrong date); for the chronology of the Hecatomnids, see Hornblower 34–51.

and successor, Artemesia, continued his policies, and the Rhodians very quickly came to realize what a comparatively light burden the Athenian alliance had been. Within a few years of the end of the Social War, probably shortly before Artemesia's death in 351/0, the Rhodian democrats were appealing for aid from their former mistress, but although their cause was championed by no less a figure than Demosthenes, the appeal fell on deaf ears.[43] Athens had too many problems of its own and had been too recently injured by the very people seeking its help to risk war with Persia on their behalf. Without Athenian aid the Rhodians had little chance of liberating themselves, and the island was compelled to remain under Hecatomnid control until Alexander's invasion.[44]

During this period of Carian domination Rhodes is heard of only twice. In 340 it joined Chios and Cos in sending reinforcements, presumably warships, to the Athenian fleet that was attempting to deliver Byzantium from siege by Philip.[45] Rhodes' participation in the defense of Byzantium is quite understandable; the city was not only an old ally from the Social War, but also the key to the crossing of the Hellespont. Keeping Byzantium out of Macedonian hands was consequently in the interests of Persia and Caria, as well as Athens, and it is precisely those naval powers in the Carian sphere—Chios, Cos, and Rhodes—that sent aid. While coming to the rescue of an old friend, Rhodes was thus also serving its Carian and Persian masters.

In the second incident the Rhodians appear to have been essentially serving themselves. In his speech *Against Leocrates,* Lycurgus states

43. Dem. 15; Diony. Hal. *ad Amm.* 1.4 (726); see also F. Focke, *Demosthenesstudien* (Stuttgart 1929) 60–64.

44. Vitr. 2.8.14–15 describes an unsuccessful attack on Halicarnassus by the Rhodians during the reign of Artemesia, but the story cannot be true; see R. M. Berthold, "A Historical Fiction in Vitruvius," *CP* 73 (1978) 129–34. Carian control during this period is reflected in a Rhodian tetradrachm of c. 340 which displays a satrapal head with Phrygian cap next to the familiar rose (G. Pollard, *Catalogue of the Greek Coins in the Collection of Sir Stephen Courtauld at the University College of Rhodesia* [Salisbury 1968] 68, no. 101).

45. Diod. 16.77.2; Front. *Strat.* 1.4.13a. Hyperides' Rhodian oration and his embassy to the island (Plut. *Mor.* 850a) are generally connected with this Rhodian aid to Byzantium; see, for example, F. Blass, *Die attische Beredsamkeit²* (Leipzig 1898) III.2, 9. The speech and trip might just as well be dated to 323, when Hyperides was seeking allies for Athens' revolt from Macedon; see below, chap. 3.

that after the battle of Chaeronea the Athenian Leocrates arrived at Rhodes with the false report that Athens was captured and the Piraeus blockaded, and that in response the Rhodians immediately dispatched warships to bring in merchant vessels.[46] Despite the fact that "κατάγειν τὰ πλοῖα" can imply the use of force,[47] however, it does not seem that in taking advantage of Athens' supposed troubles the Rhodians were acting in any piratical manner. Granted it was in their interest to divert cargoes to the island, but given the news about Athens, it was in the interest also of those captains whose vessels were intercepted. If Philip was blockading the Piraeus, what better place to dispose of cargo than at the emporium at Rhodes? And in the same passage Lycurgus in fact mentions that merchants already at the island when the news arrived decided to unload there rather than sail on. In any case, the Athenians could hardly complain; in the years that led up to Chaeronea their own navy had been increasingly engaged in overt acts of piracy.[48]

After 338 there is no mention of Rhodes again until its surrender to Alexander, but in these last years of the Persian empire two individual Rhodians, the brothers Mentor and Memnon, are found in the service of the Great King. At the head of the Persian army Mentor had reconquered Egypt in the 340s, and more recently he had begun to organize the defenses of Asia Minor, but this task was interrupted by his death in 338. Carrying on his brother's work, Memnon waged an excellent campaign against Philip's generals in 336 and 335 and after Granicus was given the supreme command in the west, but before he could launch his planned naval offensive against Greece he died suddenly in 333, a great bit of good fortune for Alexander.[49] Mentor and Memnon were two of Rhodes' greatest sons, but ironically so, since the brothers were also two of Persia's most valuable assets in the struggle against the power that would ultimately bring liberation to the island.

---

46. Lycur. 18.

47. See Harpoc. s.v. κατάγειν τὰ πλοῖα.

48. See Ormerod 117–20. On the commercial development of Rhodes before 323, see below, chap. 2.

49. On Mentor and Memnon, see H. W. Parke, *Greek Mercenary Soldiers* (Oxford 1933) 128, 166–69, 178–82.

Although almost all of Asia Minor, including Caria, had fallen into Macedonian hands, because of the continued existence of the strong Persian fleet in the Aegean, Rhodes remained nominally loyal to the Great King. Once Issus had been fought, however, the fleet began breaking up as the Macedonian army moved south through Phoenicia, and in early 332 the Rhodians sent ten ships to offer formal submission to Alexander before the walls of Tyre. The submission was accepted, a Macedonian garrison was installed on the island, and Rhodes began its last decade of foreign domination.[50]

Unfortunately, the sources have virtually nothing to say about Rhodes during this crucial period when democrat and oligarch were finally reconciled, and one is forced to draw conclusions on the basis of analogies and indirect evidence. As a Greek state Rhodes must certainly have been freed from the control of the satrap of Caria and made directly responsible to Alexander, but whether or not it was enrolled in the League of Corinth, as were a number of other liberated islands, is impossible to say.[51] Rhodes thus became theoretically autonomous, but the presence of the Macedonian garrison and the ultimate power of Alexander made that autonomy hollow. The harsh truth of Rhodian dependence was demonstrated by the arrest of Harpalus' treasurer by Alexander's agent Philoxenus in 324 and even more clearly by the arrest and deportation, probably also by Philoxenus, of the Rhodian brothers Demaratus and Sparton, who seem to have been charged with political offenses.[52]

Much more important and much less clear are the internal developments on the island and the role played in them by Alexander. When Rhodes submitted, it was, as far as can be seen, still governed by the Carian-supported oligarchs, while at the time of Alexander's death nine years later it already possessed the democratic government of the Hellenistic period.[53] The possibility certainly exists that the Rhodian

---

50. Arr. *Anab.* 2.20.2; Curt. 4.5.9, 8.12; Just. 11.11.1; Diod. 18.8.1. The Rhodians presented Alexander with a costly cloak (Plut. *Alex.* 32.6).

51. Chios was certainly a member: *Syll.*[3] 283 (= Tod 192).

52. Paus. 2.33.4; Plut. *Phoc.* 18.4–5; Ael. *VH* 1.25. See H. Hauben, "Rhodes, Alexander, and the Diadochi from 333/332 to 304 B.C.," *Hist.* 26 (1977) 310–11, esp. n. 23.

53. Contrary to the belief of many, the Hellenistic government was certainly democratic; see below, chap. 2.

democrats, perhaps at the time of the submission, were solely responsible for the change of government, but in view of Rhodes' history, it
would be somewhat surprising to find there an indigenous democratic revolution that resulted not in the usual smoldering bitterness
of the oligarchs, but rather in their harmonious cooperation with the
new government. Since Alexander was very much concerned with
the problem of internal political harmony and stability in the Greek
states,[54] this newfound political tranquility at Rhodes also suggests
the hand of the Conqueror, and this suggestion is supported by the
maintenance of a garrison on the island. True, Rhodes did occupy a
strategic position in the Aegean, but once the Persian fleet had disintegrated, it could hardly be a serious threat to Alexander, and the
continued presence of the garrison might be at least partially understood as a safeguard against the nuisance of factional strife.[55]

There remains the question of what part Alexander might have
played in the final determination of the constitutional structure of the
Rhodian state, but in the absence of any pertinent evidence the answer
to this question must be conjectural. That the essential constitutional
machinery was established sometime before the death of Alexander
seems certain, since there is no sign of any major constitutional re-
form in the period after 323. The most fundamental constitutional
elements, those necessary for the change to a unified island government, must of course have followed soon after the synoecism, while
the first democratic machinery and probably also the introduction of
the deme system must have come after the democratic revolution of

54. Alexander intervened in Chios (*Syll.*[3] 283 = Tod 192) and Ephesus (Arr. *Anab.*
1.17.10–13) to prevent factional strife, and the exiles decree (Diod. 18.8.2–5; Curt.
10.2.4; also *IG* xii.2 6 = Tod 201; *Syll.*[3] 306 = Tod 202), whatever its other aims and
its outcome (see E. Badian, "Harpalus," *JHS* 81 [1961] 25–31), was directed toward
internal political harmony; see H. Berve, *Das Alexanderreich auf prosopographischer
Grundlage* (Munich 1926) I, 234–35; A. Heuss, "Antigonos Monophthalmos und die
griechischen Städte," *Hermes* 73 (1938) 134–41. Arr. *Anab.* 1.18.2 suggests Alexander's involvement, but no more, since this was not so much a general policy as a
political expediency; see A. B. Bosworth, *A Historical Commentary on Arrian's History
of Alexander* (Oxford 1980) I, 134–36.

55. Van Gelder 99. According to Curt. 4.8.12–13, the Rhodians "de praesidio
querebantur" and their request was granted. What this means is not known. Perhaps
the conduct of the garrison was changed or the size reduced; see Hauben, *Hist.* 26,
309–10.

395. But whether the constitution of 395–55 was identical to that of the restored democracy of 332 cannot be determined, although it would be very surprising if the Rhodians had not learned something from eighty years of political oscillation.[56] That there was perhaps a change to a more moderate democracy in the Alexander period is suggested by the fact that the Hellenistic constitution, while clearly democratic, had a definite aristocratic tone and avoided the usual ill of a rampant all-powerful assembly, though it should be noted that other factors also contributed to the stability of the Hellenistic state. What Alexander had to do with these developments is impossible to know, but at the very least he indirectly affected the final development of the Rhodian constitution through the presence of his garrison. The Macedonian peace imposed moderation on the democrats and compelled the oligarchic elements to cooperate with the democracy if they wished to play any political role in the state, and the way was thus paved for the reconciliation of the factions.

The fourth century had been a time of unending political strife and foreign intervention for the young Rhodian republic, but the struggles had seemingly served a useful purpose. To some degree the factional hostility within the state had been exhausted, and all Rhodians had learned a bitter lesson about the involvement of foreign powers in their internal disputes. Further, the growing economic strength of the island, especially toward the end of the period,[57] must have suggested to the Rhodians what prosperity might be theirs were they independent and at peace with themselves, and increasing wealth undoubtedly contributed to the moderation and harmony that grew out of the Alexander period. The imposed stability of these nine years provided for compromise and the emergence, presumably, of

---

56. This last suggestion is made by J. Schneiderwirth, *Geschichte der Insel Rhodus* (Heiligenstadt 1868) 159. It is extremely difficult to date constitutional changes at Rhodes because of the dearth of pertinent inscriptional material for the fourth century, but there is in any case no evidence for any major constitutional development in the Alexander period; see P. Fraser, "Alexander and the Rhodian Constitution," *Par. Pas.* 7 (1952) 199–201. As far as the democratic machinery is concerned, the introduction of the deme system after 395 is likely but cannot be proved, and the question of when the democratic elements of the Hellenistic constitution were introduced must remain open. On the demes and constitution in general, see below, chap. 2.

57. See below, chap. 2.

the more moderate men of both factions, and the final unity was thus achieved. Rhodes had at last come of age, and when news of Alexander's death arrived, it was not the democrats or the oligarchs that expelled the Macedonian garrison and declared the state free, but rather the Rhodians.[58]

58. Diod. 18.8.1. Diod. 20.81.3 states that Alexander honored the Rhodians by depositing with them his will, but no such thing existed, as even Diodorus' own narrative indicates. The will also appears in the Alexander romance, in the section titled "Testamentum Alexandri" (Psd.-Call. 3.30–33; *Epit. Mett.* 87–123). Among other things, Alexander is said to have specifically freed Rhodes and put it under the care of Ptolemy, while granting it leadership of the islands. Clearly the Rhodians had a hand either in composing the "Testamentum" or interpolating passages into it, but it is not at all clear when they did so, and consequently it is also unclear whether the motivation was an early defense of Rhodes' independence or a much later enhancement of its prestige. See Fraser, *Par. Pas.* 7, 202–3; R. Merkelbach, *Die Quellen des griechischen Alexanderromans* (Munich 1954) 54–55, 108–11, 145–51; Hauben, *Hist.* 26, 311–15.

CHAPTER 2

The Rhodian State

"THE best-governed city of the Greeks"—so Diodorus describes Rhodes, and this praise was echoed by other writers in antiquity, reflecting the high repute in which the island was held.[1] The foundation of this renown and the measure of Rhodes' success in foreign affairs was the moderation of its government, which, though democratic, avoided the problems usually associated with an all-powerful assembly. The highest civil organ of the state was the Council, which was composed of an unknown number of paid members, who were elected from the entire body of citizens and who sat for six months. The prime functions of the Council were to serve as the probouleutic organ of the assembly, to provide the day-to-day leadership of the government, and generally to represent the Rhodian state; it was this body that dispatched and welcomed embassies and that received the reports of high civil and military officials. The Council apparently also possessed some judicial power in capital cases, but the extent of its jurisdiction is unclear.[2] Also elected from

---

1. Diod. 20.81.2; Polyb. 33.16.3; Strabo 14.2.5 (652); Dio Chrys. 31.146; Psd.-Arist. 43.

2. Polyb. 16.15.8, 27.4.4, 28.17.13, 29.11.1–5; Diod. 20.94.5; Dio. Chrys. 31.102; Cic. Rep. 1.31.47, 3.35.48; IG xii.1 53; Inscr. Lind. 707. The judicial power is mentioned by Cic. Rep. 3.35.48: "et in theatro et in curia res capitalis et reliquas omnis iudicabant iidem." On the calendar, see Chr. Börker, "Der rhodische Kalender," Zeit. f. Pap. u. Epig. 31 (1978) 193–218. On the Rhodian government in general, see van Gelder 234–49.

the citizen body and serving for half a year were the five prytanes, who presided over the Council and probably also the assembly, and who apparently had the unusual power of appointing envoys. One of these five, it would seem, was elected to serve as overall president of the state, but the relationship between this individual and the remaining magistrates is unknown.[3] The ultimate decision-making body and source of authority in the state was of course the assembly, which was comprised of all Rhodian citizens and which met regularly at least once a month. The assembly possessed full freedom of discussion, but, as was typical of Greek democracies, it appears to have lacked the power of initiation, which consequently placed a good deal of influence in the hands of the Council and prytanes.[4]

In view of this commanding power of the executive and the Council, it has been suggested that although Rhodes is described as democratic by most ancient authors and in several official inscriptions,[5] it was not in fact so, but rather "an aristocracy disguised as a democracy."[6] This judgment depends, of course, on how one understands

3. Polyb. 15.23.4, 27.7.2, 7.13; App. *B.C.* 4.66; Livy 42.45.4; Strabo 7.5.8 (316). All of these passages speak of a single prytanis, implying some sort of presidency, while inscriptions and other passages (see van Gelder 239–40) speak of prytanes. On the number of prytanes, see S. Selivanov and F. Hiller von Gaertringen, "Über die Zahl der rhodischen Prytanen"; M. Holleaux, "De prytanum Rhodiorum numero," *Hermes* 38 (1903) 146–49, 638–39 (= Holleaux I, 399–400). For the influential position of the prytanes, see esp. Polyb. 15.4.4, 22.5.10, 27.4.4, 7.13, 29.10.4 (appointing envoys; J. O'Neil, "How Democratic Was Hellenistic Rhodes?" *Athen.* 59 [1981] 471, has noted the atypical nature of this arrangement). They apparently had direct military control only when the city was immediately threatened (Diod. 20.88.3, 98.7 [siege of 305–4]).

4. Polyb. 27.7.2–4, 7.13, 29.10.1, 11.2–5; Cic. *Rep.* 1.31.47, 3.35.48; *IG* xii.1 3; *Ath. Mitt.* 20 (1895) 228, no. 2. The enacting agent in the state was either "the Demos" or "the Demos and the Council" (e.g., *IG* xii.1 65, 83, 89–92). Cic. *Rep.* 3.35.48 indicates the strong influence of the Council and prytanes: "tantum poterat tantique erat, quanti multitudo senatus." It may be noted that the judicial system was democratic and the jurors were paid (Dio Chrys. 31.102; Psd.-Sall. *ad Caes.* 2.7.12); see P. Fraser, "Notes on Two Rhodian Institutions," *BSA* 67 (1972) 119–24.

5. Polyb. 27.4.7; Diod. 20.93.7; Cic. *Rep.* 1.31.47; Tac. *Dial.* 40.3; Dio Chrys. 31.6; *Syll.*[3] 581; *SGDI* 3749; *Ath. Mitt.* 20 (1895) 386, no. 5. Ael. Arist. 44 (831 D) reports that in his day there was a saying that the Rhodians would even refuse immortality unless eternal democracy came with it.

6. E.g., M. Rostovtzeff, *CAH* VIII (1930) 633; Strabo 14.2.5 (652): "The Rhodians are concerned for the people, although they do not have a democratic government."

"democracy"; that Rhodes was not in practice the radical democracy of late-fifth-century Athens is clear, but it may be judged democratic by standards accepted both today and in the age of Polybius.[7] Formulation and execution of policy might be given over to the prytanes and Council, but the people retained and exercised the ultimate power to accept or reject that policy and to determine the composition of the executive and Council in twice-yearly elections. This last is the key democratic institution, for although it is probable that an "aristocracy" of ability and influence continually supplied candidates for the Council and magistracies,[8] the people held the power to overturn this group at the next election. It is in this respect that the Rhodian constitution differed from the Roman, to which it has been compared; the similarity of "the Council and the Demos" to "Senatus Populusque" may be striking, but the Roman senators were elected (indirectly) for life, their Rhodian counterparts for a brief half year. Not only did the Rhodian nobility thus have no permanent lease on power, but they were especially checked by the unusually short tenure of the high civil offices, and their direction of the state's affairs was accepted only by virtue of the prosperity and security it produced. And conversely, the extensive executive power of the prytanes and Council—normally controlled, it may be assumed, by the upper class—could temper the exuberance and potential excesses of the Rhodian people in their assembly.[9]

The prytanes, Council, and assembly, backed up by the usual array of minor officials,[10] made up the national government of Rhodes and together with the military officials described below provided for the

7. See K. von Fritz, *The Theory of the Mixed Constitution in Antiquity* (New York 1954) 8, 184–85, 340–43. Polybius also considered the Achaean League democratic (Polyb. 2.38.6, 41.5, 44.6).

8. Knowledge about officeholders in Rhodes is almost nonexistent, though it seems a fair assumption that those groups or families with financial or political influence generally supplied the candidates, as in fifth-century Athens before Pericles' death. The limited number of names appearing in lists of officeholders and ambassadors supports this notion.

9. See, for example, the political crisis of the Third Macedonian War. (below, chap. 9).

10. See van Gelder 256–88; F. Hiller von Gaertringen, "Rhodos," *RE* Supp. V (1931) 67–68; Maiuri no. 20.

direction of the state. In the area of domestic affairs the national government was supplemented by the governments of the three old cities of Rhodes, whose political structures had survived the synoecism to become the centers of local administration on the island. Each of the cities had a board of elected officials and a local council or senate and looked after the management particularly of social and religious affairs, as typically occurs when the real political and military power has moved away.[11] The cities also served as the titular heads of the demes into which the Rhodian state was divided, but this tripartite grouping of the demes seems to have played no part in political matters. The deme, as in Attica, was the basic territorial division and probably also the fundamental political unit of the state, but the deme system and its relation to the *ktoina,* an older and distinctively Rhodian division, is in general very poorly understood.[12]

The territory of the Rhodian state, it should be noted, was not confined to the island of Rhodes itself, but in time came to include a number of small nearby islands and parts of the neighboring mainland. The islands of Carpathus, Chalce, and Syme were apparently already Rhodian territory before the synoecism, and although they were detached from Rhodes by the Athenians, they were all reincorporated by the end of the fourth century. Megiste was incorporated by the middle of the fourth century, Casus, Nisyrus, and probably also Telos by the end of the third, and it is very probable that Sarus

11. The local senators were called *mastroi* (Hesych. s.v. μάστροι). Local decrees were generally enacted in the name of the senate and the Lindians, Ialysians, or Camirans (e.g., *IG* xii.1 677, 696, 761), though other formulas are found (e.g., *IG* xii.1 694, 890).

12. There is no evidence that the demes existed before the synoecism, and the existence of an older unit, the *ktoina,* suggests the creation of the deme system after the synoecism. On the demes, including those in the Peraea, see F&B 79–82; G. Pugliese Carratelli, *Studi class. e orient.* 2, 69–74, "Ancora sui *damoi* di Rodi," *Studi class. e orient.* 6 (1957) 62–63, 71–75. I am grateful to Peter Fraser for some thoughts on the question of Rhodian demes. The *ktoina* survived as one basis for local administration, especially for religious affairs; see Momigliano, *Riv. Fil.* 14, 57–60; G. Pugliese Carratelli, "La formazione dello stato rodio," *Studi class. e orient.* 1 (1951) 84–86, 6, 67–71. As Dorians the Rhodians were also divided into three tribes, but the tribal names were taken from the three major cities, a circumstance that suggests that the original colonists settled the island according to tribal division; for discussions on the tribes, see esp. Pugliese Carratelli, *Studi class. e orient.* 1, 78–80, 2, 74–78.

and some smaller unknown islands were also incorporated in the course of these two centuries.[13] On the mainland much, if not all, of the Loryma peninsula southwest of Physcus appears to have been Rhodian before the synoecism, and in the course of the fourth century this incorporated area was extended to include all the territory west to the Cnidian frontier at modern Bencik, north to Cedreae and east to some point just beyond Physcus. Added to this territory, probably also in the fourth century, was the isolated enclave of Daedala, on the coast some forty miles east of Physcus.[14] All of this territory comprised the incorporated Peraea and together with the incorporated islands formed an integral part of the Rhodian state. The inhabitants of these areas were full citizens, politically equal to those who lived on Rhodes, and the land was divided into demes, each of which came under the titular leadership of one of the three old cities of Rhodes (the deme of Physcus in the Peraea, for example, was Lindian).[15] This was the extent of the republic; other mainland acquisitions, all of them after the death of Alexander, were not incorporated, but rather were ruled by Rhodes as subject territory and are known collectively as the subject Peraea.[16]

Of the military establishment of Rhodes the far more important arm, naturally enough, was the navy. Because of Rhodes' naval skill and the need to protect its merchantmen, the composition of the fleet tended toward lighter vessels, and the primary capital ship was the quadrireme, backed up by smaller units, such as the trireme and triemiolia, an extremely fast warship specially developed by the Rho-

---

13. On the islands, see esp. F&B 54, 138–54. There is no evidence for the islet of Sarus, but inasmuch as Carpathus and Casus were incorporated, Sarus undoubtedly was also; Telos is found in alliance with Rhodes shortly after 300 (*SEG* xxv.847).

14. On the incorporated Peraea, see esp. F&B 51–70, 94–98. The Loryma peninsula comprised the Rhodian "Chersonese" and the incorporated territory to the north (except Physcus) the "Aperaea" (F&B 65–69).

15. On the administration of the incorporated territory, which was organized primarily along military lines, see below, chap. 4. For evidence that the demes of the Peraea were treated somewhat differently from those of the island, see F&B 125–26.

16. The distinction between "incorporated" and "subject" Peraea is modern terminology, recognizing what is not explicitly stated in the sources; in the incorporated areas Rhodian names are followed by a demotic, if anything, and in the subject, which was not part of the deme organization, simply by Ῥόδιος.

dians for the pursuit of commerce raiders.[17] The standing military fleet in the Hellenistic period numbered probably less than forty, but it must be remembered that the term "standing fleet" is somewhat misleading, as warships were generally commissioned only when they were needed. The real index of naval power was the capability of quickly putting a fleet to sea, and while it is likely that Rhodes did increasingly keep a small fleet in being as its commercial thalassocracy and antipirate activities developed, the real strength lay in its shipyards and their ability to augment considerably the existing squadrons. Rhodes' fleets were still small by fifth-century Athenian standards (the highest number of capital ships sent out in a single year seems to have been about seventy-five in 190),[18] but the Rhodians relied not on numbers but on a skill at sea that was literally proverbial.[19] In an age when naval warfare was more and more becoming an affair of grappling and boarding, they practiced the tactics of ramming, especially the dreaded *diekplous*.[20] The essential lack of Rhodian vessels heavier than the quadrireme bears witness to their dependence on speed and maneuverability. The seamanship of Rhodes' citizens lay at the heart of its naval power; while other states might be able to launch larger fleets, Rhodes was, especially after the decline of Ptolemaic sea power, the only one that possessed the capability of rapidly launching a considerable force and manning it with a constant supply of highly skilled sailors.

Most of the warships were skippered by a trierarch, usually a wealthy citizen who outfitted the vessel and paid its crew in anticipation of reimbursement by the state.[21] Because of the strong naval

17. On the triemiolia, see L. Casson, *Ships and Seamanship in the Ancient World* (Princeton 1971) 127–31; the Rhodians did occasionally use quinqueremes.

18. See appendix II. Dio Chrys. 31.103 speaks of an expedition of 100 or more ships, but this is clearly an exaggeration.

19. Psd.-Diogenian. *Paroemiogr.:* "If we have ten Rhodians, we have ten ships." Cic. *Leg. Man.* 18.54. The only known instance of a Rhodian fleet being wrecked by the weather occurs in 48, long after Rhodes had passed its prime (Caes. *B.C.* 3.26–27).

20. The *diekplous* involved breaking through the enemy line, shearing off oars in the process, then turning and ramming the disabled vessels; see Polyb. 16.4.13–14; W. W. Tarn, *Hellenistic Military and Naval developments* (Cambridge 1930) 144–49.

21. Arist. *Pol.* 5.5 (1304b.27–31). The evidence is from the fourth century, but the trierarchy is found in the Hellenistic period.

tradition, the Rhodian trierarch usually assumed the actual command of his ship, but if he did not, or if he had financed more than one vessel, the command passed to the *epiplous* or vice-captain.[22] Likewise, the *epiplous* would also become captain in the event that the trierarch was placed in command of a squadron of smaller vessels. A squadron leader was known as an archon of whatever type of vessels he commanded (trireme, *aphraktos,* triemiolia, etc.), and his command varied from three ships, which was apparently the basic tactical unit of the navy, to much larger squadrons sent out on specific expeditions. In time of war the overall command of the fleet was in the hands of the nauarch, who seems to have been an extraordinary magistrate elected at the outbreak of war to serve as admiral for the duration. Possessing the power to conclude treaties, the nauarch was also a high political officer and was on occasion elected during peacetime to serve in a diplomatic capacity as a minister plenipotentiary.[23] The command structure of the peacetime navy is unclear; very likely the small squadrons that policed the Aegean and pursued pirates were commanded by experienced trierarchs, who probably bore the title of archon, but whether these squadron leaders reported directly to the civil government or to a peacetime admiral (of whom there is no word) is unknown.

The importance of the navy to the prosperity and security of Rhodes can hardly be overestimated, and evidence of Rhodian concern for naval affairs is found at every turn. The dockyards were the scenes of heavy security, designed to protect the ships from sabotage and to preserve the secrets of certain technical achievements, for the Rhodians were great shipbuilders as well as great sailors.[24] With a few exceptions, the crews of the warships were composed entirely of

22. On the officers and crews of the Rhodian warships, see esp. Maiuri nos. 5, 18; M. Segré, "Dedica votiva dell' equipaggio di una nave rodia," *ClRh* 8 (1936) 225–44; Casson, *Ships* 306–9.

23. Polyb. 4.50.5, 16.15.8, 18.1.4, 2.3, 21.7.1, 30.5.4–5, 33.15.3; Livy 45.25.8; App. *B.C.* 4.66; Diod. 20.88.6; Arr. *Success.* F 1.39 (Roos-Wirth); on the last two examples, see below, chap. 3. Duration: Polyb. 18.1.4; Livy 31.46.6, 32.16.6 (Acesimbrotus); Polyb. 21.7.1; Livy 36.45.5, 37.10.2 (Pausistratus). A nauarch fatally wounded in action apparently could appoint his own successor (Polyb. 16.9.1).

24. Strabo 14.2.5 (653); see van Gelder 425–26.

Rhodian citizens, though nothing is known of the terms of service.[25] The great majority of Rhodians, then, at some point in their lives must have served in the fleet, and this service is carefully recorded in numerous inscriptions by men of both high and low station. Whereas service in the army, including the holding of important commands, was generally given only brief mention in an individual's *cursus,* Rhodians who had attained the highest posts in the state proudly recorded their beginnings as lowly ratings in the fleet.[26] Ex-sailors, very often the officers and men of a single ship, formed associations to preserve the ties that had bound them together during their service, and the crews of warships engaged in a variety of lively competitions, promoting efficiency and stimulating patriotism and the military spirit.[27]

Inasmuch as Rhodes is an island, the navy was the essential shield of the state, but the security of the continental possessions required land forces as well. Little is known about the army, however, since it played a minor role in Rhodian affairs and was accordingly paid small attention by Rhodians in the inscriptions recording their careers. Although evidence is lacking, it is very likely that Rhodes kept a small standing army as a police force in the Peraea before 188, and it certainly did so afterward, when the area of the subject Peraea had been tremendously increased by the acquisition of Caria and a rebellious Lycia. The higher army officers were of course Rhodians, but the rank and file seems to have been almost exclusively mercenaries, recruited especially in Crete and Anatolia.[28] Rhodian citizens were perfectly capable of bearing arms, as the great siege of 305–4 demonstrates, but like the Carthaginians, they were disinclined to interrupt

25. See, for example, *IG* xii. 1 766.

26. See, for example, the career of Polycles: Maiuri no. 18; further dedications by sailors: Maiuri no. 5; *Lindiaka* 7 (1938) nos. 32, 40.

27. See van Gelder 366–67; M. Launey, *Recherches sur les armées hellénistiques* (Paris 1949–50) II, 1003–6, 1018–22.

28. The only Rhodian army about which any information exists is the 3,700-man force that faced Philip V in the Peraea in 197; see below, chap. 6. For Cretan mercenaries, see the treaty with Hierapytna: *Syll.*³ 581; see further G. T. Griffith, *The Mercenaries of the Hellenistic World* (Cambridge 1935) 90–92. For a survey and prosopography of Rhodian soldiers in the Hellenistic period, see Launey I, 240–46, II, 1149–50.

their affairs with service in the army. This attitude was undoubtedly fostered by the general naval orientation of the state and by the fact that in times of war the fleet drew very heavily on the manpower of the citizen body. As the land forces required were relatively small, it was convenient for Rhodes to use a portion of its great wealth to hire the soldiers necessary for the security of the Peraea.

The supreme command of the army was in the hands of a board of ten strategoi, the most important of which were the "strategos of the island" and the "strategos of the Peraea."[29] The former was responsible for the security of the island of Rhodes itself, and subordinate to him were three hegemones, one for each of the three old territories of Rhodes. Each of these officers commanded in turn an epistates, who probably held a post in the city in his particular territory, while the hegemon looked after the general security of the rural areas.[30] In similar fashion of the strategos of the Peraea was also supported by a hierarchy of hegemones and epistatai, but here distinction must be made between the officials in the incorporated Peraea and those in the subject. Inasmuch as the incorporated Peraea was part of the Rhodian state, the duties of the hegemones and epistatai presumably duplicated those of their colleagues on the island and were essentially

29. στραταγὸς ἐπὶ τᾶς χώρας (τᾶς ἐν ταῖ νάσωι): *IG* xii.1 701, 49 (= *Syll.*[3] 619); Maiuri no. 21; *ClRh* 2 (1932–39) nos. 18, 19, 22; *Inscr. Lind.* 153, 172. στραταγὸς ἐπὶ τὸ Πέραν: see below, chap. 4. Board of ten: *IG* xii.1 42, 49; Maiuri no. 18. *IG* xii.1 50, which is later than the other inscriptions (first century), lists twelve names; if these twelve are indeed strategoi, possibly a new division of duties resulted in the addition of two members to the board. There is the problem of the στραταγὸς ἐκ πάντων: *IG* xii.1 700, 701, 1036; *Syll.*[3] 673; Maiuri no. 18; *ClRh* 2 (1932–39) no. 18; *Inscr. Lind.* 151, 222. It cannot mean "general over all," since this interpretation strains the meaning of ἐκ πάντων and since the phrase is found together with ἐπὶ τᾶς χώρας and ἐπὶ τὸ πέραν. The phrase probably refers to a special mode of election, one that ignored the presumed usual selection by division (tribe or whatever) and drew from all the citizens (*Syll.*[3] 586, n. 5; Hiller 768). For a similar practice at Athens, see Arist. *Ath. Pol.* 61.1. στραταγὸς ἐκ πάντων is often found together with κατὰ πόλεμον, suggesting that the office was a special wartime measure; this is the case in Ptolemaic Cyrene: *SEG* ix.1. My thanks to Tony Raubitschek for a conversation about strategoi.

30. This arrangement of a hegemon and epistates for each territory is actually attested to only in the case of Lindus. Hegemon: Maiuri no. 18; epistates: *Inscr. Lind.* 200, 202, 209, etc, It is assumed that a similar arrangement existed in the other two territories.

military, though in a much more real sense, as the mainland territory was actually exposed to attack. In the subject Peraea, on the other hand, these officers not only served in a military capacity but also provided the administrative structure of Rhodian rule in the area, and the epistatai (and possibly also the hegemones) consequently had civil as well as military powers.[31] All of these officials were elected by the Rhodian assembly and possibly paid by the state, and the commands were probably annual, at least in the case of the strategoi.[32] What the other eight strategoi of the board did is not at all clear, especially considering that the only sizable bodies of troops were stationed in the Peraea; very possibly these eight had by the Hellenistic period assumed essentially nonmilitary functions, such as supervision of state finances.[33] In any event, the Rhodian army basically served as a garrison force, providing for the external and internal security of the mainland possessions; the active military potential of the state lay on the seas.

The strength behind the military, the real might of Rhodes, lay in trade and the wealth it brought. The republic had commodities to export, notably fruits, honey, grape and olive products, and some fish and minerals, but the natural resources of the island and the Peraea were limited, and the Rhodians had an ever-increasing need for imported goods, especially grain and timber for shipbuilding. Rhodes was fortunately situated, however, lying midway between the Greek Aegean and the oriental ports of Cyprus, Syria, and

31. See below, chap. 4.
32. Elected: Maiuri no. 18; *Inscr. Lind.* 193, 209, 224. A period of less than the customary year seems too short to be practical, especially for the military/administrative posts in the Peraea. The possibility of pay stems from an interpretation of a number of inscriptions (*SGDI* 4275; Maiuri no. 18;*ClRh* 2 [1932–39] no. 19) which mention a hegemon *amisthos;* if a hegemon is specifically designated as *amisthos,* the indication is that such men normally were paid. There is also mention of an epistates *amisthos: Inscr. Lind.* 224 (second half of second century).
33. Van Gelder 253–54. Strategoi in Athens (see W. S. Ferguson, "Researches in Athenian and Delian Documents III," *Klio* 9 [1909] 317–23) and Erythrae (*IG* xii.1 6) had assumed nonmilitary duties. A connection between strategoi and finances makes sense, especially considering the nature of the Rhodian military—fleets and mercenaries. This supposition is supported by *IG* xii.1 42, which records the erection of a statue by οἱ συνάρξαντες στραταγοὶ καὶ ταμίαι.

Egypt,[34] and it was thus from very early times involved in commerce. Given the strategic position of the island, the carrying trade became especially important, and Rhodes consequently built up its own merchant marine, rather than relying on foreign bottoms, as did Athens.[35] This strategy not only multiplied tremendously the profits available to the Rhodians, but also provided them with more direct control over their trading network. At the same time, of course, the possession of this merchant fleet also increased Rhodes' commitment to the security of the seas and thus served as a further spur to the development of its navy and of maritime laws.[36]

Information on Rhodian commercial activities for the period before 323 is extremely scarce, but there are some indicators of the direction and extent of the pre-Hellenistic trade. In the sixth and early fifth centuries Lindus and Ialysus minted their coins on the Phoenician standard, indicating a commercial orientation to the east, as is only to be expected, given the position of the island. Despite liberation from Persia and enrollment in the Athenian empire, these ties persisted, and a Rhodian proxenos is found at Naucratis at the end of the fifth century.[37] Athenian rule brought the Attic standard to the coinage of the island, but with the defeat of Athens in 404 Rhodes adopted the Chian standard, which subsequently spread among the states of the eastern Aegean. It is impossible to know the precise role played by Rhodes in the spread of this coinage weight, but it is probable that the increasing popularity of the new standard was due in large part to the growing commercial importance of the recently unified republic, a conclusion supported by the fact that the weight quickly became better known as the Rhodian rather than the Chian

34. The Rhodes–Egypt route was navigable even in winter: Dem. 56.30. For examples of sailing times from Rhodes to important ports, see Casson, *Ships* 286–89, 293.

35. See, for example, Lycur. 15; Dem. 56.21; Polyaen. 4.6.16; Diod. 26.8.1; Polyb. 5.88.7, 89.8.

36. There is no direct evidence on a Rhodian maritime code, but later Roman sources indicate that Mediterranean sea law was commonly known as "Rhodian"; see H. Kreller, "Lex Rhodia," *Zeitschr. f. d. ges. Handelsrecht u. Konkursrecht* 85 (1921) 257–367.

37. Proxenos: *Syll.*[3] 110; see also E. Schwyzer, *Dialectorum Graecarum Exempla epigraphica potiora* (Leipzig 1923) nos. 278, 279.

standard. By the advent of Alexander, the new Rhodian standard had been accepted by most of Ionia, including the dynasts of Caria, and by many of the states of the Cyclades and the Propontis, and when Alexander adopted the full Attic standard the Rhodian was the only other Greek weight able to maintain its position.[38] This fact certainly suggests a well-developed sphere of commercial activity, and in fact Lycurgus, in a speech dated to 330, describes the merchants of Rhodes as men "who sail the entire civilized world for trade."[39] Especially important were the old ties to the southeast. Both Lycurgus' oration and one from the Demosthenic corpus picture the island as an important emporium for the Egyptian trade, and this picture is supported by the fact that Cleomenes, Alexander's governor in Egypt, selected Rhodes as the center for his grain operations.[40] Cleomenes' decision is a sure indication that the disposal of Egyptian grain had become to a good extent a Rhodian affair even before Alexander, and given the huge output of the Nile valley, it stands as telling evidence of the growth of Rhodian commerce in the fourth century.

With the passing of Alexander, Rhodian commercial enterprises blossomed. In order to understand the economic underpinning of the state and its policies it is worthwhile to step out of the chronological context and survey briefly the Hellenistic trade. The almost explosive growth of the Rhodian economy is reflected in the great siege of 305–4; within a generation of Alexander the island had already grown strong enough to attract and resist successfully the attentions of the most important power in the Greek world. Moreover, in the midst of the struggle Antigonus was moved to issue a proclamation of safety to the Rhodian merchants in Pamphylia, Cilicia, and Syria, thereby

38. Pre-Hellenistic coinage and the Rhodian-Chian standard: Head 635–39, Rhodian and Chian standard, q.v.; Head, *Greek Coins of Caria, Cos, Rhodes, etc.*, British Museum catalogue (London 1897) c–cvi, 223–34; Babelon II.1, 459–78, II.2, 141–42, 973–76, 1001–32, 1037–42, 1053–58.

39. Lycur. 15.

40. Dem. 56; also Arist. *Oec.* 2.33 (1352a.16–b.25). On the pre-Hellenistic trade, see also E. Ziebarth, "Zur Handelsgeschichte der Insel Rhodus," *Mélanges Gustav Glotz II* (Paris 1932) 910–12; V. Grace, "Stamped Wine Jar Fragments," *Hesp.* supp. 13 (1956) 119, 138–41.

underscoring the extent of their activity in those areas.[41] This growth continued, and in the course of the next century Rhodes became the clearinghouse and banker of the eastern Mediterranean. Rhodian merchants and financiers were found in all the great commercial centers, while the island in turn played host to a growing body of foreign businessmen.[42] A telling indication of the economic importance attained by Rhodes in this period is found in the wake of the disastrous earthquake of 228, when scores of small states and virtually every important monarch in the Greek world contributed to the relief of the stricken island.[43] Such unparalleled unanimity of action on the part of the ever-contentious Hellenistic powers can be understood only as a response essentially to hard political/economic interests, and as such illustrates Rhodes' economic importance. The catastrophe on the island probably caused a sharp fear of widespread financial crisis to run through the international banking and trading community, and this fear penetrated to the council chambers of the contributing states, all of which were involved to varying degrees in the Rhodian commercial network.

The scope of the Hellenistic trade can be seen to some extent in the impact and distribution of Rhodes' coinage,[44] but far more revealing are the huge numbers of its stamped amphora handles found throughout the classical world. It is no exaggeration to say that there is hardly a site in the Mediterranean where Rhodian handles have not appeared, and these finds show commercial ties stretching from the Nile to the Crimea and from Mesopotamia west to Illyria, southern

41. Polyaen. 4.6.16.

42. Rhodes' position as a clearinghouse is clearly indicated in the correspondence of Zenon (*PRyl* 554). Rhodian financiers: Ziebarth 916–21. For a discussion of the Rhodian state bank, see Fraser, *BSA* 67, 113–17; on Rhodian banking in general, see R. Bogaert, *Banques et banquiers dans les cités grecques* (Leiden 1968) 213–16.

43. See below, chap. 4.

44. See Head 639–41, Rhodian and Chian standard, q.v.; K. Regling, *Die Münzen von Priene* (Berlin 1927) 128–30; S. Noe, *A Bibliography of Greek Coin Hoards* (New York 1937) passim; T. Hackens and E. Lévy, "Trésor hellénistique trové a Délos en 1964," *BCH* 89 (1965) 504–34; T. Hackens, "La circulation monétaire dans la Béotie hellénistique: Trésors de Thèbes, 1935 et 1965," *BCH* 93 (1969) 701–22; M. Oeconomides, "Thēsauros nomismatōn ek Thessalias 1968," *Arch. Eph.* (1970) 13–26.

Italy, Sicily, and Carthage.[45] Within this trading sphere by far the most important areas were Ptolemaic Egypt and the Black Sea, the two breadbaskets of the East. Of the great variety of goods that passed through the harbors of Rhodes, the most essential was grain.[46] Innumerable Rhodian handles are found in Alexandria, almost to the complete exclusion of those from other areas of Greece, and it seems clear that disposal of the tremendous grain output of Cyprus and the Nile Valley became virtually a Rhodian monopoly after the death of Alexander.[47] The number of Rhodian handles found in the Black Sea region is second only to that found in Egypt, and it appears from this and other indications that in the course of the third century the important trade from the Pontic granary also fell largely into Rhodian hands. Much of the Pontic grain, of course, was sold directly to Aegean customers and never passed through Rhodes, but Rhodian financiers are even found behind many of these deals.[48] Rhodes'

45. To the bibliography on Rhodian handles in Rostovtzeff III, 1486, n. 97, add P. C. Sestieri, "Bolli anforari rodi d'Albania," *Epigraphica* 3 (1941) 284–91; V. Grace, "Standard Pottery Containers of the Ancient World," *Hesp.* supp. 8 (1949) 175–85 (general on amphorae); "Timbres amphoriques trouvés à Délos," *BCH* 76 (1952) 517–19, 525; "The Eponyms Named on Rhodian Amphora Stamps," *Hesp.* 22 (1953) 116–28; *Hesp.* supp. 13, 138–44; J. H. Kent, "Stamped Amphora Handles from the Delian Temple Estates," *Studies Presented to D. M. Robinson on His Seventieth Birthday* (St. Louis 1953) II, 127–34; M. Lenger, "Timbres amphoriques trouvés à Argos," *BCH* 79 (1955) 484–89; D. Levi and G. Pugliese Carratelli, "Nuove inscrizioni di Iaso," *Annuario* 39–40 (1961–62) 605–17; N. G. L. Hammond, *Epirus* (Oxford 1967) 639; see also below, n. 48. For a further discussion of the meaning of the stamps, see D. Sippel, *Rhodes and the Nesiotic League,* diss. (Cincinnati 1966) 120–25.

46. On the grain trade, see esp. Casson 168–87.

47. On Rhodian handles in Egypt, see esp. Grace, *Hesp.* supp. 8, 183. The importance of Egypt to Rhodes is attested to by Diod. 20.81.4. In one of the harbors of Alexandria was an island called Antirrhodos: Strabo 17.1.9 (794). *SEG* ix.2 records a large shipment of grain from Cyrene to Rhodes. For a calculation of the amount of grain exported by Egypt, see A. Segré, "Note sull'economia del'Egitto ellenistico nell'età tolemaica," *Bull. Soc. Arch. Alex.* 29 (1934) 289–97.

48. To the bibliography in *CAH* VIII (1930) 791 and Rostovtzeff III, 1485, n. 93, add J. Kruškol, "Principle Points and Routes of Trade between the North Black Sea Area and Rhodes in the Hellenistic Epoch," *VDI* 62 (1957) 110–15 (in Russian); D. Šelov, "Towards a History of the Ties between the Hellenistic Bosporus and Rhodes," *Sov. Arch.* 28 (1958) 333–36 (in Russian); E. Solomonik, "Epigraphical Documents of Scythian Neapolis," *Num. i. Epig.* 3 (1962) 40–44 (in Russian); V. Eftimie, "Imports of Stamped Amphorae in the Lower Danubian Regions and a Draft

dealings with the western granary, Sicily, were far less extensive, but some part, at least, of Sicilian grain was also carried in Rhodian bottoms.[49]

Given Rhodes' position and financial resources, it naturally dealt in more than just grain, and every kind of commodity could be seen on its wharves, including slaves and luxury goods from the East.[50] It also exported its own products, chiefly its wine, but these exports must have comprised only a fraction of the island's commercial enterprises, and probably the great numbers of jars that are found contained not only domestic products but also foreign goods being disposed of by Rhodian merchants.[51] Whatever the exact extent of these other activities, however, it is clear that the grain trade was at the heart of the island's commerce; here Rhodes had virtually no rivals in the East. Athens' commercial position had already been slipping in the fourth century, and although in the third the city still imported large quantities of grain, it was to feed Attica; Athens' role as a grain dealer seems to have been negligible.[52] The same may be said of Delos; though Delos grew in importance as a commercial center in the Hellenistic period, it seems never to have played any significant part in the grain business. Its harbor facilities were not adequate for the large grain transports, and its location was not really suitable for the distribution of Pontic supplies to the important customers of the north Aegean and Anatolian littoral. There is word of various grain

---

Corpus of Amphora Stamps," *Dacia* 3 (1959) 198–211; A. Sadurska, "Timbres amphoriques de Mirmeki" *Griechische Städte und einheimische Völker des Schwarzmeergebietes: Eine Aufsatzsammlung* (Berlin 1961) 109–11; J. Badalyants, "Rhodian Amphora Stamps from Nymphaeum," *VDI* 113 (1970) 113–26 (in Russian); V. F. Gajdukevič, *Das bosporanische Reich*[2] (Berlin 1971) 103–4, esp. 182, n. 37, 308, n. 2 (with a bibliography of Rhodian trade with the northern Black Sea area).

49. Polyb. 5.88.7; Diod. 26.8.1; but see Polyb. 28.2.17.

50. See J. Kruškol, "Some Basics on Slavery at Rhodes in the Hellenistic Epoch," *VDI* (1947) 231–32 (in Russian). The extent of Rhodes' network is suggested by the famous anecdote of Mysta; see below, chap. 4.

51. See F. Bleckmann, *De inscriptionibus quae leguntur in vasculis Rhodiis,* diss. (Göttingen 1907) 29–30. Rhodian wine was held in fair repute at Athens and Rome: Aul. Gell. 13.5; Athen. 1.31e, 33e; Vir. *Geo.* 2.101–2; Psd.-Aesch. *Epit.* 5.2.

52. See F. Heichelheim, "Sitos," *RE* supp. 6 (1935) 851–52; Casson 168–69; Gajdukevič 97–99.

transactions on the island, but the evidence suggests no more than that Delos served as a local market for the neighboring islands and that Rhodians were in fact often instrumental in the deals that were made there.[53]

The immediate result of Rhodes' commercial activities was to make it probably the richest state in the Hellenistic East after the three great monarchies. Statistical evidence is, as usual, in short supply, but there are a few indicators of the immense wealth of the island. In the early second century the yearly income from the harbor dues alone amounted to about a million drachmas, and if the customery 2 percent duty is assumed, this means that some 50 millions' worth of goods yearly passed through Rhodes' harbors in this period.[54] Since the bulk of these goods would either have been carried in Rhodian bottoms or have been subject to the manipulation of Rhodian businessmen, the amount of money earned by the private sector must have been enormous, especially considering that the 50 millions represents only the goods that actually passed through Rhodes. The only other known income figure concerns the subject Peraea: in the second century the two cities of Caunus and Stratonicea returned an annual 720,000 drachmas to Rhodes.[55] A further idea of the magnitude of Rhodian resources may be had from its ability to launch and maintain large fleets and from the extent of its foreign aid. In 219, for example, an appeal from Sinope was met with 140,000 drachmas' worth of war material and cash, and at an unknown date Argos was granted an interest-free loan of 600,000 drachmas, indicating the maintenance of large financial reserves by the Rhodian state.[56] In the last analysis it is impossible to calculate even approximately the gross national product of the island, but Rhodes was clearly an extremely wealthy state, so wealthy that more than two centuries after it had passed its prime,

---

53. See J. A. Lenzmann, "On the Grain Trade of Delos from III to II Centuries B.C.," *VDI* (1946) 89–96 (in Russian); Casson 174–79. Rhodians involved in Delian grain deals: *IG* xi.4 1055 (= *Syll.*³ 493), 1116; *Insc. de Délos* 442A, 100–105.

54. Polyb. 30.31.12.

55. Polyb. 30.31.6–7.

56. At the end of the third century the maintenance of a trireme cost 10,000 drachmas a month: *Syll.*³ 581. Sinope: Polyb. 4.56.2; Argos: G. Vollgraff, "Novae Inscriptiones Argivae," *Mnem.* 44 (1916) 220–21.

Dio Chrysostom could still describe the Rhodians as "richer than any other Greek people."[57]

Because of wise government, the effect of this prosperity on Rhodes' internal affairs was soothing rather than aggravating, and throughout the Hellenistic period the republic displayed a domestic harmony uncharacteristic of important Greek states, especially those with democratic constitutions. Granted, knowledge of Rhodian domestic politics is slight, especially for the third century, but nevertheless the only known instance of serious dissension comes amid the foreign-policy crises that heralded the end of Rhodes' independence, and even this trouble passed quickly.[58] This is not to say that wealth automatically solves social and political problems; more often it creates them. But when wisely managed, prosperity can ease the frictions among economic classes, and such was the case in Rhodes, where the needy were supplied with food by the state and through liturgies undertaken by wealthy individuals.[59] Such practices, together with the brilliantly successful foreign policy, serve to explain the internal harmony enjoyed by the Rhodians in the years after Alexander. They also contributed something of an aristocratic flavor to the democracy, and this patrician quality was further nurtured by the survival of the old gentilic groupings of the people, such as the *patrai*. Though no longer important in the functioning of the state, these old associations continued to play an important role in cult and social affairs and thus helped lend an aristocratic air to the republic.[60]

The persistence of the gentilic groups was also a manifestation of Rhodian exclusiveness and passion for associations,[61] characteristics undoubtedly fostered by the relatively large numbers of aliens who lived within the bounds of the republic. Drawn by the cultural and, much more important, commercial activities of Rhodes, outsiders

57. Dio Chrys. 31.100; also 31.55.
58. See below, chap. 9. There are scattered signs of dissension after 164, especially during the period of the Roman civil wars; see below, chap. 11.
59. Strabo 14.2.5 (653); see further van Gelder 275–77.
60. On the *patrai,* see esp. *IG* xii.1 695; G. Pugliese Carratelli, "Per la storia delle associazioni in Rodi antica," *Annuario* 20 (n.s. 1–2) (1939–40) 198–200.
61. On associations, see esp. Pugliese Carratelli, *Annuario* 20, 168–200; K. M. Kolobova, "Rhodian ΣΥΝΝΟΜΑΙ," *Studies Presented To G. Tomson on the Occasion of His Sixtieth Birthday* (Prague 1963) 141–47 (in Russian), n. 27.

flocked to the island, and foreign businessmen very rapidly became a vital part of the economic machinery. They came from all areas of the Mediterranean, but most traveled along Rhodes' eastern connections, from Asia Minor, Syria, and Egypt, with a smaller number coming from Athens and the islands. At the same time the growing demands of the Rhodian economy brought in a steady stream of public and private slaves, most of whom came also from the east and from the Black Sea region. All these strangers were naturally excluded from the ancestral associations reserved for citizens, but they enjoyed their own clubs and organizations, and many wealthy foreigners participated directly in Rhodian social life by undertaking state liturgies.[62] The legal status of the resident aliens varied and the terminology of the inscriptions is unfortunately unclear, but most seem to have fallen in the category of *metoikoi*. Others are designated as having received *epidamia,* and though the exact status of these individuals is disputed, it appears that they were superior to the more common *metoikoi* and closer to the citizenship. The offspring of a Rhodian citizen and a foreigner had a special status as a *matroxenos,* but seems nevertheless to have been a citizen, probably with some minor distinctions.[63] The proportions of citizens, aliens, and slaves, as well as the overall population of the republic itself, are unknown; in 304 some 6,000 citizens and 1,000 alien residents were able to bear arms in deference of the city, but there is no indication of what fractions of the total populations of the city and states these figures represent.[64] Suffice it to say that Rhodes was in the top rank of

---

62. Aliens in general: Rostovtzeff II, 690–91, III, 1484, n. 87; D. Morelli, "Gli stranieri in Rodi," *Studi class. e orient.* 5 (1956) 126–28. Slaves: Kruškol, *VDI* (1947) 231–32; Morelli 137. Origins: *IG* xii.1 480–676; Maiuri nos. 136–241; Pugliese Carratelli, *Annuario* 20, 172–73; Morelli 136, 141–85.

63. The terminology applied to aliens in Rhodes is bewildering; in addition to *metoikoi* there were *paroikoi* and *katoikeuntes.* For discussion, see esp. Pugliese Carratelli, *Annuario* 20, 174–75, and "Sullo stato di cittadinanza in Rodi," *Studi in onore di V. Arangio-Ruiz nel XLV anno del suo insegnamento* (Naples 1953) IV, 485–91; Morelli 128–35, 139, n. 1.

64. Diod. 20.84.2. Obviously 6,000 is too few for the entire citizen body and must represent males of prime fighting age, possibly those of hoplite status. K. J. Beloch, *Die Bevölkerung der griechisch-römischen Welt* (Leipzig 1886) 226–27, suggests 24,000 citizens out of 30,000 free and 100,000 total population in the city during the siege. If the 6,000 were hoplites and Rhodes had approximately the same ratio of hoplites to

cosmopolitan communities and that the foreigners and slaves in its population far outnumbered the native Rhodians.

The site of probably the highest concentration of foreigners and the economic and political heart of the republic was the city of Rhodes. Founded in 408/7, allegedly by Hippodamus, the capital of the new Rhodian republic came to be known as possibly the most beautiful city in the Greek world and was certainly among the busiest.[65] The city was situated at the strategic northeastern tip of the island, where Rhodian engineers improved upon the already favorable topography and with the construction of protective moles created two magnificent harbors on the eastern shore.[66] From these basins with their famous dockyards the city swept up into the hills on the western side of the island, forming a kind of vast amphitheater and creating serious drainage problems; three times in the course of the fourth century the lower levels of the city were flooded as water running off the upper terraces was trapped by the city walls. In the last inundation, in 316, complete disaster was averted only when the fortifications collapsed under the pressure of the rising waters, and henceforth drainage channels through the walls were kept clear.[67] The walls themselves were kept in good repair and completely encircled the city, running along the crest of the hills and down to the harbors, where they followed along the line of the shore. Thus the harbors were outside the city walls, but they could be defended by artillery and naval units, and the

---

total citizen body as Athens in the fifth and fourth centuries (12 to 15 percent), then the Rhodian citizen body numbered perhaps 40,000.

65. Beauty: Strabo 14.2.5 (652); Ael. Arist. 44; Lucian *Am.* 8; Aul. Gell. 15.31.1. Strabo 14.2.9 (654) says the city was founded by the architect of the Piraeus, but uses the expression ὡς φασίν. In view of his age it is highly improbable that Hippodamus actually participated in the founding. The association probably stems from the Hippodamian plan of the city. For an examination of the city plan, see J. D. Kondis, *Symbolē ek tēn meletēn tēs rymotomias tēs Rodou* (Rhodes 1954) 3–31, and "Zum antiken Stadtbauplan von Rhodos," *MDAI* 73 (1958) 146–58.

66. Strabo 14.2.5 (653); Dio Chrys. 31.163; Psd.-Arist. 43 (797–98, 810 D). For a description of the harbors, see K. Lehmann-Hartleben, *Die antiken Hafenanlagen des Mittelmeeres* (Leipzig 1923) 128–29. The present Bay of Akandia apparently did not serve as a regular harbor in antiquity, being too rocky and exposed, but its mole provided added protection.

67. Diod. 19.45.1–8. On the drainage systems, see J. D. Kondis, "Ta archaia teichē tēs Rodou," *Arch. Delt.* 18A (1963) 76–78.

smaller military harbor to the north could be closed off by a boom. As the great siege by Demetrius would demonstrate, the static defenses of the city were exceedingly strong. Like so many other aspects of Rhodes, they were famous throughout the Greek world.[68]

The physical beauty of Rhodes, apart from the attractiveness of the natural setting, was firmly rooted in the immense wealth of the republic, and it was the merchants that were ultimately responsible for the fine buildings and objects of art that filled the cities of the island. More important than decoration, however, this commercial wealth also provided Rhodes with the means to power far out of proportion to the size of the state. Its tremendous assets allowed the erection of outstanding fortifications, the hiring of mercenaries, and, most crucial, the maintenance of an excellent navy, which was able to provide the island republic with a measure of security generally unknown among the small states of the Hellenistic world. In addition to these direct mechanisms of power, Rhodian commercial activity also furnished the state with no small measure of political influence in the form of the island's key role in the economic life of the eastern Mediterranean. Not only did Rhodes have the resources to support an ad hoc program of foreign aid in the form of gifts and loans, but its dominant position in the carrying trade, especially in the distribution of grain, provided it with economic leverage among the smaller Greek states. Even powerful Egypt had at least to consider the island's interests in its decisions, inasmuch as virtually all the grain exported by the Ptolemies traveled in Rhodian bottoms. For all its wealth and economic importance, Rhodes was of course still no match for one of the great powers, but its economic and naval power made it leader of the second rank of Greek states in the period after Alexander and a potential valuable ally for the constantly warring monarchies.

Besides providing it with access to the pursuit of a meaningful foreign policy in the Hellenistic arena, Rhodes' wealth, because of its mercantile nature, also dictated the broad lines that that policy had to follow. Naturally, the prime objective of Rhodian policy had to be

68. Strabo 14.2.5 (653); Paus. 4.31.5; Dio Chrys. 31.163. On the fortifications see below, chap. 3.

the security and independence of the state, but the continued attainment of the goal rested squarely on the fruits of Rhodian commerce. At the root of Rhodes' independence in the face of the superior might of some of its neighbors was the simple fact that it was an island, but the means of capitalizing on this geographical asset, the fortifications and especially the navy, were afforded by the wealth generated by commercial activity. The maintenance and development of commerce was consequently vital to Rhodes' long-term security, and, as will be seen, concern for these mercantile interests would determine the basic strategic objectives of the island in the eastern Mediterranean, specifically, the suppression of piracy, the promotion of peace, and the preservation of a balance of power among the great monarchies. War and the activities of pirates could of course only be harmful to trade and prosperity, while any serious upset to the strategic balance among the large states, particularly the emergence of a single dominant power, would threaten not only trade but also the security of the republic. Accordingly, after the death of Alexander Rhodes carried on an unrelenting war against pirates while pursuing a course of studied neutrality in order to avoid potentially embarrassing entanglements and preserve independence of action. As the source of so much of Rhodes' wealth, Egypt of course played a special role in the island's strategy, but the goal was to maintain, so far as possible, friendly and thus profitable relations with all its neighbors and in the event of a conflict to apply itself according to its own interests.[69] Until the Roman legions overturned the Hellenistic order of things, this policy proved eminently successful.

69. Polyb. 30.5.8; Diod. 20.81.4.

CHAPTER 3

The Diadochi
and the Great Siege

WHEN word of Alexander's death reached Rhodes in June 323, the Rhodians promptly seized the opportunity created by this unexpected event to eject his garrison and declare the island independent.[1] Presumably they calculated that it would be some time before a new king was securely in power, and that during this initial period of struggle the main contenders would have their attention turned to other, more critical areas. Rhodes would thus, it was hoped, have the time to secure its defenses, at least to the point where an assault on the city might be prohibitively expensive in time and resources for any power that still had other enemies left to deal with. The Rhodians could not, of course, count on the continued fluidity of the political situation, but with the city's defenses in any sort of reasonable shape, the island's independence might stand a good chance of surviving any new power structure that did not preserve Alexander's empire intact.

Though declaring their autonomy, the Rhodians quite wisely decided against joining the general revolt being organized by Athens in the Balkan peninsula. Athens may well have considered Rhodes an important enough ally to send Hyperides himself with the appeal,[2] but a reciprocal view clearly did not prevail on the island. The Rho-

---

1. Diod. 18.8.1.
2. Hyperides' Rhodian oration and embassy to the island (Plut. *Mor.* 850a) are generally dated to 341 (see above, chap. 1), but they might also be dated to 323; see Hauben, *Hist.* 26, 317, n. 54.

dians must have had doubts about the final success of operations against the formidable military strength that Antipater could ultimately mobilize and undoubtedly saw little reason to dissipate their own resources in a struggle that, even if victorious, would not necessarily safeguard the position of the island. It was seemingly more profitable to look only to their own security and hope that their neutrality might buy some advantage from the Macedonians. If the Lamian war should fail, Rhodes would thus be free of embarrassing entanglements; if it succeeded, Rhodes could nevertheless still benefit from the Macedonian defeat in the west. And finally, involvement in the revolt would be an acceptance of Athenian leadership, something that, at least in the economic sphere, most Rhodians would have resisted. In fact, so long as Rhodes was able to defend its own position, the defeat and subjugation of its commercial rival to the northwest would be nothing short of wonderful.[3]

The strategic assumptions of the Rhodian leadership proved to be correct, and for eight years the island was ignored by the great Diadochi in their struggle for power. During this period Rhodes was, however, forced to suffer the attentions of a minor figure, Attalus, brother-in-law and naval commander of the regent Perdiccas. When the latter was killed during the first part of 321, Attalus sailed north with his fleet and a remnant of the army and attacked Caunus, Cnidus, and Rhodes, presumably with the intention of capturing bases astride the main northwest–southeast sea route. Whether or not Attalus was successful against Caunus and Cnidus is not clear, but in any case his fleet was soundly defeated by the Rhodian navy under the nauarch Damaratus, the earliest known holder of that office. This repulse not only preserved the safety of the island but also persuaded Attalus to abandon the sea and turn his attention inland.[4]

This episode demonstrated clearly the Rhodians' intentions of defending themselves, at least against the advances of the less powerful. Attalus was relatively small fry, condemned to death after the fall of Perdiccas, and the Rhodians could thus oppose him without fear of

3. As van Gelder 101 has already noted.
4. Arr. *Success.* F 1.39 (Roos-Wirth); H. Hauben, *Het vlootbevelhebbershap in de vroege Diadochentijd (323–301 voor Christus)* (Brussels 1975) 19–24, 26–27.

bringing upon themselves one of the stronger powers. Whether the republic would or could resist one of the Diadochi was another matter. The navy had proved itself against Attalus' fleet, but skill could carry the Rhodians only so far in the face of the massive resources that might be mobilized for a major assault on the island. There was little doubt that serious pressure would sooner or later be brought to bear, and Attalus' attack only underscored what the Rhodian leadership already knew: the importance of Rhodes to any established naval power in the eastern Mediterranean.

The island could also be important for an aspiring naval power, and in 315 Rhodes' isolation from Diadochian affairs was finally ended when Antigonus decided to challenge Ptolemaic sea power. The ambassadors Moschion and Idomeneus came to the island seeking aid for the Antigonid cause, and the Rhodians agreed to build warships from timber imported from the king's Syrian possessions. As a result of this agreement, ships from Rhodes are subsequently found taking part in Antigonus' siege of Tyre (spring 314–summer 313), brought there, along with contingents from the Hellespont, by the king's nephew Dioscurides. Another Rhodian-built squadron, this one commanded by the Antigonid admiral Theodotas, never reached Tyre; while sailing east from Patara it was ambushed off the Cilician coast by Ptolemaic forces and completely routed.[5] In 312 the Rhodians were further involved in the third Diadochian war when Antigonus obtained from them an alliance and ten warships "for the liberation of the Hellenes." Inasmuch as Diodorus' brief mention of this alliance is sandwiched between the report of the dispatch of Polemaeus' expedition and that of its arrival in Greece, it is likely that the Rhodian squadron joined Polemaeus' fleet, though nothing more is heard of it.[6]

Nothing more is heard of Rhodes, either, until 306, when Anti-

5. Diod. 19.57.4, 58.5, 61.5, 62.7, 64.5–7. Whether or not 62.7–8 is a reiteration of 61.5 (Hauben, *Hist.* 26, 324–25), there were still only two Rhodian contingents, since the ships in 61.5 are not added to those in 62.8 and μεταπεμψάμενος may be read simply as "summoned." The conventional chronology of the period has been convincingly revised by R. M. Errington, "Diodorus Siculus and the Chronology of the Early Diadochoi, 320–311 B.C.," *Hermes* 105 (1977) 478–504.

6. Diod. 19.77.3; *Staats.* III, no. 426.

gonus again sought aid from the island. In the spring of that year he instructed Demetrius to break off his operations in Greece and prepare an assault on Cyprus and Ptolemaic naval strength. Following his father's orders, Demetrius sailed to Caria and from there sent an embassy to Rhodes, requesting the republic to conclude an alliance and supply ships for the war against Ptolemy. Antigonus was probably as much interested in depriving Egypt of possible Rhodian support as he was in gaining it for himself, but in any case the Rhodians refused, and Demetrius sailed for Cyprus.[7] Antigonid reaction to the Rhodian refusal was delayed until the end of the year by the events in the south, but after the failure of the Egyptian expedition the king turned his attention again to the island, determined now to force it into his camp. The potential military distraction involved in coercing Rhodes seemed justified by the rewards: acquisition of the island would not only dramatically improve Antigonus' naval position but also allow him to apply economic pressure to Rhodes' chief business associate, Ptolemy. Antigonus' first move, in fact, was to send a squadron to seize merchantmen on the Rhodes–Egypt run, a maneuver that would obviously injure the Rhodians, but that might be justified to Greek opinion as a measure necessary to prevent the succor of a declared enemy, Egypt. The Rhodians immediately countered by driving off the enemy warships, and Antigonus, undoubtedly prepared for such an eventuality, declared himself unjustly attacked and threatened Rhodes with a siege. Voting the king various honors in hope of appeasing him, the Rhodians sent an embassy asking that they not be compelled to war against Ptolemy "contrary to the treaties," but Antigonus was hardly to be moved by votes of the Rhodian assembly, and in the summer of 305 Demetrius appeared off the island with a huge force. The Rhodians promptly agreed to submit to Antigonus' demands, but they were informed by Demetrius that there were now two further conditions: they must surrender a hundred hostages and allow the Antigonid fleet into their

---

7. Diod. 20.46.5–6, 82.1; Plut. *Demet.* 15.1. As Hauben, *Hist.* 26, 328, points out, these may be two versions (Hieronymus and Zenon?) of the same embassy, but two embassies are possible.

harbors. The Rhodians responded by shutting their gates and preparing for a siege.[8]

In the introduction to his account of the hostilities between Rhodes and Antigonus, Diodorus briefly sketches Rhodian policy and emphasizes that the island had established friendly relations with all the powers, while showing particular favor to Egypt because of the economic connection.[9] Diodorus is unfortunately vague about the precise nature of Rhodes' friendship with the other powers, nor does he indicate when these pacts (if such they were) were established. Further, it is not immediately clear that this policy can be squared with Rhodian actions in the decade before 305, and the suspicion is aroused that Diodorus' sources are guilty of extrapolating third-century policy back into the fourth. And if this is indeed the case, can any sort of consistent policy be found behind Rhodes' activities in the years before the siege?

Diodorus makes no mention of any treaty arrangements behind the shipbuilding deal of 315, but it has nevertheless been suggested that elements of the Rhodian fleet actually took part in the Tyre operations.[10] This seems extremely unlikely. The contingents from Rhodes were commanded by Antigonid officers, something unthinkable for the Rhodian navy, and they are nowhere identified with the ethnic adjective or noun generally employed by Diodorus to indicate nationality. It is easier to understand the arrangement made between Rhodes and Antigonus in 315 as being essentially a business deal with political overtones, an agreement by which the Rhodians, for reasons discussed below, contracted to supply arms to the king. A formal treaty is certainly possible but not at all necessary, and Diodorus does not mention one. By the same token, some sort of neutrality clause regarding Rhodes is also possible but unnecessary, since the Rhodians' action was umambiguous. They were building ships for Antigonus and nothing more, and Ptolemy and his allies would have to judge them on that basis.

8. Diod. 20.82.2–3: παρὰ τὰς συνθήκας; Paus. 1.6.6.
9. Diod. 20.81.2–4; see also Polyb. 30.5.8.
10. Hauben, *Hist.* 26, 326–27; the only serious flaw in a good article.

It was equally clear to everyone, however, that those vessels being constructed in the Rhodian yards would be used against Ptolemy, and the question remains: why, if Rhodes had a special economic regard for Egypt, did it undertake this action, and why especially at a time when Antigonus was weak at sea and no direct threat? It is true that Rhodian-Egyptian relations were not as developed in 315 as they would be a decade later, but though this fact would help to explain why the Rodians might be reluctant to cross Ptolemy later, it hardly explains why they would do so now.[11] It should of course not be forgotten that Rhodes was a commercial state, always keeping an eye out for economic gain, and it is very probable that, foreign policy aside, the island did reap a profit from the deal. Almost certainly it imposed its customary duties on the imported timber, and it is hard to believe the completed ships were delivered free of charge. But for all that, it is unlikely that a successful business deal, even of this magnitude, would be sufficient cause for the Rhodians to stray from the strictest neutrality and supply warships to Egypt's enemy.

The major factor behind Rhodes' concessions to Antigonus was unquestionably fear. It was not, however, fear for the safety of the island, which the fleetless monarch could not at the moment seriously threaten, but rather concern for two more vulnerable areas. One was the incorporated Peraea, that part of the state which lay across the straights on the mainland and which was open to assault by Antigonid forces in Greater Phrygia and Lycia; the other was Syria-Palestine, where the Rhodians had trading interests.[12] In both regions Antigonus could with little effort apply pressure to the island, and while the occupation of the Peraea and the closing of the Syrian markets would hardly force the Rhodians to their knees, they would nevertheless hurt. Besides, a little threat was all that was needed, since it was only a little concession that Antigonus desired. By building the ships the Rhodians could avoid serious trouble with a powerful neighbor while probably making a profit, and they must have sus-

---

11. Ibid. 335. His other explanation, the disastrous flood of 316 (Diod. 19.45.2–8), holds water no better than the city walls did.

12. See above, chap. 2; Polyaen. 4.6.16 (Antigonus' proclamation to Rhodian merchants in Pamphylia, Cilicia, and Syria).

pected they could do so without really jeopardizing their position with Ptolemy. They knew that the Egyptian monarch was a realist and a hardheaded businessman, and that two important facts could hardly escape his attention: the importance of Rhodes to the Egyptian economy and the potential importance of the island and its fleet to Antigonus. They must have calculated that even if Ptolemy had little sympathy for their difficulties, he could clearly see that far worse things could happen than the Rhodian yards' building some warships for his enemy. Ptolemy had already shown himself to be ever the rational strategist in the struggle of the Diadochi, and it would have seemed to the Rhodians extremely unlikely that he would risk any action that might really drive them into the enemy camp, especially as they were only acting under pressure from Antigonus.

The situation in 312 is similar. Antigonus now controlled most of Syria-Palestine and Asia Minor, including Caria, and his possession of a large fleet and his control of the Asiatic side of the Hellespont threatened also Rhodes' access to the Black Sea. Once again the pressure was on the island and the Rhodians took the line of least resistance, though undoubtedly they were increasingly concerned over the growing Antigonid ascendancy, especially at sea. This time the monarch required an alliance, and though Diodorus does not specify the nature of the agreement, he does say that the ten Rhodian ships were for the liberation of the Greeks, and the circumstances make it almost certain that the alliance spoke only in those terms. The fact that the Rhodians contributed only ten vessels indicates that Antigonus' goal was the neutralization of the island rather than its serious support, and this goal would have been achieved by an alliance that simply committed Rhodes to the liberation of the Greek cities. Such would satisfy Antigonus' needs without unduly disturbing the neutral stance of the Rhodians, who could claim that they were bound not to a particular monarch but to a policy—one in fact which suited Rhodian aims and which would become a facet of their own foreign policy. Strictly speaking, of course, Rhodes had surrendered its neutrality, since the alliance committed it to fight against Cassander, who was an ally of Egypt. As in 315, however, Ptolemy could appreciate the position the Rhodians were in and indeed be glad that they had not been pressed to do more than contribute a token force for Antigonus' campaign in Greece, which after all injured Ptolemy's ally more than himself.

There is no problem at all in understanding Rhodes' actions in 306–5, and it is unnecessary to postulate stronger ties with Ptolemy in order to explain why the republic should resist now, when Antigonus was far stronger and Ptolemy far weaker than in 315 and 312. Rhodian-Egyptian relations probably were in fact better, especially since the successful Ptolemaic campaign in Caria and Lycia in 309/8,[13] but the crucial fact behind Rhodes' refusal was that this time it was being asked to participate directly in a war against Ptolemy. The Rhodians would not do so unless serious pressure were applied, and when Antigonus applied that pressure by threatening to besiege the city, they acquiesced. Egypt was special to the republic, but certainly not worth its ruin. The final decision to resist had nothing to do with Egypt. When Demetrius demanded access to the Rhodian harbors, the question ceased to be one of foreign policy and became one of basic survival, since an Antigonid presence in the harbors meant an end of Rhodian independence. All other considerations were minor compared to this, and the Rhodians were ready to fight to prevent a return to the misery of foreign domination.

Less easy to understand is the precise nature of Rhodes' legal relationship with its neighbors. The language used by Diodorus in his sketch of Rhodian policy suggests strongly that Rhodes had established actual pacts of friendship with all the powers and that the special regard for Egypt was not embodied in any formal agreement.[14] The most likely time for the establishment of these friend-

---

13. Diod. 20.27.1–3; J. Seibert, *Untersuchungen zur Geschichte Ptolemaios' I* (Munich 1969) 158–86. It is tempting to see a connection between the new lower-weight Ptolemaic silver and the Rhodian standard (as do Rostovtzeff I, 394; Hauben, *Hist.* 26, 337, n. 34), but the fact remains that the new Ptolemaic standard was still heavier than the Rhodian; see rather E. Will, *Histoire politique du monde hellénistique (323–30 av. J.-C.)* (Nancy 1966–67) I, 155–60.

14. The two key phrases are: πρὸς ἅπαντας κατ' ἰδίαν συντιθεμένη τὴν φιλίαν and πρὸς πάντας . . . συντεθειμένοι τὴν φιλίαν. That συντίθεμαι τὴν φιλίαν is a technical term for concluding a treaty is demonstrated by numerous passages: *Syll.*[1] 171 (*Staats.* III, no. 492); Polyb. 7.9.12 (*Staats.* III, no. 528); Diod. 16.87.3 (*Staats.* III, no. 402); Diod. 20.46.1 (*Staats.* III, no. 446); App. *Syr.* 55 (*Staats.* III, no. 441); Plut. *Pelop.* 29.6 (*Staats.* II, no. 212).

ship treaties appears to be at the time of or immediately following the common peace that ended the third Diadochian war in 311. This would have been the perfect opportunity for the Rhodians to re-establish friendly relations with all the warring states, and they did in fact mention a common peace in their first refusal to Antigonus, suggesting at least a temporal link.[15] But the evidence does not permit much beyond conjecture, and the whole question is relatively unimportant anyway, because whatever the exact nature of Rhodes' diplomatic agreements, its motivations and policy in the years that led up to the great siege are perfectly clear. It may be true that the policy statement of Diodorus 20.81 is an extrapolation from the third century, but with the exception of the statements regarding naval affairs, it nevertheless also describes the island in the last decades of the fourth century.[16] Given the circumstances in which Rhodes found itself, it acted quite consistently in these years and attempted to maintain friendly relations with all the powers, while showing a special regard for Egypt. That Rhodes was on occasion forced by events to depart momentarily from a position of absolute neutrality hardly invalidates this notion, any more than does the island's participation in a number of wars, including one against Egypt, in the next century.

Once the Rhodians had refused his ultimatum, Demetrius gathered his forces at Loryma, in the Peraea, and prepared for the siege. He had 200 warships of varying sizes and more than 170 auxiliary vessels for the transport of almost 40,000 infantry and an unknown number of mounted troops. This regular force was joined by a host of pirates and by almost a thousand craft belonging to merchants and others drawn by the hope of rich plunder.[17] With these ships assembled into a kind of grand naval parade, designed to undermine the morale of the

15. Diod. 20.46.6. See Hauben, *Hist.* 26, 332–34.

16. The importance of the Rhodian navy is exaggerated for the fourth century. Demetrius' pirate allies were not responding to Rhodian police activity, but rather were after plunder; Diod. 20.82.5 says as much.

17. Diod. 20.82.4–5. Diodorus' account of the siege must be based on a Rhodian source, possibly Zenon, to reflect such details of events within the city as acts of the prytanes; see W. Nietzold, *Die Überlieferung der Diadochengeschichte bis zur Schlacht von Ipsos,* diss. (Dresden 1904) 40–46; Seibert, *Untersuch.* 81–82.

defenders, Demetrius crossed to the island and disembarked his troops a little to the south of the city. While the irregular forces pillaged the island, the army ravaged the suburbs and from trees felled in the neighborhood constructed a fortified camp just out of missile range of the walls. A safe harbor was then created for the fleet, probably in the gulf of Ialysus, and protected by a rampart.[18] During these operations Demetrius demonstrated his respect for the arts by taking measures for the protection of the painter Protogenes, who was caught in the suburbs applying the final touches to his masterpiece "Ialysus"—while Ialysus itself was left to the tender mercies of Demetrius' irregular allies.[19]

Meanwhile, the Rhodians, perhaps only now really comprehending that the final showdown was upon them, looked to the defenses of the city. Artillery and other equipment was repaired and strengthened, and various measures were taken to put the population in fighting trim. Those aliens who were unwilling to join in the defense were expelled as unnecessary mouths and possible threats, while provisions were made for the children of the fallen and for the emancipation and enfranchisement of slaves who fought for the city. A count revealed about 6,000 citizens and 1,000 aliens able to bear arms, but this number must refer strictly to free males of prime fighting age, probably of hoplite status, who formed the military heart of the city's defenses. Backing up these troops would be thousands of other able-bodied Rhodians, who would not only provide the all-important logistical support but also help man the warships and serve as light-armed troops.[20]

18. Diod. 20.83.1–4. The camp had to be south of the city as there was not enough room on the north point for the camp or for an advance on a four-stade front (Diod. 20.91.8); see Map. 1. The expedition probably landed on the west coast, in the gulf of Ialysus; this is where the Turks landed in A.D. 1480.

19. Plut. *Demet.* 22.2–3, *Mor.* 183a–b; Gell. *NA* 15.31.3–5; Pliny *HN* 7.38.126, 35.36.104–6.

20. Diod. 20.84.2–5. The fortifications of 305 were for the most part pre-Alexandrian and not the postearthquake works praised by later authors and described by Philon of Byzantium; see below, chap. 4. Among the engineers on the Rhodian side were Dionysius of Alexandria, who developed the repeating catapult (Philon *Bel.* 73); Diognetus of Rhodes; and Callias of Aradus (Vitr. 10.16.3–8). The women of the city gave their hair for torsion instruments, if Front. 1.7.3–4 and Psd.-Arist. 43 (809 D) refer to this siege.

In the midst of organizing the city for the siege, the Rhodians also took some offensive action. Envoys were dispatched to seek aid from Antigonus' enemies, Ptolemy, Cassander, and Lysimachus, and three swift raiders were sent out to create havoc among the shipping scattered about the island. The appeals to the monarchs brought nothing for the moment, but the warships, appearing unexpectedly, sank or burned many merchantmen and returned with prisoners for ransom. By arrangement with Demetrius, these captives, like any Rhodians taken by Demetrius, would be ransomed back at the rate of 1,000 drachmas for a free man and 500 for a slave, an agreement seemingly more beneficial to the Rhodians, since it allowed them to regain valuable manpower. Antigonus, on the other hand, promised at the outset of the siege to guarantee the safety of Rhodian merchants and sailors caught in Antigonid ports, so long as they did not attempt to return home, a measure clearly intended to aid in choking off the movement of men and matériel into the city.[21]

Demetrius' first assault was directed against the harbor area, since he realized as well as the Rhodians that the ultimate fate of the republic would probably depend on whether or not the harbors could be captured and the city cut off from outside help.[22] To this end two four-story towers and two large penthouses containing artillery were built and mounted on cargo ships, and a floating boom was prepared to protect these machines from ramming. At the same time a number of light craft were decked over and equipped with artillery and Cretan archers and immediately sent into the harbor to harass with missile fire the men working on the defenses in that area. The Rhodians meanwhile, besides increasing the height of the harbor walls, also placed penthouses and artillery on the mole, on ships near the boom of the small harbor, and on cargo vessels at anchor in the large harbor.[23]

Rough seas thwarted Demetrius' first attempt to bring his floating siege engines into the harbor, but shortly afterward he used the cover of darkness to seize the end of the mole in the large harbor and land

21. Diod. 20.84.1, 5–6; Polyaen. 4.6.16.
22. Diod. 20.88.1.
23. Diod. 20.85.1–4. Part of the problem in following Diodorus' narrative is that he is not careful about identifying to which mole and to which harbor he is referring.

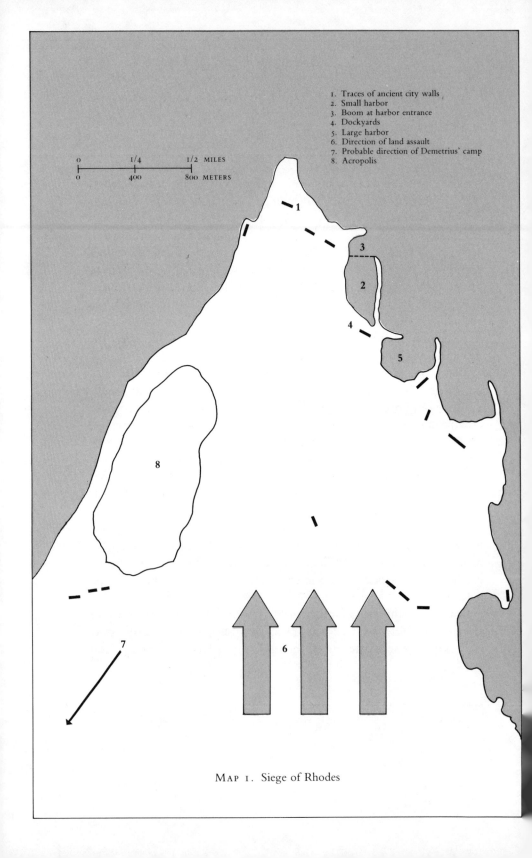

1. Traces of ancient city walls
2. Small harbor
3. Boom at harbor entrance
4. Dockyards
5. Large harbor
6. Direction of land assault
7. Probable direction of Demetrius' camp
8. Acropolis

0   1/4   1/2 MILES

0   400   800 METERS

MAP 1. Siege of Rhodes

artillery and a force of 400 men, who immediately fortified their beachhead, only 500 feet from the city walls. At daybreak the big engines and missile-firing boats were brought into the harbor and concentrated their fire on the Rhodian fortifications on the mole, destroying some of their machines and severely damaging the wall. Reinforcements from the city enabled the Rhodians to defend the position, however, and after a day of heavy fighting and causalties Demetrius towed his engines out of the harbor, unsuccessfully pursued by Rhodian fireships. For the next six days the operation against the harbor continued, together with a diversionary land attack, but though the harbor fortifications were breached and the walls scaled at several points, the Rhodians were successful in repelling the assault. With heavy casualties and damage to his machines, Demetrius finally withdrew to repair and regroup, leaving the defenders to rebuild their damaged defenses.[24]

After a week Demetrius renewed his assault on the harbor, pounding the wall with his artillery once again and attacking the anchored Rhodian warships with fire bolts. With the situation becoming critical, the prytanes decided on a desperate action and sent out three ships with picked crews under the nauarch Execestus. Aided probably by the surprise caused by such a bold tactic, the warships were able to penetrate the rain of missiles, break through the boom, and sink two of the large siege machines. Incredibly, two of the ships actually managed to escape the swarm of enemy vessels that surrounded them, and though Execestus and the trierarch of the third vessel were captured with the ship, most of the crew swam to safety. The favor of Helios notwithstanding, the incident dramatically reveals the great disparity in skill between the Rhodians and Demetrius' sailors.[25] Though undoubtedly impressed, Demetrius was not daunted and constructed a new machine, three times the size of those that had been sunk. While this machine was being towed to the harbor, however, a storm blew up from the south and swamped it, and the Rhodians immediately seized the opportunity to sally forth

24. Diod. 20.86.1–87.4.
25. Diod. 20.88.1–6. A fire bolt was apparently a cylinder filled with oil or naphtha. On Execestus, see Hauben, *Vloot.* 34–36; his title of nauarch is undoubtedly correct, as the passage goes back to a Rhodian source.

against the troops on the mole. As Demetrius could not reinforce the position because of the weather, the 400 men were ultimately compelled to surrender, and the mole was again in Rhodian hands. Topping off this success was the arrival soon afterward of help in the form of 150 soldiers from Knossos and more than 500 from Ptolemy, some of whom were Rhodian mercenaries.[26]

It was now early 304, and Demetrius decided to switch his main attack to the land walls, constructing for this purpose the "helepolis," one of the largest mobile siege machines ever built. Designed by the architect Epimachus of Athens, the wheeled pyramidal tower was almost 150 feet high, armored and divided into nine stories loaded with artillery that fired through shuttered ports. At the same time numerous penthouses and covered galleries were built to carry rams and protect those filling the moat, while crews from the fleet cleared a space four stades wide before the walls. In all some 30,000 men were involved in these preparations, which would allow Demetrius to assault the fortifications along a front covering seven towers and six curtains.[27] The wall would be shaken by mines, rams, and artillery in the helepolis and smaller machines, while the superior height of the helepolis would allow a devastating covering fire to be directed against the Rhodian ramparts.

All of this activity was of course observed by the Rhodians, who took two countermeasures. Preparing for the worst, they tore down the encircling wall of the theater, adjacent houses, and even some temples in order to obtain the material to build a second wall inside that area of the fortifications being threatened by Demetrius.[28] In a more positive vein, three squadrons of three ships each were sent out in different directions to raid enemy shipping, and all met with tremendous success. The group under Damophilus sailed to Carpathus, where it sank or burned a number of enemy vessels, and returned to Rhodes with captured crewmen and several merchantmen laden with grain for Demetrius' army. The three triemioliai under Menedemus

26. Diod. 20.88.7–9.

27. Diod. 20.91.1–8; Plut. *Demet.* 21.1–2; Vitr. 10.16.4; Athen. Mech. 27.2; Amm. Marc. 23.4.10; Athen. 5.206d. On the helepolis, see also E. W. Marsden, *Greek and Roman Artillery,* Technical Treatises (Oxford 1971) 84–85.

28. Diod. 20.93.1.

headed for Patara, on the Lycian coast, and there burned one vessel and captured many merchantmen loaded with provisions for the army and a quadrireme carrying a royal outfit from Demetrius' wife, Phila; the freighters were sent to Rhodes and the robes to Ptolemy. The third squadron, under Amyntas, cruised the islands and sank or captured a good number of cargo ships carrying war matériel, returning home with a special prize of eleven engineers noted for their skill in artillery fabrication.[29] The complete success of these commerce raiders can be explained by two facts: at no time did Demetrius have enough warships to attempt to blockade the island and protect the extensive shipping necessary to supply his army, and at this particular time a sizable portion of his crews was at work on preparations for the land assault. At the same time, however, though the Rhodians apparently had little trouble slipping ships out of the harbor, only during lulls in the siege could they spare the manpower necessary for the crews of even a small number of warships, and consequently commerce raiders were sent out on only two occasions.

While all this activity was taking place, Demetrius' sappers were busy tunneling under the walls and preparing mines; but the Rhodians were informed by a deserter and quickly answered with countermines to foil the enemy operation. The mines did, however, provide Demetrius a channel of communication into the city, and through them his men attempted to bribe the mercenary Athenagoras, guard commander at the Rhodian end. But Athenagoras only pretended treachery, captured a high-ranking Macedonian, and was rewarded for his loyalty with a golden crown and five talents of silver.[30] A second incident that occurred during the calm before the assault says something about the character of the Rhodian democracy. It was proposed at a meeting of the assembly that the statues of Antigonus and Demetrius erected before the siege be torn down; but rather than receiving the overwhelming approval one might have expected given the circumstances, the motion was met with anger and its sponsors were censured. Keeping the statues and other hon-

29. Diod. 20.93.2–5; Plut. *Demet.* 22.1. On the commanders, see Hauben, *Vloot.* 9–11, 24–26, 69–70. Damophilus' ships are called *phylakides,* which were probably light fast craft similar to the triemioliai.
30. Diod. 20.94.1–5.

ors, it was thought, would remind Antigonus and the world of the injustice of his war against his friends and possibly also ease Rhodes' situation should the city be taken. Such sober considerations regarding a potentially emotional issue are not characteristic of democratic assemblies under great pressure.[31]

Once the construction was done, Demetrius positioned his machines and forces for an all-out assault. The helepolis was stationed in the center of the cleared space and flanked by eight penthouses that would protect sappers and two mammoth movable sheds that housed rams over a hundred feet long. In order to strain Rhodian manpower as much as possible, infantry was assigned to attack other sections of the walls, and the fleet was positioned for a renewed offensive against the harbors. When these dispositions had been made, the signal was given and the city was assaulted from all sides. Before anything of consequence was achieved, however, an embassy from Cnidus showed up seeking a truce and a renewal of negotiations, and Demetrius broke off his attack. For several days the envoys shuttled back and forth in an attempt at arbitration, but the negotiations failed, probably foundering on the issue of access to the harbors, which was completely nonnegotiable so far as the Rhodians were concerned. Demetrius resumed his assault, and soon one of the strongest towers and an entire section of curtain were knocked down, throwing the Rhodians back on their second wall.[32]

At this critical point Rhodian morale was lifted by the arrival of help from Ptolemy in the form of a large number of cargo ships loaded with provisions. A favorable wind had aided the freighters in running the blockade, such as it was, and they were able to deliver to the city 300,000 artabai of grain and legumes. Cassander also sent the Rhodians 10,000 medimni of barley, and Lysimachus delivered 40,000 medimni each of barley and wheat.[33]

31. Diod. 20.93.6–7.

32. Diod. 20.95.1–5. For a detailed description of the ram built by Hegetor of Byzantium, see Athen, Mech. 21.2–26.1; Vitr. 10.15.2–7. An embassy from Cnidus is easily understood; with its territory adjoining the Rhodian Peraea and its economy employing the Rhodian standard since 400 (see Head 615–16), Cnidus was completely in the Rhodian economic sphere and must have suffered considerable economic difficulties during the siege.

33. Diod. 20.96.1–3.

Heartened by the arrival of the food supplies, the Rhodians decided to strike back at Demetrius' machines. Collecting a large supply of fire-bearing missiles and bringing as many of their machines as possible within range, they chose a moonless night to lay down a tremendous artillery barrage. While the smaller machines kept up a devastating antipersonnel fire, the larger ballistae and catapults directed a hail of balls and fire bolts at the helepolis, dislodging some of the iron plating and starting several fires. Surprised by the sudden attack and fearing for the safety of the machine, Demetrius was compelled to have it dragged back out of range of the walls. The following day he had the Rhodian missiles collected in order to estimate the resources of the defenders and was amazed to find that during the relatively short time of the barrage the Rhodians had fired more than 800 fire-bearing missiles and some 1,500 catapult bolts.[34]

The helepolis was not destroyed, but the damage suffered by it and the other machines and the casualties inflicted on Demetrius' forces bought the Rhodians time to repair their own defenses. A third wall was constructed behind the damaged sections of the city fortifications, and a deep ditch was dug behind the fallen portions to hinder any sudden assault by the enemy. At the same time the opportunity presented by the lull to send out another group of raiders was not ignored, and Amyntas was ordered to the Peraea with a squadron of fast ships. There he captured a number of merchantmen loaded with grain and three strong *aphraktoi* led by Demetrius' ally the archpirate Timocles, and under the cover of darkness these prizes were led into Rhodes.[35]

Demetrius had meanwhile repaired his machines, and once more he assaulted the Rhodian defenses, this time battering down two adjoining curtains with his rams. The Rhodians, however, fought fiercely for the intervening tower, and in a series of hard-fought encounters the strategos Ananias and a good many of his soldiers were slain. Meanwhile a second convoy arrived from Egypt, bringing another 300,000 artabai of provisions and, to the relief of the

---

34. Diod. 20.96.3–97.2. Vitr. 10.16.7 does not fit into Diodorus' narrative and is unlikely.

35. Diod. 20.97.3–6; see Hauben, *Vloot.* 106.

weary Rhodians, 1,500 soldiers under the command of one Antigonus. Demetrius, on the other hand, was visited by an embassy of
more than fifty envoys from Athens and other Greek cities who
persuaded him to establish another truce. But these negotiators were
no more successful than those from Cnidus, and after a time the siege
was resumed.[36]

Demetrius now decided on a night attack through the breaches in
the walls, and having prepared the rest of his forces for a general
assault, he stationed a picked group of 1,500 for the push into the city.
At the signal the assault group stormed through the breaches and past
the moat. Overcoming Rhodian resistance, they were able to penetrate into the city and occupy the area of the theater. This surprise
intrusion, coming under the cover of darkness, threw the city into
confusion, as Demetrius undoubtedly had hoped, but the prytanes
were prepared for such a crisis. Ordering the men on the fortifications
to hold their posts, they attacked the intruders with their emergency
reserve and the troops from Egypt. By dawn the assault group had
been contained and apparently cut off, and though Demetrius
launched a general attack by land and sea, his men in the city were
doomed. The fighting around the theater was long and bloody, and
many men fell on both sides, including the prytanis Damoteles and
the two enemy commanders, Alcimus and Mantias. In the end only a
handful of the intruders were able to escape back out of the city, and
Demetrius called off the assault.[37]

Without realizing it, the Rhodians had won the siege, for though
Demetrius began to prepare for another assault, he soon received
instructions from his father to obtain the best terms possible and
break off the operation. Antigonus could not wait any longer for
Rhodes to fall; the situation in Greece was deteriorating rapidly and
Seleucus was threatening from the east. Ptolemy, meanwhile, had

36. Diod. 20.97.7–98.3. According to Plut. *Demet.* 22.4 the Athenian embassy
came at the end of the siege and provided the pretext Demetrius was seeking.

37. Diod. 20.98.4–9; Plut. *Demet.* 21.4. An immediate question arises from this
section of Diodorus: what happened to the third wall if it was the second that was
breached before the helepolis was pulled away? It must be assumed that if the walls
were in fact raised one behind the other, as Diodorus' narrative indicates, the third
wall, possibly hastily and poorly built, was breached during the final assault that
carried Demetrius' men into the city.

promised the Rhodians more grain and 3,000 troops, but had advised them to make peace should Demetrius offer acceptable terms. Like Cassander and Lysimachus, Ptolemy had supported the Rhodians partly because every day that Demetrius was tied up at Rhodes was another day his massive resources could not be used against Egypt or Greece. That his support was somewhat slow in coming and was limited mostly to provisions can be explained by Egypt's momentary weakness after Salamis and Ptolemy's fear of risking troops in a beleaguered city before he had some idea of the odds in his favor.[38] In the final analysis, however, it was utterly crucial to Ptolemy that Rhodes not become an Antigonid naval base, and it was undoubtedly this fear that led him to advise the acceptance of reasonable terms, by which he clearly meant any settlement that would guarantee the island's autonomy. The Rhodians had demonstrated well their capacity to resist, but in recent months Demetrius had come perilously close to overcoming the city's defenses, and Ptolemy could not take the risk of its falling. Knowing that the pressures were growing for Antigonus also, he consequently advised a settlement in the hope that Demetrius would give in on the autonomy issue; but should Demetrius refuse, Ptolemy was prepared to throw several thousand soldiers into the city, so vital to him was its survival. With the major parties thus inclined, the arrival of a peace embassy from the Aetolian League served as a catalyst for negotiations and a settlement was reached. Rhodes would be autonomous and ungarrisoned and enjoy its revenues, but would be an ally of Antigonus, except when he went to war against Ptolemy. To guarantee this arrangement, the Rhodians would surrender to Demetrius a hundred hostages to be chosen by him, officeholders excepted.[39]

And so after a year-long siege the Rhodians rejoiced. Honors and prizes were awarded to the fallen and the brave, and those slaves who had proved themselves in the battles were granted freedom and citizenship. The walls and the theater and other damaged buildings were repaired, and in accordance with a vow, the temples that had been

38. Seibert, *Untersuch.* 229–30.

39. Diod. 20.99.1–3; Plut. *Demet.* 21.4; *Mar. Par.* B23 (= *FGH* 239); *Staats.* III, no. 442. The hundred hostages were freed when Lysimachus' general Prepalaus took Ephesus in 302 (Diod. 20.107.4).

cannibalized for building materials were reconstructed on a grander scale. As for their benefactors, Cassander and Lysimachus were honored with statues, but for Ptolemy there was something more. A mission was sent to the oracle of Zeus-Ammon at Siwah to ask if it would be right to honor the Egyptian monarch as a god, and receiving a positive reply, the Rhodians established a cult of Ptolemy Soter. A sacred precinct, the Ptolemaeum, was built in the city, and a yearly festival was to be celebrated in honor of the new deity.[40] The average Rhodian did not, of course, seriously believe that Ptolemy was divine, but in a very real sense the monarch warranted the epithet "Soter." Rhodes' survival of the siege was attributable first to its excellent defenses, the will of its people, and Demetrius' failure to close the harbors, but these advantages might well have been for naught were it not for the aid from Egypt, limited though it was. It may be that the Rhodians could have captured enough supplies to sustain themselves and could have won the battle of the theater alone, but Diodorus' Rhodian sources certainly suggest that the food and soldiers sent by Ptolemy played a crucial role. The Rhodians apparently believed this to be the case and honored the king according to the latest fashion.

Demetrius had been thwarted by Rhodes' excellent fortifications and even more so by the unusual quantity and quality of the city's artillery, which provided the Rhodians with a crucial means of defense against the enemy siege machines. The key element in Demetrius' failure, however, was his apparent inability to close the Rhodian harbors and cut the city off from the outside world, something that a naval blockade, as was amply demonstrated, could not do. Demetrius fully realized as much at the onset of the siege, but after his failure to storm the harbor fortifications he switched the focus of attack to the landward walls, leaving the Rhodians free to

40. Diod. 20.100.1–4; Paus. 1.8.6. Athen. 15.696f–97a (= *FGH* 515 F9) mentions a paean sung in Ptolemy's honor. A Lindian inscription from the end of the third century names a priest of the cult (M. Segré, "Epigraphica VII. Il culto rodio di Alessandro e dei Tolemei," *Bull. Soc. Arch. Alex.* 34 [1941] 29–31). Ptolemy also found his way into the legends preserved in the Lindus Temple Chronicle (D. III.95–115); see C. Habicht. *Gottmenschentum und griechische Städte* (Munich 1956) 109–10, 233–34.

import critical food supplies, both from their allies and through commerce raiding. Why Demetrius acted as he did is not easy to understand, since it is reasonable to suppose that the energy and resources expended in the land assault could have meant success in shutting the ports; at the very least he might have closed the harbor mouths with blockships and rubble fill if need be. It might have been the increasingly inclement weather, which in fact thwarted his last assault on the harbor, or it may be that, aware of the importance of time, he decided to try for a quick victory against the landward walls, where more of his tremendous resources could be brought to bear for a decisive blow. But though he achieved some successes there, the progress was gradual, and the Rhodians, supplied and reinforced through their harbors, showed every sign of being able to keep pace and counter each enemy advance.

The siege of Rhodes turned out to be one of the greatest failures of Antigonid foreign policy, gaining the One-eye nothing but an ironic enhancement of his son's reputation as "the Besieger." With his unprovoked attack on a small and hitherto friendly state, Antigonus seriously undermined his credibility as liberator of the Greeks, and his embarrassing failure to capture the city after a year could only mean a decline in military prestige. Far worse, not only had Antigonus lost opportunities for more profitable employment of Demetrius' forces, but during the year of the siege he also suffered serious setbacks in Greece and Asia, having in effect provided his opponents with something of a grace period. To show for all this the king now had a qualified alliance with Rhodes, which was less than what the Rhodians had been willing to submit to before the siege, and this alliance, so expensive to Antigonus, would never bring his cause a single ship or man.

For the Rhodians the siege was an unqualified triumph. They had defended their independence against the strongest of the Diadochi and had compelled Antigonus to accept their special relationship with Ptolemy, demonstrating to the world and to themselves the viability of their policy of neutrality. At the same time the siege revealed to the Rhodians that although they could defend themselves against a first-class power, they could not do so completely alone and must depend on other first-class powers for support, in the form of either direct aid

or "second front" operations. Rhodian policymakers would consequently have to concern themselves with the ebb and flow of power
among the big states and attempt, within the bounds of the republic's
other goals, to influence events toward the maintenance of some
balance among the monarchies. Rhodes also emerged from the siege
with the foundation of an international reputation that would grow
rapidly in the following years. Its heroic stand against the superior
strength of Demetrius, together with its nonaggressive policies, established the republic as potential leader of the small states of the
Aegean, and in the course of the next century its developing position
as peacemaker and defender of Greek autonomy would make that
leadership actual.

The siege was in a sense a turning point for Rhodes, marking the
end of its trial period as an independent state. Its defenses having been
tested, its autonomy and independence of action now seemed secure
for the foreseeable future, while its navy showed every sign of developing into an efficient instrument of defense and policy. The dramatic growth of its commerce and wealth continued, epitomized perhaps
by its trade discussion with Rome about 306, the first known official
contact between a Greek state and the Italian republic.[41] Appropri-
ately, with the money realized from the sale of Demetrius' siege train
the Rhodians began construction in 304 of a monument befitting their
emergence as the strongest of the second-rank Hellenistic powers.
Built by Chares of Lindus, this was a colossal bronze statue of
Helios. When completed eleven years later, it towered more than a
hundred feet above the city. Standing beside the harbors that were at
the heart of Rhodes' prosperity and watching over the coming and
going of the ships that were its strength, the bronze god was a perfect
symbol of the island republic as it entered the third century and the
days of its greatness.[42]

41. See appendix I.
42. Philo Byz. *de Sep. Orb. Spec.* 4.1–6; Strabo 14.2.5 (652); Pliny *HN* 34.18.41;
Plut. *Demet.* 20.5, *Mor.* 183b; Vitr. 10.16.8; H. Maryon, "The Colossus of Rhodes,"
JHS 76 (1956) 68–86; D. Haynes, "Philo of Byzantium and the Colossus of Rhodes,"
JHS 77 (1957) 311–12; P. Moreno, "Cronologia del Colosso di Rodi," *Arch. Class.*
25–26 (1973–74) 453–63. The date is obtained by counting back 66 and 12 years
(Greek style) from the earthquake of 228 (see below, chap. 4).

CHAPTER 4

The Third Century

THE increasing political and economic stabilization of the Greek world after Ipsus could only enhance the position of Rhodes, and the third century saw the steady rise in the republic's power and prestige, leading ultimately to its greatest triumphs and final tragedy in the second century. Unfortunately, the third century is also the darkest period of Greek history since the early Archaic age, and knowledge of Rhodian affairs is limited to a few scraps of evidence in the literary and archaeological records. When these scattered clues are arranged and examined, it is possible to construct only the barest framework of the island's history as a basis for speculation on the general course of Rhodes' development during those years.

The first quarter of the century yields isolated references to Rhodians and Rhodian activity. Three Rodians are found in the service of the monarchs, hardly a surprising fact considering the constant demand for military and administrative talent and the Rhodian tradition of condottieri. The first, Nicagoras, son of Aristarchus, appears in 299 as an ambassador of Demetrius and Seleucus to the city of Ephesus, where he was granted Ephesian citizenship and various other honors. The second is Telesphorus, a friend of Lysimachus, who probably served the king in a military capacity, though this presumption is nowhere stated. What is known is that for some slight Lysimachus had Telesphorus mutilated and kept in a cage, and because of this episode the Rhodian survived in literature as an example of royal cruelty and the strength of the human spirit. The final example, Theodotas, was unquestionably a mercenary, and according to Lucian he was the tactician responsible for Antiochus' victory over the Galatians in 275.[1] It is hardly possible to draw any important conclusions from these notices of Rhodians in foreign service, but they do demonstrate what might be expected: because of Rhodes' limited military activities, it still had talent to export, despite its rapid growth.

The second group of references from this period illustrates various aspects of Rhodian activity and policy. About 300 the Ephesians honored the Rhodian Agathocles, son of Hegemon, for importing into the city 14,000 *hekteis* (about 3,300 bushels) of grain, and this same merchant was also honored by Arcesine on Amorgus, probably for another grain deal.[2] Agathocles is thus a perfect example of Rhodes' already well-developed position as middleman in the Aegean grain trade. At about the same time Rhodes is found lending money to exiles from Priene for their struggle against Hiero, under whose tyrannical rule their city was suffering.[3] Such an act not only helped build for the republic a growing reputation as an enemy of oppression, but also guaranteed its merchants increased influence in Priene once the tyrant was removed. In the same vein, sometime in the period 278–72 100 talents were lent to Argos for the improvement of its walls and cavalry; this loan helped, at least, to secure Argive autonomy, whether the threat came from Antigonus, Pyrrhus, or Ptolemy.[4] It was this kind of aid that made Rhodian propaganda credible, in contrast to the declarations of the monarchs, for whom

---

1. Nicagoras: *OGIS* 10; Olshausen no. 76; Telesphorus: Sen. *de Ira* 3.17.3–4, *Epist.* 70.6; Athen. 14.616c; Plut. *Mor.* 606b; Theodotas: Lucian *Zeuxis* 8–11; Polyaen. 4.9.4; H. Bengtson, *Die Strategie in der hellenistischen Zeit* (Munich 1937–52) I, 225; see Launey 241–43.

2. *Syll.*³ 354; *IG* xii.7 9; Ziebarth 916. On inscriptions honoring Rhodians, see further below, n. 55.

3. *Inscr. Priene* 37; also *Syll.*³ 363; Paus. 7.2.10.

4. Vollgraff 220–29. Val. Max. 2.10 ext. 1 reports that sometime around 300 Seleucus sent Athens the statues of Harmodius and Aristogeiton stolen by Xerxes, and that while the boat carrying them was stopped at Rhodes, the tyrannicides were honored by the Rhodians. If this episode actually happened (according to Arr. 3.16.8, Alexander sent them back in 311), it was in the nature of a publicity stunt for Rhodes.

Greek freedom generally meant the expulsion of an opposing king's forces and the installation of their own.

Of somewhat greater importance during this period was the acquisition of the pre-Apamea subject Peraea. Unfortunately, information in this area is limited to Livy's brief narrative of its recapture from Philip V in 197/6 and a group of almost identical dedications by one of the generals during that war, Nicagoras, son of Pamphilidas. From this scant evidence it is possible to discern only that Rhodes possessed a tract of Carian territory extending north from the Ceramic Gulf to the vicinity of Stratonicea and including the towns of Pisye, Idyma, Cyllandus, and Tendeba.[5] The date of this acquisition is also obscure, though it was very probably sometime between Alexander and the battle of Corupedion, since central Caria was controlled by the Hecatomnids before 333 and by one or another of the Hellenistic monarchs after 281. Further, Rhodes' best opportunity to seize the area would have come in the years between Ipsus and the fall of Demetrius in 286, a poorly documented period during which Caria was only vaguely controlled by the unpopular Lysimachus.[6] Having taken advantage of the fluid power situation to capture the territory with its meager military forces, Rhodes was then left undisturbed by the Seleucids, presumably because this tiny piece of Asia Minor was a small price to pay for Rhodian goodwill, especially considering the island's normal inclination toward Egypt.

Rhodes acquired only two other pieces of mainland real estate before Apamea, the cities of Caunus and Stratonicea. Caunus presents no problems; it was purchased for 200 talents from the generals of Ptolemy V about 191.[7] The date and circumstances of the acquisi-

---

5. Livy 33.18.1–22; *IG* xii.1 1036 (= *Syll.*[3] 586); *Inscr. Lind.* 151; *SGDI* 4269. On the understanding of *recipere,* see below n. 9. Idyma was at the head of the Ceramic Gulf and Pisye to the north; Tendeba was in the area of Stratonicea, but its exact site is unknown. F&B do not locate Cyllandus, but Magie II, 879, n. 2 and map, places it northwest of Idyma; see also F&B 71–78.

6. F&B 99–101, who also suggest that it must have come before the acquisition of Stratonicea, as otherwise the city would have been isolated in Seleucid territory; this suggestion speaks against the only other period of possibly sufficient confusion for the Rhodians to seize territory, the last years of Antiochus Hierax.

7. Polyb. 30.31.6, which places the purchase before 189; Livy 33.20.11–13 places it after 196; App. *Mith.* 4.23 places it about 191. It is impossible that Astymedes could

tion of Stratonicea, however, are impossible to pin down with any
certainty, since the only bit of evidence is the statement of the Rhodian envoy Astymedes to the Roman Senate in 166: "We received
Stratonicea as a great favor from Antiochus and Seleucus."8 The
question, of course, is which Antiochus and Seleucus are meant.
Antiochus III and Seleucus IV may be rejected as candidates, since
according to Livy the city was *recaptured* with Seleucid aid in 197.9
The remaining possible pairs are Antiochus I and his son Seleucus and
Seleucus II and his brother Antiochus Hierax. Though there is something to be said for and against each of these choices, the second
appears the more likely.

The order in which Astymedes presents the names more readily
suggests Antiochus I and his son, who were corulers from 279 to 268,
but there are two apparent difficulties with this choice. As Stratonicea
was probably founded by Antiochus I, it would have had to be given
away very soon after its founding; yet Strabo says of Stratonicea that
"it also was adorned with expensive constructions by the kings,"
suggesting that the city was a Seleucid possession for a longer period
of time.10 Further, since Rhodes, though friendly to Antiochus, was
definitely inclined toward Egypt in those years, it is difficult to see
why the Syrian monarch would present a gift to the special friend of
his worst enemy.

The second pair, Seleucus II and Antiochus Hierax, present less
difficulty and have been generally identified as the rulers named by
Astymedes. As they were corulers in the late 240s, Stratonicea would
have been Seleucid for a sufficiently long time and the transfer would

tell a blatant lie concerning something the Senate could easily check, so ἐπὶ τῷ
'Αντιόχου πολέμῳ must either mean during the war or simply be wrong; F&B 105–6.

8. Polyb. 30.31.6. Niebuhr's emendation to 'Αντιόχου τοῦ Σελεύκου has been
almost universally rejected. The statement of Valerius Antias (Livy 33.30.11) that
Rome gave Straonicea to Rhodes in 196 is clearly false.

9. Livy 33.18.19: "recipi eam urbem"; 18.22: "nec recipi nisi aliquanto post per
Antiochum potuit." This evidence has been ignored by several authors. Briscoe 283
maintains *recipere* does not necessarily mean "regain"; even if this interpretation is
correct, it ignores the ἀνακτησάμενος of the Nicagoras inscription, strong evidence
that in this instance Livy means "regain."

10. Strabo 14.2.25 (660); an inscription from the area of Stratonicea (J. & L. Robert,
"Deux inscriptions de Carie," *Mélanges Isidore Lévy* [Brussels 1955] 553–68) indicates
very strongly that Straonicea was built after 276, making it even less likely that
Antiochus I and Seleucus are the pair in question.

have occurred after the Second Syrian War, when Rhodes had actually fought against Egypt. The period during which the brothers could be considered corulers of any sort runs from 245 to about 241, when Antiochus was viceroy in Asia Minor, and from about 241 to about 229, when he claimed royal status. Since during this time Seleucus was never in possession of Caria, Antiochus would have been the one who actually handed the city over to the Rhodians, and the order of the names may well recall this circumstance, regardless of what the official arrangement was. Or it may be, if the gift followed his revolt, that in the documents that record the transfer Antiochus placed his name first as part of his campaign to assert his position as equal or sole ruler of the Seleucid empire. The circumstances of the War of the Brothers would also provide a reason for the gift: Antiochus was attempting to win Rhodian favor and recognition of his position. The Rhodians would not hesitate long to accept such an offer, since it would cost them nothing and would cover their position should Antiochus retain control of Asia Minor. If, on the other hand, Seleucus should win the civil war, there was not much to fear in the way of reprisal, since the king already had enough troubles in the east and south without also alienating the Rhodians. It is most likely, then, that Rhodes acquired Stratonicea from Antiochus Hierax in the years around 241, and though Antiochus' kingdom rapidly disintegrated, for the rest of the century the situation in Asia Minor was fluid enough so that no ruler had sufficient reason or opportunity to revoke the gift.

Rhodes' reason for acquiring the territory that came to make up the subject Peraea can only be speculated upon. Stratonicea and Caunus are perfectly understandable; not only were both tremendous financial assets picked up at bargain prices, but also the former provided a strongpoint at the northern edge of the Peraea and the latter a good harbor and access to the fertile region north of the city. The remainder of the subject territory was probably also acquired because of the revenue it would bring the Rhodians, who probably calculated that the expense of occupying the area would be more than offset by the income derived from it.[11] It has been suggested that because of its

---

11. In the second century the two cities returned an annual 120 talents to Rhodes (Polyb. 30.31.7). See Magie I, 50–51 for the products of Caria.

rapidly growing population in the period after Alexander, the island seized the Carian territory in an effort to achieve self-sufficiency in foodstuffs,[12] but although the Rhodians probably considered the additional food supplies, it is unlikely this was the real motivation. The parts of Caria acquired by Rhodes did not include, so far as one can tell, the two really fertile regions of the country, and even those areas produced mainly fruits, rather than cereals. Further, it is improbable that a state with such a firm grip on the grain trade as Rhodes would worry unduly about its food supply; in the event of widespread shortages, its own trading network would ensure that the island was fed. The only serious drawback to the acquisition of the subject Peraea was that Rhodes was thus gaining territory that it could not really defend against any serious mainland power, but since it already faced the same problem with the incorporated Peraea, the addition of the Carian possessions did not materially alter its situation in that regard.

The administrative system imposed on the subject territory was virtually identical to that of the incorporated Peraea. The entire mainland was under the jurisdiction of the strategos of the Peraea,[13] and subordinate to him were three hegemones: one for the incorporated Peraea, one for the city of Caunus, and one for the subject Peraea. After the settlement of Apamea, a fourth hegemon was created for the administration of the Lycian territory.[14] Subordinate in turn to

12. Er. Meyer, *Die Grenzen der hellenistischen Staaten in Kleinasien* (Zurich 1925) 54; F&B 101 point to Rhodian importation of grain from Cyrene (*SEG* ix.2) during a year of shortages, but this simply shows that even during the lean years Rhodes had no trouble importing grain. Livy 45.25.12 may be true: "includi se insulae parvae et sterilis agri litoribus, quae nequaquam alere tantae urbis populum posset"; but the connection of this fact with the Peraea may easily be Livy's own inference.

13. στραταγὸς ἐπὶ τὸ or εἰς τὸ or ἐν τῶι Πέραν; *Syll.*[3] 586, 619 (= *IG* xii.1 1036, 49); *Inscr. Lind.* 151; *SGDI* 3789; *ClRh* 2 (1932) 188, no. 18, 192, no. 20; *JHS* 16 (1896) 221, no. 15; Maiuri no. 18; F&B 48–49, no. 49, 82–83; see also above, chapt. 2. The section on the administration of the Peraea is, with some differences, essentially a condensation of the invaluable work of Fraser and Bean.

14. ἀγεμὼν εἰς Ἄπειραν καὶ Φύσκον καὶ Κερσόνασον, ἐπὶ Καύνου, ἐπὶ Καρίας and ἐπὶ Λυκίας; *Syll.*[3] 619 (= *IG* xii.1 49), 819 (cf. *Inscr. Lind.* 189); *SGDI* 4267; *ClRh* 2 (1932) 192, no. 20; F&B 2–3, no. 1, 25, no. 13, 83–86; H. van Gelder, "Ad inscriptiones quasdam Rhodias observationes," *Mnem.* 23 (1895) 83–89. The title of hegemon of the incorporated Peraea does not include the isolated enclaves of Daedala and Megiste, and it is not clear if they were under the jurisdiction of this hegemon or

these officials were numerous epistatai, who were apparently located in the individual communities and strategically important places and represented the bottom rung of the governmental structure.[15] Information concerning the duties of these officials is almost nonexistent, but it appears that with one exception they were primarily military, the entire administration in fact being organized along military lines. Certainly the hegemones and epistatai of the incorporated Peraea filled an essentially military role, since as part of the Rhodian state this territory already possessed organs of civil administration. Presumably their duties were parallel to those of their counterparts on the island, though more serious because of the much greater threat of military activity.[16] The epistatai of the subject Peraea, on the other hand, did have civil powers, and their functions probably corresponded generally with those of the Seleucid officials of the same name; indeed, the office of epistates may well have been borrowed from the Seleucids.[17] For general civil administration in the subject territory Rhodes also made use of the machinery of the previously existing associations of villages or towns, the koina, a practice that both facilitated Rhodian administration and contributed to the tranquillity of the subject population.

Consideration of Rhodes' treatment of its subject Peraea must be limited to the Carian territories, since for most of the period during which Lycia was under Rhodian control it was in revolt and Rhodian activities in the area are thus of an exceptional nature.[18] As usual, information is at a premium, but it appears that with the likely exception of the larger cities, Rhodian rule was not really oppressive or especially unpopular. As might be expected, Rhodes attempted to

---

directly under the strategos; a ἁγεμὼν ἐν Μεγίστη is recorded in *SEG* iv. 178 (= F&B 45–46, no. 2), but it is a wartime appointment. *SGDI* 4275 mentions another hegemon: ἁγεμὼν ἄμισθος ἐπί τε ᾽Αρτούβων καὶ Παραβλείας, but it seems best to accept the suggestion of F&B 89 that the appointment of a hegemon for these two unknown localities was temporary and due to some local crisis.

15. *SGDI* 4276, 4330–32; *Tit. Asiae Min.* ii. 163; Michel 479; *Rev. Bibl.* 14 (1917) 291, no. 12, 293, no 23; see also Holleaux I, 412–17; F&B 86–88. Cnidus, acquired after Apamea (see below, chap. 8), seems to have been governed by mercenary *phrourarchoi* instead of Rhodian citizens, but this situation is unclear (F&B 93).

16. F&B 91–93.

17. Michel 479; Holleaux I, 412–13; F&B 93.

18. See below, chap. 8.

bind its subjects closer to it through the introduction of the cults of Helios, Rhodos, and the Rhodian demos and various Rhodian constitutional and social institutions,[19] but at the same time it refrained from any undue interference with the native Carian koina. Instead, these ancient political and social units were granted some degree of independence,[20] and it is possible, in view of the large number of koina found, particularly in obscure places, that the organization was systematized by Rhodes and occupied a position comparable to that of the deme in the incorporated Peraea.[21]

The liberal treatment of the koina was accompanied by a harder attitude toward the large cities, where the Rhodian presence was much more overt. As natural strongholds and points of potential insurrection, the cities of Caunus and Stratonicea, and probbly others, were garrisoned,[22] Caunus having in addition its own hegemon. These two cities also paid a stiff tribute, together returning 120 talents annually, and it is safe to assume that the other dependent cities were taxed, though it is impossible to know how heavily.[23] In general, it is perhaps indicative of Rhodian treatment that during the fifteen years in which revolt raged in Lycia there is no word of unrest in Caria, and when Rhodian authority was completely undermined in 167, only Caunus revolted.[24] Caria's tranquillity might of course in part be a reflection of Rhodian control, but it is also at least suggestive of some

---

19. See F&B 128–37. The cult of the Rhodian demos seems to have been confined to the subject territory and was perhaps in some ways similar to the worship of Dea Roma and Urbs Roma. Examples of particularly Rhodian institutions: a semestral calendar at Stratonicea (*BCH* 11 [1887] 85, no. 10, 87, no. 11, etc); an honorand at Antiphellus given meals in the *hierothyteion*, rather than the usual *prytaneion* (L. Robert, "Hellenica," *Rev. Phil.* 65 [1939] 215–17); a koinon of *eranistai* found at Hyllarima (L. Robert, *La Carie* [Paris 1954] II, 309).

20. For example, the koinon of the Panamarans near Stratonicea could pass decrees, such as awards of *politeia*, without the need of formal ratification in Rhodes (*BCH* 28 [1904] 348–50, nos. 4–5; see F&B 91–92). On the native institutions of Caria, see A. Mastrocinque, *La Caria e la Ionia meridionale in epoca ellentistica* (Rome 1979) 212–26.

21. F&B 50.

22. Polyb. 30.21.3.

23. Polyb. 30.31.7; 30.31.4 describes Lycia and Caria together returning πρόσοδοι πολλοί.

24. Polyb. 30.5.11–15.

measure of contentment. Further, sometime after 167 the now independent city of Ceramus, which for two decades had been under
Rhodian control, voluntarily struck a defensive alliance with the island, certainly a sign that for this city, at least, Rhodian hegemony
had not been so intolerable as to poison subsequent realtions.[25]

From these poorly known decades of the mid–century there comes
further notice of Rhodian activity. Recorded in the Lindus Temple
Chronicle is a dedication that reveals the surprising fact that Rhodes
was at war with Ptolemy II Philadelphus, and this inscription is
complemented by an anecdote in Polyaenus which describes a victory
of the Rhodian fleet led by Agathostratus over the Ptolemaic admiral
Chremonides before Ephesus.[26] It can hardly be doubted that these
passages refer to the same war, which would fall sometime between
about 262, when Chremonides fled from Athens, and 246, when
Ptolemy II died. There is an addition a strategem in Frontinus describing the joint capture of Ephesus by the Rhodians and Antiochus,
and this has generally been coupled with Polyaenus' battle and accepted as proof that Rhodes was a Seleucid ally in the Second Syrian
War.[27]

As has been recently reaffirmed, however, the anecdotes of Polyaenus and Frontinus cannot refer to the same action.[28] Most important, in Frontinus' passage Ephesus is Egyptian, but in Polyaenus' it
must already be Seleucid; why otherwise would Chremonides land
his vessels in an exposed area, rather than in the harbor of the city,
where they would be protected from just the kind of surprise that was
sprung on them? Frontinus is thus describing a different action, and
this presents something of a problem, since Ephesus was Seleucid in
267 and in 253 and there is no word of its changing hands in the

25. Michel 458. Hula-Szanto, *SB Wien. Akad.* 132 (1895) 9, no. 1, seems to record a
similar appeal to Rhodes from Euromus; see F&B 110–11.

26. *Lind. Temp. Chron.* 37; Polyaen. 5.18. Agathostratus, son of Polyaratus, was
honored, probably for his part in the battle of Ephesus, with a statue by the Nesiotic
League (*IG* xi.4 1128 [= *Syll.*³ 455]). He is also mentioned as a trierarch in an earlier
inscription (*Inscr. Lind.* 88; see Blinkenberg and Kinch II.1, 48–55).

27. Front. *Strat.* 3.9.10. For a full treatment of the literature on Ephesus, see J.
Seibert, "Die Schlacht bei Ephesos," *Hist.* 25 (1976) 45–61, who also disposes of the
passages in Myron and Teles thought by some to have a bearing on the battle.

28. Ibid. 48–50.

intervening years.[29] The events surrounding the mysterious Ptolemy "the son" provide no evidence, since there is no mention of Ephesus' involvement in his defection, and his death in that city is now to be placed after 246.[30] The assumption that the Antiochus named by Frontinus was Hierax rather than his father or that he was a Ptolemaic official known to have been operating in Cilicia in 245[31] accommodates the known facts, but in each case sufficient motivation for Rhodian involvement is lacking. The Rhodians, normally so reluctant to resort to military means, would have had little to gain by supporting Hierax against the legitimate king or by helping a strong Egypt against a Seleucid state in the throes of a civil war.

It may be well that Frontinus is simply wrong, but aside from the fact that it is bad form thus to dismiss a source, it is in fact possible to locate the incident in the Second Syrian War if one unrecorded event is assumed: the capture of Ephesus by Ptolemy at the very outset of the war.[32] Inasmuch as Antiochus was initially busy with Eumenes and Ptolemaic naval forces were operating in the area, it seems quite reasonable to suppose that the strategic city was suddenly captured; this event would have provided even more reason for the Rhodians to step into the fray. Frontinus consequently describes the Seleucid recovery of the city and Polyaenus its subsequent defense against an Egyptian counterattack. Given the sorry state of the sources for this period, it is hardly overly bold to postulate an event of which there is no record, and to do so certainly seems preferable to inventing Rhodian wars that cannot at all be explained in terms of the island's traditional policies.

However one deals with Frontinus, it is nevertheless obvious that the Temple Chronicle and Polyaenus must refer to Rhodian participation in the Second Syrian War. This is the only occasion during the period 262–46 when Rhodes could have had allies against

29. *OGIS* 222, 225.

30. Trog. *Prol.* 26: "Ut in Asia filius Ptolemaei regis socio Timarcho descriverit a patre"; Athen. 13.593a–b; J. Crampa, *Labraunda,* Swedish Excavations and Researches VIII.1: Inscriptions (Lund 1969) no. 3.

31. See Bengtson, *Strat.* III, 172–74.

32. This assumption has of course been explicitly or implicitly made by all those who interpret the Polyaenus as showing Egyptian control of the city; e.g., Crampa 117 and n. 21.

Ptolemy, and it is inconceivable that the island would have gone to war alone against Egypt. There is no known instance of the republic's taking on a major power singlehanded, and it is difficult to imagine a *casus belli* so sudden and serious that the Rhodians, having waited out the Second Syrian War, would then have declared war on an Egypt free to devote all its attention to its small adversary.

It is, on the other hand, possible to understand Rhodian involvement in the Second Syrian War. By the outbreak of that conflict Ptolemy had become by far the strongest of the monarchs, especially at sea, and a serious dislocation of the balance of power threatened the Greek world. Most of the Ptolemaic gains had been at the expense of Antiochus I, who had been forced to conclude an extremely disadvantageous peace at the end of the First Syrian War, and more recently the old king had been hard pressed in Asia Minor by the sudden hostility of Pergamum under its new ruler, Eumenes I. The young Antiochus II inherited a kingdom in serious trouble, and it was not at all in Rhodian interests to see a further dissolution of the Seleucid state. Nor, despite their special relationship with Egypt, did the Rhodians wish to see Ptolemy recreate the empire of Antigonus Monophthalmos. And his use of pirate squadrons in the First Syrian War,[33] in addition to being very annoying, must have been an uncomfortable reminder of Poliorcetes.

It is at least clear that despite their long friendship and extremely important economic ties, the Rhodians would fight even Egypt if they perceived their interests to be threatened. Exactly why they went to war with Ptolemy is of course a matter of speculation, but given the circumstances of the war and the apparently consistent rationality of Rhodian policy for a century and a half, the reason can be nothing other than the threat to Hellenistic political stability. The Seleucid empire seemed to be tottering, while Philadelphus appeared on the road to becoming master of the eastern Mediterranean. Rhodes might well have concluded that it could ride to greater power on the cloak of its old friend and exist comfortably under a Ptolemaic hegemony, but the island's policy makers were farsighted enough to realize that the predominance of any one power, even Egypt, would

33. Paus. 1.7.3.

almost certainly mean the end of the republic's autonomy and influence. It is a clear sign of the maturity of Rhodes' leaders that they not
only resisted the temptation to join the Ptolemaic bandwagon, but in
the interest of long-term policy goals were also willing to shoulder
the burden of a war with their most important trading partner.

There is no word of Rhodes again until 228, when the island was hit
by a tremendous earthquake that severely damaged the city and toppled the Colossus and most of the old walls.[34] The response of the
Greek world, however, was of such a magnitude that the relief afforded the republic by its neighbors allowed it to emerge from the
calamity with undiminished strength, an enhanced reputation, and
renovated fortifications.[35] The list of contributors reads like a survey
of Hellenistic royalty: Antigonus Doson, huge quantities of lead,
pitch, and timber, 100,000 medimni of grain, and 100 talents of silver;
Seleucus II, timber, hair, and resin, 200,000 medimni of grain, ten
equipped quinqueremes, and exemption from Seleucid custom duties; Ptolemy III, large amounts of timber and other shipbuilding
materials, 450 paid builders and masons, 1,000 talents of coined
bronze, 300 talents of silver, 3,000 talents of bronze for the Colossus,
and over 1 million artabai of grain; Hiero II and Gelo of Syracuse, 50
three-cubit catapults, 100 talents of silver, and exemption from
custom duties; and similar gifts from Prusias and Mithridates II, from
the dynasts Lysanias, Olympichus, and Limnaeus, and from cities
"too numerous to mention."[36] It is interesting to note that missing

34. Polyb. 5.88.1–90.2; Diod. 26.8.1; Strabo 14.2.5 (652); Pliny *HN* 34.41; *Chron.
Pasc.* 1 (331 Bonn); Euseb. *Chron.* II 122–23 Schöne (wrong date). Holleaux I, 452–57
established 226 (death or Seleucus) as a terminus ante quem, and an inscription from
Iasus has fixed the quake in 228; see G. Pugliese Carratelli, "Supplemento epigrafico
di Iaso," *Annuario* n.s. 29–30 (1967–68) 437–86, no. 2, 445–53; M. Guarducci, *Epigrafica greca* (Rome 1962) II, 120.

35. The fortifications are described by Philon of Byzantium (*Par.* 1.17–18 [80
Thev.]); see Kondis, *Arch. Delt.* 18A, 76–78, 84–85, 89–91.

36. The 3,000 talents of bronze (the word "bronze" is added) for the Colosus is six
times the amount said by Philon to be used in the original construction; the figure is,
however, much closer to the 100 tons of copper used in the Statue of Liberty. In any
case, the Rhodians were directed by an oracle not to repair the statue, and the figure
lay where it fell until the metal was sold in A.D. 653 (Const. Porphyr. *de Admin. Imp.*
20–21). The customs exemptions granted by Seleucus and Hiero were possibly also an
attempt to direct more Rhodian trade to their ports (Walbank I, 618). Olympichus

from this list is Attalus I, and unless Polybius has slipped, an unlikely assumption, the absence of the Pergamene strongly suggests that there existed already between the king and the Rhodians the cool relations that are evident eight years later during the Rhodian altercation with Byzantium.[37]

This unparalleled unanimity of action was hardly born of great humanitarian motives; they presumably played some role, but at heart the response was directed by hard economic interests. All of these states were involved in the commercial activities of Rhodes, and many were dependent on it to some extent for imports and the shipping and marketing of exports. The degree of concern of course varied, but the well-being of the island was crucial to those who relied on the Rhodian-dominated network of grain distribution, from the small Aegean importers to such big exporters as the normally tight-fisted Ptolemy, whose lavish gifts show the particular importance of Rhodes to his country. Further, there was probably also a general fear in the international banking community of a widespread financial crisis should the Rhodian economy be seriously disrupted. There are in fact few more impressive signs of the extent of Rhodian economic influence than the reaction to the earthquake and the seeming ease with which the Rhodians elicited the simultaneous support of the ever-contentious Hellenistic powers.

From about 220 on, information about Greek affairs begins to become more plentiful again, and it is possible to construct a more coherent picture of Rhodian activity. From the first years of this period come three instances of Rhodian diplomatic success, all of which illustrate various facets of the island's policies and interests. In 220 the Black Sea city of Sinope was threatened with a siege by Mithridates II of Pontus and appealed to Rhodes for aid. With Cos aiding in the negotiations, the Rhodians granted a loan of 140,000 drachmas, which was used to supply the matériel needed by the Sinopeans: 10,000 jars of wine, 300 talents of hair, 100 talents of bowstring, 1,000 suits of armor, 3,000 gold pieces, and four catapults

---

was dynast of Alinda in Caria and is later connected with Philip V (see below, chap. 5); the other two are unknown.

37. On Rhodian-Pergamene relations, see below, chap. 5.

with crews.[38] This prompt response is easily understood; Sinope was one of the primary economic centers and probably the most important carrier on the Black Sea, and the Rhodians had extensive commercial commitments in this region, particularly in grain.[39] The Sinopeans were well aware of this situation and also of the island's reputation as protector of the small states, and presumably concluded that the Rhodians would come to their aid out of self-interest. The conclusion was correct, and the Rhodians decided that the security of their trading partner was worth at least the risk of investing capital in the requested supplies. As it happened, this relatively small amount of aid was sufficient to deter Mithridates from attacking the city,[40] and Rhodes was thus able to defend its interests without resorting to military action.

In the summer of the same year Rhodes' attention was also called to another part of the Black Sea, where a much more critical situation had developed. Hard pressed by an annual tribute exacted by neighboring Gauls, the city of Byzantium appealed to other Greeks for help. Receiving no response, it took the desperate measure of imposing a duty on vessels passing through the straights. This action gained the immediate attention of the states that traded through the Bosporus, and they turned for help to the acknowledged leader of the maritime cities, Rhodes. The Rhodians, whose own vital interests were also being injured, promptly sent an embassy to Byzantium, and when it was rebuffed they declared war, a vivid sign of just how important they considered free passage of the straights. Having taken this unusual and serious step, the Rhodians nevertheless still attempted to resolve the problem without actually resorting to military action. They sent envoys to Prusias of Bithynia, inviting him to settle

38. Polyb. 4.56.1–9, who is clearly drawing on a Rhodian source, either Zeno or the actual decree; H. Ullrich, *De Polybii fontibus Rhodiis,* diss. (Leipzig 1898) 27. Cos: R. Herzog, *Jahr. deutsch. arch. Inst.* 18 (1903) 198; *Ath. Mitt.* 30 (1905) 182. The participation of Cos is a further example of its extremely close relationship with Rhodes. The money is assumed to be a loan, since this appears to have been Rhodes' normal practice.

39. Sinope: Magie I, 183–84, II, 1074–77, nn. 18–23; D. M. Robinson, "Ancient Sinope," *AJP* 27 (1906) 134–44. On Rhodes in the Black Sea, see above, chap. 2.

40. There is no direct evidence for this statement, but as Sinope was not captured until 183, it may be assumed to be true.

his own grievances against the Byzantines, and he agreed to undertake the war by land while the Rhodians fought at sea.[41] They then sent the nauarch Xenophantus with six Rhodian and four allied ships to Sestus, from which place Xenophantus sailed alone to Byzantium to find out if the city would now back down.[42] The Byzantines, however, had scored their own diplomatic successes and gained the promised support of Attalus of Pergamum and Achaeus, the Seleucid governor who had become king in Asia Minor. They also summoned from Macedon Tiboetes, Prusias' uncle and a strong pretender to the Bithynian throne. With this support they were little minded to acquiesce to Rhodian demands, and Xenophantus left for Rhodes with his squadron.[43]

Inasmuch as Attalus was confined in Pergamum by Achaeus, it was clearly the latter who was the key to Byzantine resistance, and the Rhodians concentrated their attention on compelling him to renege on his promise of support. Their mechanism for achieving this aim was Achaeus' father, Andromachus, who was a prisoner of Ptolemy IV and who may well have been the reason for Achaeus' involvement in the war.[44] It is difficult to understand how, in terms of real power, Achaeus could hope to benefit from his support of Byzantium, for it brought no real advantage and instead earned him the enmity of Bithynia and Rhodes, at a time when he could count on a reckoning with Antiochus III. It is consequently possible that Achaeus seized the opportunity presented by the war and made promises to Byzantium simply as a way of pressuring Rhodes into using its influence to obtain the release of his father. This notion is supported by the facts

41. Polyb. 4.45.9–47.7, 49.1–5; *Staats.* III, no. 514. One or more small states joined Rhodes in a declaration of war, as four "allied" ships joined the Rhodian squadron.

42. Polyb. 4.50.5–6. The Xenophantus, son of Hagestratus, in *IG* xii.1 40 is probably this individual.

43. Polyb. 4.48.1–13, 50.1, 7–9. Tiboetes may be an error for Zipoetes; see Magie II, 1196, n. 36. B. Niese, *Geschichte der griechischen und makedonischen Staaten seit der Schlacht bei Chaeronea* (Gotha 1893–1903) 385–86, n. 6, suggests that Xenophantus returned to Rhodes because of the appearance of Demetrius and his pirates in the Aegean. This interpretation would explain why he took the entire squadron back with him.

44. For the positions of Attalus and Achaeus, see H. H. Schmitt, *Untersuchungen zur Geschichte Antiochos' des Grossen und seiner Zeit* (Wiesbaden 1964) 158–65.

that Achaeus apparently never made a single move toward actually helping Byzantium and that the Rhodians had in fact requested Andromachus' release before, presumably at the urging of Achaeus. Further, it is not likely that Ptolemy—or the Rhodians, for that matter—would surrender such a potentially valuable pawn without some assurances that something substantial would result from the action, suggesting that the Rhodians knew that all Achaeus really wanted from the war was his father.

In any case, Ptolemy surrendered Andromachus to the Rhodians, who returned him to Achaeus, and the latter withdrew his support from Byzantium. This alone would probably have been enough to sway the Byzantines, but in addition Tiboetes died on the way from Macedon, and Prusias hired Thracians to harry the city on the European side while he ravaged Byzantine territory on the Asian side. The Byzantines clearly now had no hope of success, and the Gallic king Cavarus was able to arrange an armistice between them and Prusias. The Rhodian envoy Aridices arrived soon after, escorted by three triremes under Polemocles, and peace treaties were concluded, probably in the autumn. Byzantium agreed not to levy any tolls on the passage of the Bosporus, and Prusias engaged to return all that he had captured except the movable booty.[45] Without lifting a sword Rhodes thus brought an end to the threat to its Pontic trade, demonstrating vividly the diplomatic skill that helped carry it through the dangerous waters of the Hellenistic world.

In the following year Rhodes' diplomatic services were requested by its old friend to the south. Caught unprepared by the sudden assault of Antiochus and the untimely defection of Theodotas in Coele-Syria, Egypt desperately needed time to prepare its defenses, and Ptolemy's government decided on negotiations with Antiochus as a way to buy that time. Consequently, Rhodes, Byzantium, Cyzicus, and Aetolia were invited to send negotiating teams, and while these envoys shuttled between the two courts, the king's ministers Agathocles and Sosibius began to assemble an army. Apparently

---

45. Polyb. 4.51.5–52.9; *Staats.* III, no. 516; Walbank I, 506–7. Why Prusias was willing to conclude a peace with such poor terms is unclear; presumably he was unwilling to cross Rhodes and feared possible trouble from Mithridates or Achaeus.

convinced that Ptolemy would not fight and concerned at least initially about Achaeus, Antiochus agreed to a four-month armistice in the late autumn, thus granting Ptolemy the time he needed.[46] The Rhodians certainly understood the real point of the negotiations from the start and were quite willing to undertake the deception in order to help protect Egypt from resurgent Seleucid power, but their role in achieving this goal should not be overstated. As recognized peacemakers in the Greek world, they presumably lent some credibility to the negotiations, but the special relationship between Rhodes and Alexandria was also widely recognized and could very well have raised suspicions. In any case, it appears from Polybius that Antiochus did not take much convincing, and it is likely that the strategy would have succeeded without the services of the Rhodians.

With the defenses prepared during the negotiations and later, Ptolemy was able momentarily to turn aside the Seleucid threat in 217, but the victory of Raphia could not hide the fact of Egypt's steady decline since the middle of the century. This could only be a growing concern to the Rhodians, for whom the fading power of the Ptolemies raised the specter of the disappearance of their oldest friend and a serious upset of the balance of power. Already the retreat of Egypt from the Aegean and the dissolution of its Nesiotic League had tremendously increased Rhodes' naval burden.[47] Egypt did retain a naval force at Samos, but there is no word of its ever taking action,

46. Polyb. 5.61.3–66.9; see W. Huss, *Untersuchungen zur Aussenpolitik Ptolemaios' IV* (Munich 1976) 47–50.

47. This is not the place to become entangled in the problems of the battles of Cos and Andros; suffice it to say that the two battles and that of Ephesus broke Ptolemaic naval power and control of the Nesiotic League. There is no mention of Egyptian officials after the 250s, and the last extant document of the league is the dedication of Agathostratus, the victor of Ephesus (*IG* xi.4 1128 = *Syll.*³ 455). While it seems clear that Egypt lost control of the islands after Philadelphus, however, it is not known what happened to the league itself. Macedonian influence was certainly paramount in the Aegean until Doson's death in 221, but there is no real evidence that the league continued to exist, though it would certainly be reasonable for Gonatus to maintain the organization as a convenient mechanism of control. There is no question that the league ceased to exist after 221 and was probably already neglected after the death of Gonatus. For a discussion of the question of the survival of the league, see W. König, *Der Bund der Nesioten,* diss. (Halle 1910) 31–40; W. W. Tarn, *Antigonus Gonatus* (Oxford 1913) 466–72; Will I, 205–7. For remnants of Ptolemaic influence in the Aegean after 220, see Huss 213–38. See below, chap. 6, for the Rhodian League.

and the ships were in fact not fitted out when Philip V took the island in 201.[48] Since Macedonian interests in the Aegean were very limited, after Doson's Carian expedition in 227, the Antigonid fleet was also allowed to deteriorate, while the Macedonian rulers, true to the tradition of Demetrius I, made alliances with pirate kings.[49] Until the rise of Pergamum and the eastern schemes of Philip at the end of the century, there was consequently a naval vacuum in the Aegean, and the Rhodian navy became the only serious organized antipirate force among the islands.

As a commercial state, Rhodes pursued a policy of unrelenting war against pirates, and unlike its neighbors never once compromised with the naval brigands. Its navy was particularly designed as an antipirate force, and as early as the end of the fourth century elements patrolled among the islands, engaging various freebooters in the Aegean area.[50] In the first half of the third century Rhodians are found fighting various western pirates, known collectively as Tyrrhenians, and in 220 they chased Demetrius of Pharus and his Illyrian raiders out of the Aegean.[51] Aetolia was a further perennial breeding ground for pirates,[52] but perhaps the greatest source of constant trouble for Rhodes was Crete. Cretans had been notorious pirates from as early as the time of Homer, and only the continual internal strife on the island prevented it from becoming the worst pirate nest in the Mediterranean. Rhodes endeavored to profit from this disunity by making alliances containing antipirate clauses with individual Cretan cities, as in the case of the treaty with Hierapytna and almost certainly also in the alliance with Knossos.[53] In 220 the Knossians

48. Polyb. 5.35.11, 16.2.9.

49. Demetrius II with Agron the Illyrian; Antigonus Doson with Demetrius of Pharus; Philip V with Dicaearchus the Aetolian.

50. On the Rhodian navy see above, chap. 2.

51. Tyrrhenians: *Syll.*[3] 1225; Psd.-Arist. 43 (540 D); Ormerod 127–30; Schmitt 43–46. Demetrius: Polyb. 4.16.6–8, 19.8. It was probably Xenophantus that did the chasing; see above, n. 43.

52. Instances of Aetolian activities: *Syll.* [3] 520, 521; *IG* xii.7 387. On the general conduct of the Aetolians, see Polyb. 4.3.1–5.10, 16.2–4, 25.1–4. Cilicia's prominence as a pirate nest came later, after the middle of the second century; see Ormerod 190–248.

53. Homer *Od.* 14.199–284; Strabo 10.4.9 (477); Polyb. 4.53.1 (Knossos); *Syll.*[3] 581; *Staats.* no. 581 (Hierapytna); see also the treaty with Olus: *Staats.* no. 582;

called on the Rhodians for aid, and responding to an old ally, who had sent them troops during the great siege, the Rhodians sent Polemo-cles with six ships. This move earned Rhodes the immediate enmity of Knossos' enemies, which in itself hardly troubled the republic, but aligned with these other cities was Philip V of Macedon.[54] Crete was thus set as a stage for a potential Macedonian-Rhodian conflict.

Shouldering the burden of policing the Aegean, though motivated by self-interest, could only enhance Rhodes' already brilliant reputa-tion among the smaller communities, and the extent of its prestige is reflected in the numerous extant inscriptions in which various cities and organizations honor individual Rhodians.[55] With the retreat of Ptolemaic naval power, Rhodes' influence grew especially strong among the islands, and it was generally recognized as unofficial leader and protector of the island states. This position was not formalized until its later resurrection of the Nesiotic League, but there is evidence that during this period the Rhodians appointed a nauarch whose duties specifically included the security of the islands.[56] As the in-scription is unique, however, it is not clear if this was a regular or extraordinary command. In any case, such was the growth of the republic's reputation that by 220 the Rhodians were ackknowledged to be "the leaders in maritime affairs."[57]

The years since the great siege had also been a steady increase in Rhodian economic strength, but the limited nature of the evidence permits only the most general statements about this development. The temporary difficulties with Egypt during the Second Syrian War

---

generally on Cretan piracy: P. Brulé, *La piraterie crétoise hellénistique* (Paris 1978) 2–29, 69–184.

54. Polyb. 4.53.1–2, 55.1–2; Polemocles came from Byzantium. On Rhodes' spe-cial friendship with Knossos see E. van Effenterre, *La Crète et le monde grec de Platon à Polybe* (Paris 1978) 214; *Num. Chron.* 13³ (1893) 12 for a Rhodian tetradrachma overstruck with a labyrinth for use at Knossos (see also R. Seager, *A Cretan Coin Hoard* [New York 1924] 10–11, 32–36 for Rhodian hemidrachmas overstruck by Cydonia).

55. See, for example, those collected in van Gelder 450–64 (from the period 230–170).

56. *IG* xi.4 596: ναύα]ρχος ἐπὶ τῆς φυλακῆς τ[ῶν νήσων καὶ] ἐπὶ σωτηρίαι τῶν Ἑλλήνων. The inscription is dated to c. 250–20; the crucial phrase τῶν νήσων is conjectural, but nothing else will fit; see F&B 158, n. 3.

57. Polyb. 4.47.1.

had been quickly repaired, and the island continued to dominate Egyptian trade and the distribution of grain in general.[58] Its share of Pontic supplies had in fact increased, as a result partly of the natural growth and development of its network and partly of the commercial decline of Athens, especially after the Chremonidian War.[59] In the Aegean area, and particularly among the islands, Rhodian economic activity and influence also increased, though documentation is sparse for this period.[60] A good example, however, is provided by Athenedorus, son of Pisagorus, a Rhodian businessman on Delos in the 230s. Athenedorus was honored by the city of Histiaea for providing an interest-free loan for the purchase of grain; the absence of any interest suggests very strongly that he was also involved in the grain deal itself. This inscription, besides illustrating Rhodian activity on the sacred island, also supports the contention that beyond serving as a local market and extension of the Rhodian network, Delos itself did not play any significant role in the grain trade.[61] Further, a romantic anecdote from the War of the Brothers reveals just how important Rhodes had become as a clearinghouse for the eastern Mediterranean. When Mysta, mistress of Seleucus, was captured and sold into slavery at Ankyra in 236, she soon appeared on the blocks at Rhodes, where she was recognized and promptly returned to the king.[62] So vital was the Rhodian market that a slave taken three hundred miles away in the interior of Asia was disposed of on the island. And finally,

---

58. For Rhodes and Egyptian grain, see above, chap. 2, and esp. Grace, *Hesp.* supp. 8, 183. As noted by Casson 173, a request to Egypt from Samothrace in the 220s to buy duty-free Pontic grain suggests that Egypt was feeling the pressure of Pontic competition; such could only place the Rhodians in an even better bargaining position with the Ptolemies. For an illustration of Rhodian–Egyptian trade at mid-century, see the discussion of Zenon's business letter (*P. Ryl.* 554) in M. Rostovtzeff, "Alexandrien und Rhodos," *Klio* 30 (1937) 72–76. The importance of Egypt to Rhodes (despite the temporary altercation in the Second Syrian War) is immediately apparent from an inscription recording a cult of Ptolemy (III) and Berenice (II) (Segré, *Bull. Soc. Arch. Alex.* 34, 29–39). For Rhodian coinage during the third century, see Head, *Greek Coins* 234–51.

59. See above, chap. 2, and esp. Gajdukevic 103–4, 182, n. 37, 308–9, n. 2.

60. See above, chap. 2. Activity in the Aegean: *Syll.*³ 354 and *IG* xii.7 9 (grain for Ephesus and Amorgus); *IG* xii. 5 1010 (grain for Ios); *IG* xii. 5 1009 (alliance with Ios); *IG* xii. supp. 120 (alliance with Lesbos, possibly later).

61. *IG* xi.4 1055 (= *Syll.*³ 493). On Delos see Casson 174–76 and chap. 10 below.

62. Athen. 13.578a, 593e; Polyaen. 8.61.

as suggested earlier, there is no more dramatic sign of the scope of the republic's economic strength than the general reaction to the earthquake of 228; the well-being of Rhodes was clearly of high importance to a great many Greeks.

In the closing decades of the third century Rhodes stood on the verge of its period of greatest prosperity and power, but this apogee would come amidst the collapse of the political structure that had for so long secured its independence. And the Fates would in fact have it thus, that the island republic would itself play an instrumental role in the chain of events that would lead ultimately to the ruin of the Hellenistic world and the end of Rhodes' autonomy.

CHAPTER 5

Philip V and
the Appeal to Rome

RHODES' initial encounter with Philip V of Macedon was quite indirect but nevertheless damaging to the island's interests. Responding to an appeal in 220, the young ruler directed the Macedonian-dominated symmachy to send military aid to a coalition of Cretan cities that were struggling against the hegemony of Knossos and Gortyn. In taking this action Philip was presumably hoping both to gain influence over the island and its valuable reserve of mercenaries and to tie up troops of the Aetolian League, which was supporting the hegemonists. Also backing Knossos, however, were the Rhodians, and for them Philip's intervention meant a potential setback for their Cretan policy, which was directed toward the suppression of piracy through alliances with key cities on the island.[1] As it happened, the anti-Knossos movement spread rapidly, and as Rhodes was unwilling to support a general war against most of Crete, peace came in 217/6, with almost all of the cities by then enrolled in a pro-Macedonian confederacy. The Rhodians thus suffered a loss of prestige and influence on Crete, while Philip, who was elected president (*prostates*) of the confederacy, gained in reputation.[2] To be sure, the

---

1. Polyb. 4.53.3–55.2. Philip sent 700 infantry. On Rhodes' Cretan policy, see above, chap. 4.

2. Polyb. 4.53.1–2, 55.3–6, 7.11.9, 14.4; Plut. *Arat.* 48.3. It was apparently in reaction to Philip's aid that the Rhodian squadron under Polemocles arrived at Knossos. Polybius and Plutarch overestimate the extent of the pro-Macedonian con-

blow to Rhodes was hardly a serious one, and Philip's office was essentially honorary, but the outcome of the civil war did leave the monarch with a channel into the Aegean and a potential mechanism for disturbing the Rhodians.

While the friends of Macedon and Rhodes were fighting it out on Crete, on the Greek mainland the Social War provided the circumstances for a direct though peaceful encounter between the two powers. In 218 embassies from Rhodes and Chios met Philip at Corinth with offers to arbitrate, and he sent them on to the Aetolians, claiming that he had always been ready to negotiate. Increasingly hard pressed, the Aetolians accepted a thirty-day truce and agreed to meet with Philip, but given new hope by the Apelles conspiracy, they subsequently postponed the date of the conference. Philip was waiting for just such a pretext to break off the negotiations, and the war continued.[3] The following year Rhodes and Chios, joined now by Byzantium and Egypt, once again sent ambassadors to the king, and he once more sent them on to the Aetolians, little inclined to peace while the war was progressing so well. Philip's mind was in fact soon changed by the news of Trasimene, but in dealing with the Aetolians he simply ignored the neutrals, and the Peace of Naupactus was consequently concluded without their involvement.[4]

The main motivation behind the peace embassies of 218–17 was unquestionably commerce. Rhodes, Chios, and Byzantium were all states with commercial interests in the Balkan peninsula, and the Social War was disrupting those interests. Further, while the neutral states were probably delighted to see the Aetolians take a drubbing, they were undoubtedly also concerned lest Philip gain too much strength and become a threat to the Aegean communities. Egypt's motivations are less clear, but it is reasonable to believe that the Alexandrian court wished to see an end to the war so that the Macedonian king might be free to serve as a potential ally against Antiochus. As it happened, all these desires were satisfied, for a peace was

federacy, since Knossos and other towns remained tied to Rhodes, while Itanus at least remained Egyptian; see Walbank II, 59. On the war in general, see Walbank I, 507–11; R. M. Errington, *Philopoemen* (Oxford 1969) 28–33.

3. Polyb. 5.24.11, 28.1–3, 29.3–4.
4. Polyb. 5.100.9–11, 102.2–4.

concluded in 217, but it was clear that the embassies had failed completely and that Philip alone had ended the war. In any case, for the Rhodians the return of peace was the important thing, and though their efforts at mediation failed, their reputation in the Greek world could only be enhanced by the attempt.

Eight years later the Rhodians are again found attempting to mediate between Philip and the Aetolians, this time amid the devastation of the First Macedonian War. In the spring of 209 delegates from Rhodes, Chios, Athens, and Egypt, joined by Amynander of Athamania, an advocate of Aetolia, caught up with Philip at Phalara and obtained his agreement to a thirty-day truce and a peace conference to be held at Aegium. At that conference the king emphasized the danger to Greece posed by Rome, which was leaving its allies to carry on the war; but with their hopes renewed by news of the arrival of Attalus at Aegina and a Roman squadron at Naupactus, the Aetolians deliberately wrecked the negotiations with unreasonable demands.[5] The following year embassies from Rhodes, Egypt, and probably also Chios met with the Aetolians at Heraclea, only to be sent on to Philip, who was now doing so well in the war that he simply dismissed them with age-old statements about willingness to accept a fair and honorable peace.[6] In 207 the neutral powers appeared twice before the Aetolian assembly to attempt to persuade it to conclude a peace, and though there is some confusion, it appears that the same states sent delegates to both meetings: Rhodes, Egypt, Chios, Byzantium, and Mitylene. Amynander was also present at the first gathering and possibly the second, while the Roman commander Sulpicius probably attended both. Polybius preserves a speech of one of the ambassadors, the Rhodian Thrasycrates, who reiterated the pointlessness of Aetolia's position and the danger from Rome, but it is not clear to which of the meetings this passage belongs.[7] In any case, at

5. Livy 27.30.4–6, 10–14. Polyb. 10.25.1–5 is usually associated with this conference at Aegium; see Walbank II, 229.

6. Livy 28.7.13–15. Chios is not mentioned by Livy, but inasmuch as Chiotes were with every other peace embassy in both wars, they were undoubtedly also with this one.

7. Polyb. 11.4.1–6.10; App. *Mac.* 3.1–4. Rhodes and Byzantium are mentioned only by Polybius, but it seems a reasonable assumption that if their envoys were at one meeting, they were also at the other; it is also inconceivable that the Rhodians should

the time of the first assembly the Aetolians were not yet desperate enough to give in, but Philip's invasion of Aetolia and the defeat of Machanidas compelled them to give the ambassadors a warmer reception at the second meeting, toward the end of the year. It is not clear, however, if the actual negotiations that led to the peace agreement of 206 sprang directly from this meeting or were handled by the neutral embassies.[8]

Rhodes' reasons for participating in this peace offensive were similar to those that moved it during the Social War; paramount among them was the severely disrupted commerce of the Greek mainland, a cause for concern also for Chios and Byzantium, and to a lesser degree for Mitylene and Egypt. Furthermore, in 208 the war spread to Asia when Philip's friend Prusias of Bithynia invaded Pergamene territory and forced the return of Attalus, thus possibly upsetting the Pontic trade.[9] There were also purely strategic considerations, as the war provided opportunities for changes in the Aegean power structure potentially harmful to the interests of the neturals. The possible growth of Macedonian strength was undoubtedly a general concern, but it must have been Attalus' participation that most specifically bothered the Rhodians. With the defeat of Achaeus, the most important check on Pergamene ambitions had been removed, and Attalus' program of naval expansion cannot have pleased any of the eastern Aegean states. Pergamene-Roman attacks on Lemnos and Euboea made clear Attalus' Aegean intentions, and his acquisition of Aegina vividly demonstrated what gains might be made in the war. Inasmuch as commercial disruptions were sufficient reason for the Rhodians to attempt mediation, it is somewhat odd that there was no

---

be absent from any peace negotiations. The speech in Polybius has generally been identified with the first meeting (see P. Meloni, *Il valore storico e le fonti del libro macedonico di Appiano* [Rome 1955] 10–24), but no real conclusion is possible. The name Thrasycrates is written in the margin in the Codex Urbinas, and J. Schweighäuser, *Polybii Megapolitani historiarum um quidquid superest* (Leipzig 1789–95) VII, 7 originally argued that from the emphasis on Rhodes in 11.4.1 the speaker was a Rhodian; the words in 11.4.7 on the unprofitableness of war indeed sound very Rhodian.

8. As pointed out by Schmitt 209, the τέλος of App. *Mac.* 3.4 reveals nothing about the length of time between the second meeting and the conclusion of a peace, and consequently it is unnecessary to move the second meeting into 206.

9. Attalus' return: Livy 28.7.10; Dio Cas. 17.58.

embassy until 209, and it is tempting to understand that first embassy as a reaction to Attalus, who was elected strategos of the Aetolian League in 210 and began moving his fleet to Greece in the early part of 209. Rhodes, Chios, Lesbos, and Byzantium all had good reason to fear this development of Attalid power, and though the king was forced to return home in 208, continuation of the war might well provide him with more opportunities and more gains.[10]

Finally there was Rome. While the war with Carthage lasted, there appeared to be little likelihood that the Romans would seriously commit themselves in the Balkans, but their ultimate intentions could not be known, and the sooner the Greeks put their house in order, the more secure they would be against possible Roman aggression. It is also likely that Rhodes and the others did not particularly care for some of the methods of the Roman legions,[11] and they must certainly have been irked by the fact that Aetolia continued to fight a war that really only served Roman interests, especially when the Romans themselves had ceased to take any real part. It is completely mistaken, however, to see in the Rhodian peace initiatives an "anti-Roman" policy;[12] the Rhodians were clearly more interested in ending a war that was devastating Greece and disrupting trade than in embarrassing Rome. Granted, the ambassador Thrasycrates had some unkind words about Roman intentions in Greece, but this single instance of expressed Rhodian hostility comes in a speech before the Aetolians, the whole purpose of which was to persuade the listeners to break with Rome. The Rhodians were undoubtedly annoyed with Rome's present posture in the Balkans, but one cannot in any case construct from a single speech a policy that would mean the apparent reversal of a century-long relationship. There is of course no evidence of how Rhodes felt about Rome in the years since the meeting at the end of the fourth century, but consideration of its interests

10. On Attalid naval development and operations, see Hansen 46–49. The concern about Attalus is reflected in Livy 27.30.10; see C. Starr, "Rhodes and Pergamum, 201–200 B.C.," *CP* 33 (1938) 66.

11. Roman reputation during the war: Polyb. 9.39.2–3, 11.5.6–7.

12. The strongest advocate of this view is M. Holleaux, *Rome, la Grèce, et les monarchies hellénistiques au IIIe siècle av. J.-C. (273–205)* (Paris 1921) 35–38, 73–74; see Schmitt 193–211 for a detailed examination of the Rhodian embassies in light of Holleaux's thesis.

would indicate that the island had probably thought favorably of the Italian republic. With their extensive commercial interests in the west and especially in Magna Graecia, the Rhodians could only have been helped by the unification of Italy and Sicily under Roman control and by the shattering of the Carthaginian naval monopoly in the First Punic War.[13] More recently, Rome's action in suppressing Illyrian piracy and imposing some order in that region must also have made a favorable impression on the Rhodians. An anti-Roman policy would clearly be detrimental to Rhodian interests, and it is hardly likely that the republic would adopt such a stance simply because of Rome's present position in Greece, a position that the Rhodians could certainly understand, if not applaud.

In the end the peace offensive of 209–7 had little more success than that of 218–17. It may be that the neutral ambassadors helped the Aetolians to appreciate fully their desperate situation a little earlier than they might have done on their own, but as in the Social War, essentially the parties made peace when they were ready to do so. Once again, however, even if Rhodes was unable substantially to hasten the conclusion of the war, the annual appearance of its mediators in the war zone could only increase its reputation and credibility as Hellenic peacemaker.

The First Macedonian War came to an end in 205 with the Peace of Phoenice, and in that year the Rhodians turned their full attention to Cretan piracy, which was apparently on the rise again. The subsequent conflict is referred to in the inscriptions as "Cretan war," but it does not appear that there was a general war; rather raids launched by the Cretans were countered by the Rhodians. The war was initiated by Rhodes in response to the depredations of a Cretan pirate squadron, and at the outset Rhodes apparently faced most of the cities of Crete, united in their pro-Macedonian association.[14] Rhodian mea-

13. Schmitt 58, n. 1, points to a statue of M. Claudius Marcellus (killed in 208) in the temple of Athena at Lindus (Plut. *Marc.* 30.4–5) as evidence of comfortable relations between Rhodes and Rome, but there is no indication when the statue was dedicated.

14. It is clear from Diod. 27.3.1 (see also Polyb. 13.4.2) that Philip had nothing to do with actually instigating the war. On the Cretan war in general, see Errington, *Phil.* 38–45; Brulé 34–56.

sures against Crete in the next several years were seemingly successful, and an envoy sent by Antiochus—the Rhodian Hagesandrus, son
of Eucrates—was able to detach a number of cities from the Macedonian group. It is clear that the united front against Rhodes was completely undermined by 200, when an Athenian embassy is found
canvassing the island for support against Philip, and the treaty with
Hierapytna, signed about this time, reveals the ascendancy of Rhodian influence on the island. The Cretan police action appears to have
been essentially over by the outbreak of the Second Macedonian War,
but sporadic raiding may well have continued through 197.[15]

The Cretan war provided the setting for the first conflict between
Rhodes and Macedon. As president of the Cretan confederacy, Philip, or at least his prestige, was obviously injured by Rhodes' action
against Crete, and the king seized the opportunity presented by this
situation to further his own plans. With his ambitions in the Adriatic
having run up against the obstacle of Rome, Philip had turned his
attention to the east and found in the Aegean circumstances that
invited Macedonian intervention. The steady decline of Egypt had
left a power vacuum in the area, and it was clearly only a matter of
time before Antiochus III, newly arrived from his eastern tour,

15. Hagesandrus: *IC* i.27.1, ii.12.21, 16.3 (= *LB-W* 63, 71, 68); Olshausen no. 135;
Athenians: Paus. 1.36.5–6; Hierapytna: *Syll.*[3] 581; *Staats.* III, no. 551. The treaty with
Olus (*Staats.* III, no. 552) is also dated to this period; see esp. van Effenterre 226–34.
The dating of Hagesandrus' mission is not clear. He was traveling with envoys from
Teos, which was seeking grants of *asylia* from various Greek states, and the replies of
the Aetolians (*LB-W* 85; *IG* ix.2[1] 192 = *Syll.*[3] 563), the Amphictyonic Council (*Syll.*[3]
564), Delphi (*LB-W* 84; *Syll.*[3] 565), and the Athamanians (*LB-W* 83) to the same
request for *asylia* have been dated to 205–3; see P. Hermann, "Antiochos der Grosse
und Teos," *Anatolia* 9 (1965) 93–100. Antiochus' support of Tean *asylia* does not mean
the city was Seleucid (nor does the decree of Rhaucus [*IC* i.27.1]); it could have been
an attempt to win favor with the city. The fact that a request was not made to the
Senate until 193 (*Syll.*[3] 601; Livy 34.57.6–59.7; Diod. 28.15.1–4; App. *Syr* 6) may be
due simply to the circumstance that Rome does not appear on Teos' diplomatic
horizon until after the war. The presence of Perdiccas, a representative of Philip (see
Olshausen no. 99), with the embassy to Crete is easily understood in terms of Philip's
great influence on the island. Hagesandrus did not actually end the war on Crete; the
Eleutherna decree (*IC* ii.12.21) says only that he was sent "for the purpose of ending
the war." For numismatic evidence of Rhodian influence on Crete, see T. Hackens,
"L'influence rhodienne en Crète au IIIe et IIe s. av. J.-C. et le trésor de Gortyne, 1966,"
Rev. Bel. Num. 116 (1970) 37–58, esp. 50–52.

would undertake operations to recover and extend Seleucid possessions in the region. For Philip this was a matter of serious concern, for
Antiochus had brought about a spectacular revival of Seleucid power
and now threatened Egypt and the Hellenistic power structure with
imminent destruction. It must have seemed to the Macedonian king
that only an extension of Antigonid power into the Aegean could
possibly thwart the apparent growing ascendancy of Seleucid
strength and allow him to face his fellow monarch on equitable
terms.[16]

An Aegean program required a fleet, which meant money, and
Philip seized upon piracy as the easiest way to obtain the necessary
funds. Rhodes' war against Crete thus not only was an assault on the
king's prestige but also ran counter to his financial plans, which
involved the encouragement of piracy. On the other hand, the Cretan
war did provide the mechanism for an indirect offensive against the
Rhodians, who could be expected to oppose his schemes, and Philip
consequently sent encouragement to the cities fighting against
Rhodes.[17] In 204 he took more direct action by sending the Aetolian
Dicaearchus with twenty ships on a plundering raid into the Aegean,
instructing him also to give whatever aid he could to the Cretans.
Operating under the guise of an independent pirate, Dicaearchus was
apparently extremely successful in extorting money from the
wealthy cities of the Troad and the Cyclades, but no details of the raid
survive.[18] About the same time Philip also sent his agent Heracleides
to Rhodes for a mission of sabotage. Pretending to be a deserter,
Heracleides managed to overcome the distrust of the Rhodian prytanes by producing an incriminating letter from Philip to the Cretans;
he was then, according to Polyaenus, able to gain access to the military dockyards and burn thirteen ships and their sheds before escap-
ing.[19] This affair certainly confirmed suspicions that Philip was a

16. F. W. Walbank, *Philip V of Macedon* (Cambridge 1940) 108–10. For events in
Egypt and Syria, see Will II, 32–36, 39–59.
17. Polyb. 13.5.1; Polyaen. 5.17.2. Piracy aside, Philip could certainly expect
Rhodian opposition to any move against the Propontis or the small Aegean states.
18. Polyb. 18.54.8–10; Diod. 28.1.1; Holleaux IV, 124–45.
19. Polyb. 13.5.1–6; Polyaean. 5.17.2. Though it is probable that Heracleides was
sent out in 204, it is not certain. It is hard to believe that Heracleides would be
permitted access to a high-security area such as the military yards, but Polyaenus'

silent partner in the activities of Dicaearchus and the pro-Macedonian
Cretans, but Rhodes nevertheless took no action. Since he had made
no overt move and could deny the authenticity of Heracleides' letter,
Philip could easily assert that he had done nothing to break the peace
with Rhodes. Further, there was little the Rhodians could do against
the land-based Macedonian power except to continue operations
against the king's friends in Crete.

Philip himself could make no move into the Aegean until his fleet
was built, and during 204 and 203 he busied himself in Illyria and
Thrace, securing his frontiers against the day when he would be
occupied elsewhere.[20] Meanwhile, in 203 Antiochus finally initiated
his assault on Ptolemaic possessions, and the Egyptian court began
actively to seek Macedonian aid against the inevitable advance into
Syria. Philip had little use for an entangling agreement with Egypt,
but kept the ambassadors dangling, since the threat of a Macedonian-
Egyptian alliance provided him with a handy diplomatic spear to
rattle in Antiochus' direction.[21] Antiochus, for his part, had no desire
to become embroiled with Philip, and the result was a secret agreement between the two monarchs in the winter of 203–2.[22]

That this agreement actually existed and was not a deliberate Pergamene-Rhodian fabrication is clear; at one point in his campaign
against Pergamum, Philip requested supplies from the Seleucid satrap Zeuxis "according to the treaty."[23] And the pact was clearly

---

account can be reconciled with the corresponding fragments of Polybius (see Holleaux IV, 136, n. 3), and it is quite possible that Heracleides was able to set his fires
without actually gaining entrance to the yards.

20. See Walbank, *Philip* 111–12.

21. See Schmitt, *Antiochos* 189–237. Egyptian appeal: Polyb. 15.25.13. A marriage
alliance was proposed.

22. Polyb. 3.2.8, 15.20.1–8, 16.1.8–9, 24.6; Livy 31.14.5; App. *Mac.* 4.1–2; Just.
30.2.8; Trog. *Prol.* 30; Hieron. *Comm. in Dan.* 11.13; Johan. Antioch. fg. 54 (*FHG* IV
558).

23. Polyb. 16.1.8. The treaty was certainly more than a local arrangement with
Zeuxis (R. Errington, "The Alleged Syro-Macedonian Pact and the Origins of the
Second Macedonian War," *Athen.* 49 (1971) 336–54), as it is inconceivable that Anti-
ochus, who was only as far away as Coele-Syria, would leave it to his satrap to
determine such important policy as reaction to the Antigonid presence in Asia Minor.
For what must be the last word on the agreement, see Schmitt, *Antiochos* 237–61.
Schmitt goes much too far, however, in accepting the pact and scheme for dividing
Egypt at face value.

aimed against Egypt, but because of the probability of exaggeration, either through rumor or deliberately by Attalus and the Rhodians, the specific details in the sources for a division of the Egyptian empire cannot be used to define the exact terms of the deal. At the very least, the agreement involved the cooperation of the rulers to the extent of temporary mutual acceptance of their respective activities in the Aegean and Coele-Syria. One can speculate that there was perhaps some discussion of the division of Ptolemaic possessions, but the serious intentions of the two kings undoubtedly did not go beyond noninterference with one another's enterprises, and only until either found it convenient to turn on the other. Anatolia was an old and important part of the Seleucids' patrimony, a territory for which they had spilled blood since the days of Seleucus I; that Antiochus, the conqueror of the east and greatest son of the dynasty since the founder, would seriously consider surrendering any part of it to the Antigonid house is incredible. This pact was an agreement of the moment. Philip undoubtedly hoped to have secured his Aegean empire before Antiochus had finished with Egypt, while on his side Antiochus probably entertained happy thoughts of Philip and Attalus wearing each other out in a protracted war and rendering Asia Minor ripe for the return of Seleucid power.

Armed with his agreement with Antiochus and with the fleet finally complete, Philip was ready in early 202 to make the opening moves of his eastern program. While preparations for the expedition were under way, he ordered his client Olympichus, dynast of Alinda, to begin to expand his power in Caria, thus putting further indirect pressure on Rhodes. When Olympichus began operations against the Greek communities in the area, the Rhodians promptly complained to Philip, who assured them of his guarantee of the security of the Carian cities. When the dynast's man Podilus subsequently attacked Iasus, the Rhodians produced Philip's letters and demanded that Olympichus cease his aggression.[24] Inasmuch as Philip is found be-

24. See Holleaux IV, 146–62, which includes the pertinent inscriptions (*SGDI* 3750). The inscriptions are dated to early 202 by mention of "friendship and goodwill" between Philip and Rhodes. A fourth inscription (*BCH* 58 [1934] 281–88) names Olympichus as strategos of Philip, but this inscription must be dated after 202; see F. W. Walbank, "Olympichus of Alinda and the Carian Expedition of Antigonus

sieging the same city in the following year, it appears that for the moment, at least, the dynast backed down, apparently unwilling to face the Rhodians without the open support of Macedon.

If Philip's posture with regard to Caria was dictated by a policy of avoiding an open break with Rhodes, that policy was certainly cast to the winds with the launching of his fleet. The target was the Propontis, and insofar as the Rhodians were concerned, the king could hardly have chosen a more sensitive area. Arriving with his fleet, Philip quickly annexed the towns of Lysimacheia, Chalcedon, and Perinthus and then joined his kinsman Prusias in the siege of Cius. Here he was met by representatives from Rhodes and other neutral cities, and in response to their entreaties on behalf of the Cians he sent a delegate to Rhodes to argue his case. Meanwhile, however, he continued the assault on the city, and news of its destruction and the enslavement of its population reached Rhodes while his envoy was assuring the Rhodians of his good intentions. This was the crowning outrage, and Rhodes promptly declared war on Philip.[25]

The reasons behind Rhodes' declaration of war are not difficult to understand. Although there was no direct evidence against the king, the Rhodian leadership could hardly fail to see that Philip was the common element in the war in Crete and the affairs of Heracleides and Olymphichus, and they could easily guess that he probably also had something to do with Dicaearchus' expedition. Such a shadowy threat to Rhodes and the small states of the Aegean was of course not enough to move the island to war, especially when Philip had provided no real pretext, but the seizure of the four Propontic towns brought the Macedonian threat out of the shadows. Most immediately Pontic trade was endangered, a cause for which Rhodes had promptly gone to war in 220, but more generally, the Macedonian expansion threatened the political position of the republic. As acknowledged leader of the independent cities, Rhodes could hardly stand by and watch Philip eliminate those cities one by one, and the treatment of Cius vividly indicated there was little hope of compro-

Doson," *JHS* 62 (1942) 8–13. Whether this Olympichus is the same man or the son of the dynast in Polyb. 5.90.1 is impossible to determine.

25. Polyb. 15.22.1–23.10, 18.3.11–12, 4.5–7; Strabo 12.4.3 (563). Lysimacheia, Chalcedon, and Cius were allied to Aetolia.

mise. Further, with a century of experience in Hellenistic power politics, the Rhodians knew that the Pontic expedition was not likely to be the end of Philip's aggressions, and though they were probably not yet aware of the secret agreements with Antiochus, they may well have had some suspicion of royal collusion. Antiochus had not raised the slightest protest over Philip's cooperation with Prusias, a natural enemy of the Seleucids, or over his annexation of Lysimacheia, to which the Seleucids had traditional claims. The Rhodians could see as easily as Philip had done that with a weakling Egypt fully engaged with Antiochus in Syria, the opportunity was ripe for a serious Macedonian move into the Aegean. Thus, with its prestige and Pontic economic interests already on the line and with the near certainty of further serious challenges from Macedon, Rhodes determined to take up the sword immediately rather than await Philip's next move.

Because of the lateness of the campaigning season and probably also because of the need to mobilize their fleet fully, the Rhodians took no action during the remainder of 202, and Philip completed his campaign for the year by treacherously seizing the free city of Thasos on his way back to Macedon. In the spring of the following year he set out with a fleet of between forty and fifty warships and 150 small cutters, or *lembi,* and, meeting little resistance, proceeded to take possession of the Cyclades and the Ptolemaic naval base of Samos.[26] By taking Samos, Philip not only eliminated a potential threat by neutralizing the Egyptian squadron, but also gained an eastern naval base and all its resources, including the Ptolemaic vessels, some of which he fitted out for his own use. Moreover, this base was excellently situated for covering Rhodes and launching a campaign in Caria, where Philip already had some influence. Operations in Caria would have the advantage of being damaging to Rhodes, because of its mainland possessions, while being less threatening to Attalus of Pergamum, who might respond militarily to further aggressions in the northeast.

26. Thasos: Polyb. 15.24.1–3; fleet: Polyb. 16.2.9; Cyclades and Samos: Polyb. 3.2.8, 16.2.4, 2.9, 7.6; Livy 31.15.8, 31.4; Walbank, *Philip* 308–9. Only Andros, Cythnos, and Paros were given significant garrisons. An inscription in honor of a Samian doctor makes it very probable that the city of Samos at least was taken by force (*Ath. Mitt.* 82 [1957] 233–41, no. 64).

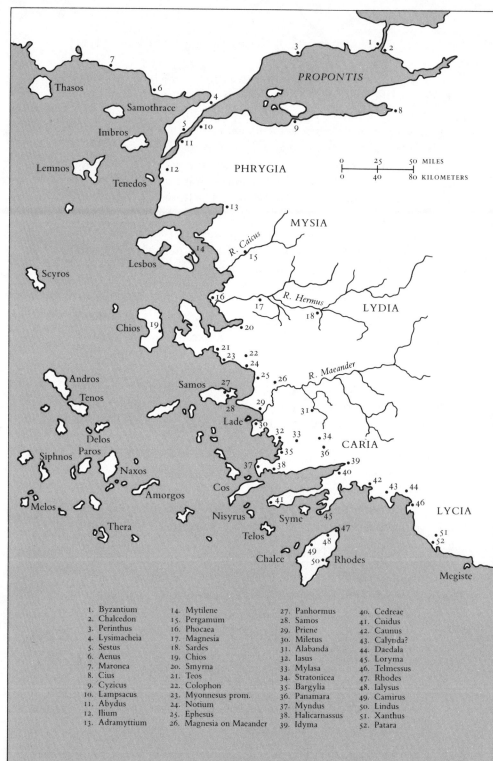

PROPONTIS

Thasos

Samothrace

Imbros

Lemnos

Tenedos

PHRYGIA

0   25   50 MILES
0   40   80 KILOMETERS

Scyros

MYSIA

R. Caicus

Lesbos

LYDIA

R. Hermus

Chios

Andros

R. Maeander

Tenos

Samos

CARIA

Delos

Siphnos
Paros

Naxos

Cos

Amorgos

Melos

Nisyrus

LYCIA

Thera

Syme

Telos

Chalce   Rhodes

Megiste

1. Byzantium
2. Chalcedon
3. Perinthus
4. Lysimacheia
5. Sestus
6. Aenus
7. Maronea
8. Cius
9. Cyzicus
10. Lampsacus
11. Abydus
12. Ilium
13. Adramyttium

14. Mytilene
15. Pergamum
16. Phocaea
17. Magnesia
18. Sardes
19. Chios
20. Smyrna
21. Teos
22. Colophon
23. Myonnesus prom.
24. Notium
25. Ephesus
26. Magnesia on Maeander

27. Panhormus
28. Samos
29. Priene
30. Miletus
31. Alabanda
32. Iasus
33. Mylasa
34. Stratonicea
35. Bargylia
36. Panamara
37. Myndus
38. Halicarnassus
39. Idyma

40. Cedreae
41. Cnidus
42. Caunus
43. Calynda?
44. Daedala
45. Loryma
46. Telmessus
47. Rhodes
48. Ialysus
49. Camirus
50. Lindus
51. Xanthus
52. Patara

MAP 2. Western Anatolia

The Rhodians responded to the seizure of Samos by sending a squadron of perhaps thirty ships to the area of Lade island to screen the city of Miletus, the most likely Macedonian objective and the door to Caria and their own Peraea. Recognizing the magnitude of the threat—Rhodes had little hope of dealing with the Macedonians on land—and the superiority of their seamanship, the Rhodians accepted an engagement against the numerically superior enemy fleet. The battle was apparently brief and ended when a stricken Rhodian vessel raised its jury mast to escape and was followed by many of the ships nearby, thus compelling the whole squadron to retire. It is not clear whether this abrupt disengagement was a sloppily executed withdrawal or the result of a misunderstanding, but in any case only two quinqueremes were lost in the affair. Having driven the Rhodians off, Philip then entered Miletus, whose cowed citizens honored him and Heracleides with crowns.[27]

At this point Attalus declared war on Philip. There was certainly no love lost between Attalus and the Rhodians; he had been almost the only monarch who did not aid the island after the earthquake and the two states had been on opposite sides during the Byzantine affair in 220. More recently, Attalus had established ties with the distasteful Aetolians, and his construction of a fleet and its use in the First Macedonian War revealed imperial designs threatening to the freedom of the Aegean and consequently to Rhodian interests. For the moment, however, mutual need overcame mutual animosity. Rhodes needed allies, and with the only other significant navy in the Aegean Attalus was a perfect candidate, especially since his own interests were also being injured or threatened. Not only was Philip building the Aegean empire that Attalus coveted, but he had also cooperated with Pergamum's enemy Prusias and had seized cities allied to the Aetolian League. It may also be assumed that in their appeals to Attalus the Rhodians were careful to point out that Philip

27. Polyb. 16.10.1, 14.5, 15.1–8. Polybius does not explicitly state that Philip took Miletus, but he almost certainly did so. Many scholars view the incident in terms of panic, but it is hard to imagine Rhodian sailors panicking, particularly in a situation in which they had lost only two ships. The order of the battles of Lade and Chios and the raid on Pergamum is disputed; see R. M. Berthold, "Lade, Pergamum, and Chios," *Hist.* 24 (1975) 150–63.

had probably also been behind Dicaearchus' raids on the cities of the Troad. The Pergamene king had hitherto hesitated to join the Rhodians, presumably out of fear of bringing Macedonian and Bithynian might upon himself, but with Philip's entry into Miletus the danger had become critical. Rhodes alone clearly would not be able to stop Philip, and the capture of Miletus raised the specter of Antigonid power in Asia and all that that meant to the security of Pergamum. Deciding that the threat now warranted decisive action, Attalus declared war and ordered mobilization of his fleet. His military preparations on land were still incomplete, but the stronghold of Pergamum would provide security while the fleet prepared for the more critical naval operations.[28] If they had not done so already, Byzantium, Cyzicus, and Cos, all of which were directly threatened by Philip, now also joined the coalition against Macedon.[29]

Philip's reaction was immediate. Leaving his fleet at either Miletus or some spot farther north, he marched his army against Pergamum, hoping to knock Attalus right back out of the war with a sudden blitz.[30] The quick defeat of Pergamum would certainly undermine the morale of the Rhodians and other allies and perhaps even drive them to seek peace. Philip may also have had in mind Attalus' excellent connections with Rome. He was able to deal with any forces that could be sent against him,[31] but he was not strong enough to take the city of Pergamum. Moreover, he had counted on feeding his army off the land, but was forestalled by Attalus, who had apparently ordered the harvest and any potential plunder to be brought into the towns. Angered by his failure, Philip vented his rage on the temples and sanctuaries in the vicinity, and then, driven by the need for provisions and plunder, moved southeast to Thyateira and back north to the

28. Polyb. 16.9.4. On Attalid policy and connections, see Starr 65–66; Hansen 46–50, 52–53. As with the Rhodians, Attalus' declaration of war technically made him the aggressor against Philip (Polyb. 16.34.5, 18.6.2; Livy 31.18.2, 32.34.7). That Rhodes appealed to Attalus for aid is only an assumption, but a reasonable one.

29. Byzantium: Polyb. 16.2.10. Cyzicus is found with the allies in 200 (Polyb. 16.31.3). Cos was heavily influenced by Rhodes and was its ally in the Cretan War (*Syll.*[3] 569).

30. So Holleaux IV, 217, 254; Will II, 107.

31. Polyb. 16.1.1: Φίλιππος . . . νομίζων οἷον αὐτόχειρ Ἀττάλου γενέσθαι; Walbank II, 500–501, *Philip* 119, n. 1, suggests this might refer to a Pergamene defeat.

plain of Thebe. Unable to supply his troops in either region, he marched southeast again, to Hiera Come, where he sent to Zeuxis, Antiochus' governor at Sardes, asking for provisions in accordance with the secret agreements. Receiving little aid from that quarter, however, he moved to rejoin his fleet, probably in the area of Ephesus.[32]

Having failed to force Attalus out of the war quickly by a land assault, Philip had now to contend with the threat posed by the Pergamene fleet, which, united with the Rhodian, would be a match for his own. Because of its position, Chios now became of key strategic importance; control of the island would bring a base ideally suited for dealing with the Attalid navy and preventing the union of the allied squadrons. He thus collected his fleet, which had been carrying on operations among the Sporades,[33] sailed north, and invested the city of Chios. Attalus and the Rhodians also recognized the importance of the island, however, and, joining their fleets, they undertook a blockade of the Macedonian forces.[34] With the siege apparently moving very slowly, Philip determined to make a sudden break for the safety of Samos, taking advantage of the loose order of the enemy, who expected him to continue the siege. The allies were surprised, but not taken completely off guard, and Philip was forced into the naval battle he clearly wished to avoid.[35]

Philip went into battle with 53 cataphracts, an unknown number of undecked vessels, and his 150 *lembi;* the allies opposed him with 65 cataphracts and 12 lighter vessels.[36] Since the allies were caught

32. Polyb. 16.1.1–9, 18.2.2, 6.4; Diod. 28.5.1; App. *Mac.* 4.1; Livy 31.46.4, 32.33.5; see Holleaux IV, 247–55; Walbank II, 500–503. The fact of the harvest makes it probable that the raid took place sometime in June; see Holleaux IV, 283.

33. Cos is attacked: *Syll.*[3] 568, 569; *Inscr. Cos.* 10, 11; Carpathus: *Syll.*[3] 570; Calymna: *SGDI* 3590. It is not clear in some cases whether the inscription refers to Philip's navy or Cretan corsairs; see Holleaux IV, 272–80. Whatever its previous relationship to Macedon, Nisyrus now definitely fell under Philip's control (*Syll.*[3] 572 = *IG* xii.3 9), only to be incorporated by Rhodes in 200 (*Syll.*[3] 673); see F&B 148–52.

34. So H. Stier, *Roms Aufstieg zur Weltmacht und die griechische Welt* (Cologne 1957) 99.

35. Polyb. 16.2.1–6; App. *Mac.* 4.1 (wrong); Plut. *Mor.* 245b–c (apocryphal?); Front. *Strat.* 3.9.8, and *Syll.*[3] 579 possibly refer to this siege.

36. Polyb. 16.2.9–10; Holleaux IV, 235–43; Walbank II, 505–7. Since Attalus had 35 heavy ships during the last war, it is likely that a little more than half of the

somewhat off guard, not all of their fleet was able to engage the enemy simultaneously, and two separate battles developed, with the Pergamene contingent of perhaps 35 of the cataphracts taking on Philip's right wing and the Rhodians and others meeting his left. The allies had the advantage in heavy warships and seamanship, but the *lembi* to some extent foiled Rhodian tactics, while the Macedonian marines had a distinct edge when it came to boarding. As it turned out, though Philip very nearly captured Attalus by driving his flagship aground, his fleet clearly got the worst of it in the battle. Polybius' figure for the allied casualties is definitely wrong, an error that in turn casts suspicion on his low number of allied ships lost: five cataphracts and two lighter vessels; in all probability the allied losses were greater, particularly among Attalus' squadron. Philip's losses are given as twenty-eight cataphracts, three lighter vessels, and half the *lembi,* heavy but believable, particularly if one supposes allied losses to be greater than those Polybius provides. So long as they avoided close contact with the Macedonian ships and concentrated on disabling and ramming tactics, as the Rhodians in fact did, the greater skills of the allies would surely begin to tell. Support for the reliability of the figures is also seen in the statistical breakdown of the Macedonian losses: with fewer ships than the Pergamene squadron, the Rhodians accounted for nearly twice the number of *lembi,* as one would expect, considering their particular tactics and skill. In the course of the struggle Philip also lost his admiral, Democrates, while the Rhodian nauarch, Theophiliscus, died of his wounds on the day following the battle.[37]

Whatever his exact losses, Philip certainly did not want a return engagement. Though claiming victory by anchoring among the

---

cataphracts were his; most of the rest of the ships were Rhodian, with a few vessels from Byzantium and probably also Cyzicus (as later at Abydus [Polyb. 16.31.3; Livy 31.17.6]) and possibly Cos.

37. Polyb. 16.3.1–7.6, 9.1–5, 14.5, 18.2.2, 6.3, 8.10; *OGIS* 283; Walbank II, 507–11. Polybius is clearly drawing on a Rhodian source; see Ullrich 36–39. Polyb. 16.7.5 records about 60 Rhodian and 70 Pergamene lives lost, but a Rhodian quinquereme went down with all hands (5.2–3), most of Theophiliscus' marines were lost (5.5), and Dionysodorus lost virtually all his men (3.15); these three instances alone would account for many more than 130 men. The reading τῶν δ' Ἀιγυπτίων in 16.7.6 seems secure; see Holleaux IV, 239–45.

wreckage, he refused the challenge when the allies sailed out from Chios on the second day after the battle and sailed instead for the haven of Samos. His navy could no longer face the united allied fleets, and the heavy casualties of the battle had depressed the morale of his men.[38] Consequently, he moved south and launched his invasion of Caria, perhaps hoping that with Macedonian attention turned toward the south, Attalus might lose interest in the war.[39] In any case, he knew that on land, at least, his forces were relatively invincible, and that by attacking their mainland possessions he could put pressure on the Rhodians which they could not resist. After an initial failure against Cnidus he rapidly subjugated most of the Rhodian Peraea by autumn, and then, moving his fleet to the gulf of Bargylia, he concentrated on northern Caria and took Iasus, Bargylia, and towns in the interior. During these last operations, however, the allies had taken a countermeasure and stationed their combined fleet at the gulf, thereby blockading the Macedonian navy. But more important for its eventual effect on the war, a diplomatic move against Philip was also decided upon, and Attalus and the Rhodians dispatched embassies to the west to seek aid from Rome.[40]

This decision must be seen as one of crucial importance in the histories of Greece and Rome, for Rome's positive response and subsequent intervention would rapidly and drastically alter the face of the Hellenistic world. Yet there remains a great deal of confusion concerning the causes and the timing of the appeal to the west, particularly with regard to the Rhodians. Why did Rhodes, whose policy had hitherto been directed toward the maintenance of the balance of power and the freedom of the Aegean, now undertake to bring a new and overwhelmingly powerful military presence into the eastern Mediterranean? Much has been made of the role of the nauarch Theophiliscus, who was allegedly the heart of the resistance to seeking western intervention, a course avidly advocated by Attalus. The nau-

38. Polyb. 16.8.1–10.
39. Walbank, *Philip* 125.
40. Caria: Polyb. 16.11.1–6, 24.1–9; App. *Mac.* 4.1; Polyaen. 4.18.1–2. For further references and a full study, see Holleaux IV, 222–24, 255–63, 272–82, 314–33; Walbank II, 512–15, 529–33; Mastrocinque, *Caria* 170–73. Embassies: Polyb. 16.24.1–3; Livy 31.2.1–2; App. *Mac.* 4.2.

arch's death at Chios thus removed the one important obstacle to the king's burning desire to bring Rome into the conflict, and the appeal was made.[41] This view, however, is based more on supposition than on evidence. Theophiliscus may well have been the dynamo of the war effort, but there is not the slightest evidence that his energies were in any way connected with the question of Roman intervention. Polybius' eulogy on the nauarch (16.9.2–4) speaks only of his role in spurring the allies to vigorous action; no mention is made of Rome.

Moreover, it is also not at all clear that Attalus was from the outset determined to seek Roman aid. He had joined Rome in the first struggle with Philip and had maintained excellent relations with the Romans,[42] but this does not mean he wanted them as partners again. It is quite reasonable to think he preferred, if possible, to settle Aegean affairs without the presence of a dominant and possibly troublesome ally.[43] It is of course also quite reasonable that Attalus, trusting in Roman goodwill, did in fact consider western intervention from the beginning, but this is very weak ground on which to erect a theory for the allied appeal and its timing.

It has been suggested that it was the revelation at this time of the secret agreement that turned the Rhodians to Rome, since they realized that Philip's operations were only part of an even greater plan of conquest and felt compelled, against their natural inclinations, to call in more powerful help.[44] But this seems hardly likely. In the first place, knowledge of the pact would surely not come as a surprise to the Rhodians, who were past masters of the Hellenistic diplomatic game and who could certainly read the signs. Inasmuch as they were at war with Philip and had possessions in Caria, they would have been following his movements on the mainland carefully. And even if they had not heard of Philip's dealings with Zeuxis, which seems unlikely, it was nevertheless plain that Antiochus was not lifting a finger to hinder the Macedonian in his Asian adventure. Moreover, it

41. E.g., van Gelder 46–52; Schmitt 59–61.
42. See Hansen 46–52.
43. So A. McDonald and F. W. Walbank, "The Origins of the Second Macedonian War," *JRS* 27 (1937) 187.
44. Ibid.; Schmitt 62–63; B. Ferro, *Le origini della II querra macedonica* (Palermo 1960) 72.

was utterly critical for Rhodes, whose autonomy for the last century had depended to a large extent on playing the great powers off against one another, to know the attitudes of those powers, especially with the outbreak of war with one of them. It is thus impossible to believe that Rhodes did not immediately extend diplomatic feelers to the Seleucid court once it was at war with Philip, even though the fragmented sources make no mention of such an approach.

The Rhodians' basic need was simply to know Antiochus' position, but it is certainly within reason to believe that they thought also of the possibilities of an alliance. Traditionally, of course, Rhodes had relied on Egypt, but in 201 Egypt was wholly absorbed in its own pressing problems, and that left only Antiochus as a possible source of support against Philip. To be sure, Antiochus was not the most comfortable of allies for the Rhodians, since he was apparently about to assault their century-old friend, Egypt, and since their Peraea was part of the territory claimed by the Seleucid house, but Philip was the threat of the moment, and the Rhodians would naturally have explored the possibility of making Antiochus the ally of the moment. Such a move would not represent simple wishful thinking on the part of the Rhodians; Antiochus might well be expected to consider it in his interest to aid the island republic in keeping a major power out of Asia Minor, even though a day of reckoning between Rhodes and himself might ultimately have to come. In any case, the actual discovery that there was indeed an agreement between the two kings would come only as a confirmation of Rhodian suspicions and would hardly cause any significant change in the island's strategic thinking.

Furthermore, even were the news of the pact to come as a diplomatic bombshell, just how drastically would this discovery alter the situation? The assumption in the argument is that the military position of Rhodes and its allies with regard to Philip by himself was entirely manageable, and that it was only the greater threat of Seleucid-Antigonid cooperation, whether active or passive, that forced their hand.[45] Examination of the military picture, however, demonstrates that this was not the case. Certainly the situation on the sea was

45. McDonald and Walbank 187: ". . . they [the allies] appeared to have the Aegean situation in hand."

favorable to the allies. The Rhodians had apparently lost only two ships at Lade, and although allied losses at Chios were clearly larger than those Polybius provides, at the end of the year the combined Pergamene-Rhodian fleet was quite able to put Philip on the defensive and blockade him in Bargylia. In addition, Rhodian military involvement in Crete appears for the most part to have ended in 201, thus freeing additional resources for the struggle with the Macedonian monarch. But the allied position on the mainland was far from rosy. Attalus had shown himself unable to defend his territory, resisting only from the stronghold of Pergamum, and Philip's troops were now in possession of most of the Rhodian Peraea, as well as northern Caria and the Cyclades. Pergamum and Rhodes simply did not have the forces necessary to face Philip in the field and prevent further conquests, let alone to regain what had already been lost. As it happened, even with Philip fully engaged in the west, the Rhodians were still battling with his general Deinocrates in Caria four years later.[46] So long as Attalus and his fleet were kept in the war, the Rhodians did not need to fear for the safety of the island, but the prospect of evicting Macedonian power from Asia must have appeared dark.[47]

Thus, word that Philip and Antiochus were scheming together made little difference to the Rhodians. The threat of Seleucid aid to Philip would not serve to convince them of the need to seek outside help for the simple reason that they were already in need of that help in order to deal with Philip alone. Besides, Rhodes had seen too much Hellenistic history to be overly concerned with the possibility of serious cooperation between Philip and Antiochus against either itself or Egypt, especially when that cooperation involved Antigonid occupation of portions of Asia Minor. And news of cooperation between the kings to the extent of Antiochus' temporarily allowing Philip a free hand in Anatolia would alter nothing, since the Rhodians must have known from the start that Antiochus, busy with his assault on Coele-Syria, was unavailable as an ally.

Pact or no pact, Rhodes faced a very dismal military situation at the

46. Livy 33.18.1–22.
47. So D. Magie, "The 'Agreement' between Philip V and Antiochus III for the Partition of the Egyptian Empire," *JRS* 29 (1939) 42 (who rejects the pact); Will II, 110.

end of 201. Most of its mainland possessions, including part of the Rhodian state itself, were in Macedonian hands, and there was no way to recover these losses without the help of some major power. But neither of the two other major Hellenistic powers was available. Egypt had been reduced almost to a state of semianarchy by native uprisings and a bloody struggle for the regency of Ptolemy V Epiphanes, and to all appearances, Antiochus was about to dismember the Ptolemaic kingdom, a situation in itself extremely dangerous to Rhodes. With literally no one else to turn to, Rhodes and Attalus followed the natural line of the latter's excellent connections and sought Roman intervention.[48]

This decision has been seen as a serious reversal of policy, undertaken only under pressure from Attalus, but this interpretation does not seem quite accurate.[49] The Pergamene dynast probably began to think of his western friends once Philip invaded the mainland, but as has been seen, it was military necessity rather than any political lassitude that turned Rhodes' head. Further, since the Rhodians did not by any stretch of the imagination have an anti-Roman policy, dealing with the Italian republic was not in itself any change of program. But the fact remains that Rhodes was inviting onto the Hellenistic stage a new and powerful player, one whose ultimate role among the Greek states was far from predictable. For a century Rhodes' policy had been concerned with the preservation of a balance of power among the great monarchies, and to all appearances it was now abandoning that policy by calling in the Romans, who must surely disturb the equilibrium. This is true, but the action must be correctly understood. The maintenance of a balance of power was not an end in itself, but only the means to the island's ultimate goals: the protection and development of its commerce and its influence in international affairs and the security and independence of the Rhodian republic. The fact is that at the end of 201 these goals were best served by calling in Rome, dangerous though that course might be to the power structure of the Hellenistic world. Unaided Rhodes could not hope to regain its mainland territories or prevent the development of the Macedonian

48. Magie, *JRS* 29, 42; Stier 101; Will II, 110.
49. E.g., Niese II, 584; van Gelder 122–24; Schmitt 60–63.

hegemony into which Philip was forcing one by one the free cities of the Aegean. Without help it could end the commercially disruptive war only by accepting heavy losses, and if Attalus and his fleet were to leave the struggle, the situation would become even more serious. Quite likely Rhodes did not like the idea of inviting into Greece a distinctly non-Greek and dangerously powerful state, but its existence as a meaningful power in a free Aegean was imperiled. Whatever danger Rome might ultimately represent to the balance of power—which Antiochus seemed in any case on the verge of dismantling—Philip was by far the more immediate and serious threat, and Roman intervention was the only apparent solution.

To accuse Rhodes of political shortsightedness in making this decision is to blame it for being unable to foretell the events of the next half century. The Rhodians undoubtedly understood as well as anyone could in the year 201 what troubles Roman intervention might bring, but much more real and pressing were the present dangers, not only for Rhodes, but also for Pergamum and scores of small states throughout the Aegean. And events, after all, proved the Rhodian decision correct. The Romans defeated Philip, but they deliberately left Macedon an unbroken power and evacuated Greece. That another generation would see the Hellenistic world falling under Roman sway is not a charge that can be laid at Rhodes' doorstep.

CHAPTER 6

Rome and the
Second Macedonian War

THE Rhodian and Pergamene embassies arrived in Rome sometime in the autumn of 201 and presented their case to the Senate. In their appeal to the *patres* presumably they dwelled on the potential threat posed to Rome by the pact between Philip and Antiochus, since no other aspect of their war with Macedon could be of any concern to the Romans. Although there is no direct evidence, it seems certain from the outcome of the consular elections at the end of 201 that the Senate responded favorably and inclined toward intervention. In those elections P. Sulpicius Galba, the Roman commander for the second half of the First Macedonian War, was elected consul and assigned Macedon as his province, a sure indication of renewed senatorial interest in the East.[1]

Exactly why the Roman Senate decided to accept the allied appeal for intervention has long been a question of intense debate, since the decision was a step of critical importance to both the Greek and Roman worlds. The resolution certainly cannot be attributed to concern for the freedom of the Greeks. Whatever philhellenic sentiment may have existed in the Senate, until this time Rome had demonstrated no concern for the welfare of Greeks, and it is hardly likely that a state that had recently been allied to Aetolia was going to risk a major war simply because of Philip's aggressions. That the decision

---

1. Polyb. 16.24.3; Livy 31.2.1, 4.4, 5.1, 6.1; App. *Mac.* 4.2.

was not simply the manifestation of an aggressive territorial-commercial imperialism is demonstrated by the final evacuation of Greece, and given the state of Italian land and capital, such a policy would have made particularly little sense in 201.[2]

A more reasonable motive is fear, but this consideration must be tempered by the rebuff handed the Aetolian embassy of 202, for the Senate, whatever its feelings of annoyance toward the league, would hardly have so harshly rejected the appeal of such a strong and strategically important ally were it seriously worried about a threat from the Balkans.[3] But in 201 Philip, embroiled in the east and defeated at sea by Rhodes and Pergamum, posed no threat to Rome, and it is difficult to believe that the Senate was so unfamiliar with eastern affairs that it was overly concerned about the possibility that Philip and Antiochus might act in concert against Rome. True, Philip might pose a danger in the future, perhaps when Rome had its hands full elsewhere; this was, after all, the man who was already responsible for the "stab in the back" during the struggle with Hannibal, and such things the Romans did not easily forget or forgive. But such shadowy fears or thoughts of vengeance or senatorial dreams of glory would not alone have brought a decision for war when the dust of Zama had hardly settled; they were not enough to prevent the unqualified rejection of the Aetolians a year earlier.

In 201, however, opportunity came calling in the guise of the embassies from Rhodes and Pergamum. Rome was being invited into Greece by one of the most reputable powers in the Greek world, and with Rhodes and Pergamum as allies the Romans could face Philip under a philhellenic banner, something all but impossible had they been allied with the Aetolians alone. In military terms the moment saw the allied coalition in possession of the dominant naval

2. For Italian land and capital, see Livy 31.13.1–9. The rebuff of the Aetolians in 202 also speaks against imperialist designs on Greece; see below, n. 3.

3. App. *Mac.* 4.2; Livy 31.29.4, 30.26.2(?). It is possible, as T. Dorey contends in "The Alleged Aetolian Embassy to Rome," *CR* 74 (1960) 9, that the rebuff was not quite so harsh as Livy makes it, but the rejection was unqualified and strong enough to result in the collapse of the policy of the league, which refused immediately to join the allies two years later. The fact that Zama remained to be fought is immaterial, for the Senate could easily have stalled the Aetolians, rather than put them off completely. On the dating of the embassy, see Walbank, *Philip* 310–11.

force in the Aegean, Philip with part of his army committed in Asia, and Rome, though weary from the Punic conflict, nevertheless with veteran armies ready at hand. In Roman eyes Philip was a force that would have to be reckoned with, and the Rhodian-Pergamene appeal made the present moment attractive enough to decide the senators, whether motivated by strategic fears or personal ambition, that the confrontation would be now.[4]

But the Roman people were tired of war, and when the question was put to the centuries at the beginning of the consulship of Galba, the new conflict was overwhelmingly rejected. Nevertheless, while the Senate mobilized its forces for a second vote, an embassy composed of C. Claudius Nero, M. Aemilius Lepidus, and P. Sempronius Tuditanus was dispatched to sound out Greek opinion and to ascertain the position of Antiochus.[5] The envoys carried the Roman ultimatum to Philip—cessation of war against the Greeks and submission of Attalus' claims to arbitration—but as they lacked the necessary *iussum populi,* their competency was limited to publishing these demands and soliciting support. Accordingly, the commission visited Epirus, Athamania, Aetolia, and Achaea, and arrived in the Piraeus in the spring of 200.[6]

4. K. Petzold, *Die Eröffnung des zweiten römisch-makedonischen Krieges* (Berlin 1940) 36–37, is the only one who has recognized this opportunistic nature of the war. How much the ambitions of individual senators and politics within the Senate influenced the decision is impossible to say, but exact Roman motivations are not important in a consideration of the role played by the Rhodians in the decision for war. The Senate could not have had serious intentions, defensive or offensive, in Greece before the Aetolian embassy, and the obvious event after that is the Rhodian-Pergamene appeal, despite Livy's lack of emphasis on it. (What patriotic historian would say that his country declared war because opportunity knocked?)

5. Livy 31.2.3–4, 6.3–4; Polyb. 16.27.5, 34.2; App. *Mac.* 4.2; Just. 30.3. These are not the stated purposes of the embassy, but they follow from the reconstruction of the ensuing events; on the precise chronology, see below, n. 6. For this confusing period up to the ultimatum at Abydus the account of McDonald and Walbank (accepted with reservations by Petzold 37–43) is generally followed.

6. Polyb. 16.25.2–6, 26.6, 27.1–5. On the question of the embassy and the *ius fetiale,* see McDonald and Walbank 192–97 and F. W. Walbank, "Roman Declaration of War in the 3rd and 2nd Centuries," *CP* 44 (1949) 15–19, against J. W. Rich, *Declaring War in the Roman Republic in the Period of Transmarine Expansion* (Brussels 1976) 56–59, 73–87, who surveys opinion on the subject. As the Roman calendar was at this time about one and a half months ahead of the Julian calendar, the consuls probably entered office and the embassy departed in late January. It is thus very

The stalemate in Asia was meanwhile broken when sometime in the early spring Philip escaped the blockade at Bargylia by means of an old ruse: through a "deserter" he leaked the information that he intended to fight the following day, then during the night lit false watch fires and slipped his fleet past the unsuspecting allies. Leaving his Asian conquests garrisoned under Deinocrates, he made his way back to Macedon with Attalus and the Rhodians in hot pursuit.[7] Awaiting him there was an appeal from the Acarnanians for aid in punishing Athens for a hostile incident of the previous autumn, and Philip, frustrated by the setbacks in Asia, foolishly but characteristically agreed to the request, sending Macedonian troops and some naval elements. Attica was then ravaged by the reinforced Acarnanians and four Athenian ships were seized, and the all but helpless Athenians responded by abolishing the tribes of Antigonas and Demetrias. Help, however, appeared in the form of the allied fleet, which put out from its station at Aegina and apparently dispersed the Macedonian squadron, the Rhodians recapturing the Athenian vessels.[8]

Hearing of the arrival of the Roman embassy, Attalus accepted an invitation from the grateful Athenians and sailed for the Piraeus, where he interviewed the three envoys. He was then escorted up to Athens and honored for his services, and when Rhodian envoys joined him a short time later, together they exhorted the Athenians to enter the struggle against Philip. Moved by the emotion of the occasion, the Athenian assembly declared war and voted the Rhodian people a golden crown and isopolity. Attalus then withdrew to Aegina and sent an unsuccessful appeal to the Aetolians, while the Rhodian squadron sailed off to begin liberating the islands from Phil-

---

reasonable that it was early spring when the Romans arrived in Athens and Philip, who arrived in Macedon about the same time, left Bargylia; although the two events can be related to one another, there seems to be no evidence to locate them precisely. The impression given by Polybius, however, is that Philip was trapped for some time in Asia, and putting the Romans in Athens in the early spring allows sufficient time for all known events to take place.

7. Polyaen. 4.18.2; Livy 31.14.11, 33.18.6. Philip had had a hard time during his confinement in Asia; see Polyb. 16.24.4–9.

8. Livy 31.14.7–11, 15.5; Polyb. 16.26.9; W. Pritchett, "An Unfinished Inscription, *IG*[2] 2363," *TAPA* 85 (1954) 159–64.

ip.[9] The Roman embassy lingered in Athens just long enough to find itself in an embarrassing situation when a Macedonian raiding party sent by an angry Philip showed up at the gates of Athens. Without the vote of the Roman people, the envoys were not actually empowered to deliver an *indictio belli,* but having advertised their ultimatum throughout Greece, they could hardly remain silent when directly confronted by Philip's troops, especially when that confrontation was before the walls of Athens. In order to preserve their credibility, the Romans consequently delivered their ultimatum to the Macedonian commander, Nicanor, and departed for Rhodes, leaving the Athenians with the problem of defending their country.[10]

Philip's response to the ultimatum was quite clear: a large force of infantry and horse was dispatched under Philocles to ravage Attica, and with no allied help in sight the Athenians probably began to wonder if perhaps their declaration of war had been a bit hasty. An embassy under Cephisodorus was sent out to seek immediate aid from Pergamum and Rhodes, as well as from Egypt, Crete, Aetolia, and finally Rome, but the appeals were unsuccessful, and Athens was forced to suffer constant raids throughout the summer.[11] Philip

9. Livy 31.14.11–15.10; Polyb. 16.25.1–26.10. Livy 31.15.7 states that the Rhodians had earlier granted isopolity to the Athenians, but there is no other record of this allegation, and it is extremely unlikely that Rhodes would ever have done such a thing. Livy puts the Rhodians at Aegina with Attalus, but Polybius says that after the Athenian meeting the fleet sailed for Ceos. The latter island would be an excellent position from which to watch the east Attic coastline, and the Rhodians might have preferred to stay elsewhere than with the Pergamene king (Thiel 233, n. 131). There is also a Cean decree (C. Dunant and J. Thomopoulos, "Inscriptions de Ceos," *BCH* 78 (1954) 338–44) which proves an alliance existed between the island and Rhodes and whose circumstances accommodate, if not support, the notion that the Rhodian fleet was stationed at Ceos; the inscription may, however, date from slightly later in the war.

10. Polyb. 16.27.1–5.

11. Livy 31.16.2; App. *Mac.* 4.1; Zon. 9.15. That the incursion of Philocles is a doublet of that of Nicanor is possible but not likely, for Livy seems to indicate that Philip knew of the ultimatum when he sent Philocles; see McDonald and Walbank 192, n. 75. The first two of the three alleged Athenian embassies (Livy 31.1.10, 5.2–6; App. *Mac.* 4.2; Flor. 1.23.7) may be rejected as reflections of the third, that under Cephisodorus (Paus. 1.36.5, supported by an inscription in Cephisodorus' honor [B. D. Meritt, "Greek Inscriptions," *Hesp.* 5 (1936) 419–28]). The embassy is also supported by the fact that at about this time the Cretan towns of Knossos, Cydonia, Gortyn, Hierapytna, Polyrrhenia, Lappa, and Priansus all struck coins bearing the

meanwhile began a new campaign in Thrace, aimed apparently at completing his seizure of the Propontis and tightening his grip on Pontic trade. Operating in connection with the fleet under Heracleides, he took Maronea, Aenus, and other towns, and by the end of the summer the Macedonians were in possession of the Thracian Chersonese and besieging Abydus, where they encountered stiff resistance. Before the town was taken, however, Philip was visited by Lepidus, the youngest member of the senatorial commission, which was still in Rhodes.[12] Perhaps about a month earlier the war question had been put before the Roman people again, and the centuries had this time voted for war.[13] In accordance with the instructions of the Senate, Lepidus was thus sent to deliver to Philip personally the ultimatum, which now correctly had the force of a *rerum repetitio*. The ante had been raised; Philip must not only cease warring against Greeks, but must also respect Ptolemaic possessions, and Rhodian as well as Pergamene claims must be submitted to arbitration. Protesting that he was not the aggressor, Philip naturally refused the demands, and with the ultimatum thus become an *indictio belli*, Lepidus returned to Rhodes, from which the Roman embassy moved on to Syria and Egypt.[14] The war between Rome and Macedon had now formally begun.

The addition of Ptolemaic possessions to the Roman demands was

---

head of Athena. Cephisodorus' embassy could have reached Rome before the second war vote was taken, a circumstance that would account for the strong tradition in Livy that an appeal from Athens played a role in the Roman decision; but as the second vote cannot really be dated, there is no way to know.

12. Livy 31.16.3–18.1; Polyb. 16.29.1–2, 30.1–34.2; Diod. 28.6.1.

13. Livy 31.6.5–8.1. The assumption of a time interval between the votes not only makes sense of the actions of the Roman envoys, but also is in itself only reasonable. If the war was so overwhelmingly rejected ("ab omnibus ferme centuriis"; but see Briscoe 71), more would have been required than simply disposing of the tribune Baebius (J. Balsdon, "Rome and Macedon, 205–200 B.C.," *JRS* 44 [1954] 38–39); rather, time would have been required for political manipulation and general propagandizing of the people, such as Galba's harangue represents. For a (perhaps too) precise chronology, see Walbank, *Philip* 314–16.

14. Polyb. 16.34.3–7; Livy 31.18.2–5; Diod. 28.6.1; App. *Mac.* 4.2. That the embassy was acting according to instructions is clear from Polyb. 16.34.2: κατὰ τὰς ἐντολάς; see also Livy 31.8.3–4. Polyb. 16.35.2 shows that a state of war did indeed exist after Abydus. The Greeks referred to in the ultimatum were probably only those of the mainland; see Walbank II, 537.

undoubtedly in answer to the king's present Thracian campaign, which was directed for the most part against towns belonging to Egypt.[15] Any estimation of Roman concern for the integrity of the Ptolemaic empire, however, must be tempered by the fact that the Senate readily accepted Antiochus' seizure of Coele-Syria. It is likely, of course, that the *patres* felt they had little choice in the matter if they wished to avoid war with both Philip and Antiochus, but the suspicion remains that Rome was at least as much concerned with backing Philip further into a diplomatic corner as with protecting Egyptian interests. The inclusion of Rhodian claims must be attributed, for lack of any other reason, to the influence of the Rhodians on the Romans during their stay on the island,[16] but the situation remains unclear. In 201 the Rhodian envoys must have apprised the Senate of their claims. Demanding the arbitration of these claims could have been no more outrageous to Philip than demanding it of Attalus', yet Attalus was included in the first ultimatum and the Rhodians were not. This might be a reflection of the greater influence of the Pergamene king, who had fought alongside the Romans in the previous war; it was he, after all, that had a private discussion with the Roman embassy and generally dominated the scene in Athens. It may also be that initially Rome was slighting the island republic, since the Rhodians had been the mainspring of the peace effort in the last war, and these efforts could certainly have been perceived by the Senate as hostile to Roman interests. In any case, the Romans altered their position while at Rhodes, and it is very likely that they did so because the Rhodians suggested that their participation in the war might be linked to an explicit statement of their claims in the *rerum repetitio*. By this time it was more or less certain that Rome and Philip were going to war, and since Rhodian participation was hardly likely to be crucial in the struggle between the two land powers, there was little reason for the island to continue its efforts without some guarantee of its specific interests. Given Rome's small concern for the affairs of Asia Minor, it was not at all certain that it would demand the evacuation of

---

15. Walbank II, 543.

16. E. Bickermann, "Les prèliminaires de la seconde guerre de Macedoine," *Rev. Phil.* 61 (1935) 174; Schmitt 66–67; Petzold 42–43; Walbank II, 543.

Caria once Philip was defeated, and there was also the strong possibility that with his superior influence Attalus might persuade his
western friends to make arrangements harmful to Rhodian interests.
It is consequently reasonable to believe that the Rhodians delivered
their own ultimatum to the Romans before the latter delivered theirs
to Philip at Abydus.

Put in its simplest terms, the Roman aim in the confrontation with
Philip was generally to humble the Macedonian king, to undermine
his authority in Greece and severely weaken his potential as a danger
to Rome.[17] If Philip had accepted the Senate's demands, this goal
would have been achieved without war, but it is doubtful the *patres*
seriously believed that he might quietly swallow them. The terms in
themselves were outrageous; that a Macedonian king should agree
unconditionally to refrain from interfering in Greece or with Egyptian possessions and to submit to arbitration the claims of two small
states, both technically aggressors against him, was unthinkable.
Were this not enough, these demands were being made by a non-
Greek power that, by virtue of the absence of any treaties with any of
the states involved, had no legal right to intervene. Though in no
position to complain about unprovoked aggression, Philip was nevertheless quick to point out that he had not violated the treaty of 205;
by what right did the Romans now venture to cast it aside?[18] The
Antigonid ruler must have foreseen the almost inevitable outcome of
a full-scale struggle with Rome, but even a cooler head than his could
hardly have refused the challenge. To have capitulated now in the
hope of fighting later on better terms would have seriously undermined the position of Macedon in Greece and provided a dangerous
precedent for Rome and for every Greek state that chafed against
Macedonian power.

17. So E. Badian, *Foreign Clientelae (264–70 B.C.)* (Oxford 1958) 66–67.
18. Philip's protests concerning the treaty of 205 (Polyb. 16.34.5–7, 18.6.2; Livy
31.18.2–4, 32.34.7; Diod. 28.6.1; App. *Mac.* 4.2) are a strong blow to the theory
(Bickermann, *Rev. Phil.* 61, 49–81, 161–76) that the Peace of Phoenice was a common
peace, to which Athens was a party, and that Philip thus provided Rome with a *casus
belli* by attacking Athens. Pergamum and Rhodes were at most only *amici* of Rome, as
well as being technically the aggressors, and thus provided Rome with no legal cause.
Rome was developing new interpretations of its fetial law; see W. Dahlheim, *Struktur
und Entwicklung des römischen Völkerrechts* (Munich 1968) 248–59.

The declaration at Abydus marks the real beginning of the "most glorious and excellent deeds" shared by Rhodes and Rome. By virtue of the contact of a century earlier, the two states were already bound by an *amicitia* of the vaguest sort, and this relationship was now officially reestablished, so that Rhodes became a recognized *amicus populi Romani*. Insofar as it also became an ally of Rome, it could also be considered a *socius,* and the vague term *socius et amicus,* whatever its origins, must have applied to Rhodes' legal relationship to Rome for the duration of the war.[19] Most important, no treaty (*foedus*) was established between the two states, so that Rome had no legal sway over its Rhodian ally. Doubtless there were arrangements and agreements regarding the aims and conduct of the war, but Rhodes nevertheless retained complete freedom of action, short of aiding Philip. If Rhodes assumed a position of neutrality, it would cease to be a *socius* but would remain an *amicus,* and Rome would have no legal cause for hostility. Such an arrangement suited Rhodes perfectly. It was left free to determine the extent and direction of its cooperation or, if the situation should warrant, to withhold that cooperation or even conclude a separate peace. Yet for all this freedom, as an *amicus* the island still had the right to take part in all negotiations with the enemy.[20] This was exactly the kind of diplomatic latitude the Rhodians had attempted to maintain throughout the course of the third century.

Rhodes' prime objective in the war, aside from the elimination of

19. Polyb. 16.35.2 (see Schmitt 67, n. 3); Livy 37.54.3, 45.25.9; see also Polyb. 21.23.11–12, 28.2.1–2, 16.7, 30.23.4, 31.17; Livy 42.19.8, 45.4, 46.6; Diod. 31.5.1, 5.3; Gell. 6.3.2, 26, 47; A. Heuss, *Die völkerrechtlichen Grundlagen der römischen Aussenpolitik in republikanischer Zeit* (Leipzig 1937) 31–32. For the previous *amicitia,* see appendix II. On *socius et amicus,* see L. Matthaei, "On the Classification of Roman Allies," *CQ* 1 (1907) 185–86, 202–3; Dahlheim 260–65.

20. Polyb. 30.5.6–8; Livy 45.25.9; Cass. Dio 20.68.3; see also Zon. 9.24. Actually, a *foedus* between Rome and an *amicus* dealt only with specific points and was not necessarily burdensome to the *amicus;* it was the *foedus* of a true *socius* that unconditionally tied a state to Rome with definite military obligations. The *amicus* was bound only to neutrality; if troops were voluntarily sent, they could remain under native command, which was not the case with *socii.* The *amicus* also had the right to take part in all negotiations with the enemy. See Matthaei 187–200. Livy 31.28.4: "Ad Rhodios quoque missi legati ut capesserent partem belli" is simply a Roman request, not a reflection of any legal obligation.

Philip as an immediate threat to its security, was the recovery of the Peraea, where Macedonian occupation meant a violation of Rhodian soil and a great financial loss to the state.[21] In addition it desired the freeing of the Carian cities of Iasus, Bargylia, Euromus, and Pedasa; the Hellespontine towns of Sestus, Abydus, and Perinthus; all the lesser emporia and ports of Asia, such Ptolemaic possessions as Philip held, and the Cyclades Islands. Inasmuch as these aims are discerned from Rhodian demands of Philip during the war, especially at Nicaea in 198, it is possible that some of the specific points emerged only as the king's position weakened, but generally these would have been the Rhodian goals from the point of Rome's entry into the war. At that time the island would have believed that Philip's situation was fairly hopeless and thus would have sought the evacuation of all his overseas possessions, a reasonable demand in the event of his defeat.[22] Finally, to these territorial objectives may be added the desire to suppress whatever piracy was engendered by the wartime conditions.

In these goals Rhodes' traditional policy as defender of the small states of the Aegean may be seen, but the roots of this policy lay in hard economic and political considerations; the smaller and more independent the political units of the Aegean, the easier the path for Rhodian commerce and influence. The culprit of the moment was Philip, but doubtless another king also figured in Rhodian policy making. One of the last things Rhodes wished to see was the Macedonian control of the places named above, particularly the Hellespont

21. Polyb. 18.2.3; Livy 32.33.6.
22. Towns: Polyb. 18.2.3–4; Livy 32.33.6–7; Pedasa is omitted in the Nicaea passages, but it is included later in Polyb. 18.44.4; Livy 33.30.3. The four Carian towns were probably under Rhodian influence, though free; see Holleaux IV, 314–21. Perinthus was to be reunited in sympolity with Byzantium. Emporia: Polyb. 18.2.4; Livy 32.33.7. These would seem to be something less than cities; see Holleaux IV, 322–23. Ptolemaic: the evacuation of Ptolemaic possessions was actually demanded by the Romans (Polyb. 16.34.3, 18.1.14; Livy 32.33.4), but it may be assumed that the Rhodians were in full agreement. There is no word of the islands, but this omission may undoubtedly be attributed to the fact that by the end of 198 all but Paros and Cythnos had been taken from Philip; it is likely that the Cyclades were considered part of "all Hellas," from which the Romans demanded Philip withdraw. That the freedom of the islands was a Rhodian objective is amply demonstrated by their immediate liberation by the Rhodian fleet.

and the islands, simply replaced with Pergamene domination. It is in fact very likely that the Rhodians added freedom for "all the markets and ports of Asia" to their demands at Nicaea in order to block Attalus, who might otherwise have sought to appropriate some of these localities once Philip was defeated. Finally, though its strategy envisaged the defeat of Macedon, insofar as that was necessary for the achievement of its aims, Rhodes, with its century-old regard for the balance of power, could not have wanted to see the Antigonid state severely crippled. The Aetolian League needed a counterpoise in Greece, Seleucid power was on the upswing, and Rome, an ally at the moment, was a potential danger in the far west—all circumstances that made a healthy postwar Macedon desirable from the Rhodian point of view.

After departing from Athens, the Rhodian fleet operated among the Cyclades, and all but three of the islands—Andros, Paros, and Cythnos—were liberated and brought into alliance with Rhodes.[23] In response to Philip's campaign in the Chersonese, the fleet sailed north in the late summer and anchored near Tenedus, where it awaited Attalus and his squadron. Before the Pergamene reinforcement could arrive, however, Philip began the siege of Abydus; and though he was presumably still outnumbered in ships, his control of the entrance to the harbor of Abydus and the middle reaches of the straights made an allied naval assault a serious gamble. Aid to the besieged city was consequently limited to 300 Pergamene soldiers, one Rhodian quadrireme, and one Cyzican trireme, all of them probably already in the city when Philip invested it. With no outside help, Abydus was doomed, and after a desperate resistance of several weeks the city fell and the allied fleet departed. Attalus apparently remained in Asian waters, and the Rhodians returned home for the winter, sending only

23. Polyb. 16.26.10; Livy 31.15.8: "in societatem acceptis." According to *IG* xi.4 751 (= *Syll.*[3] 582), a Rhodian fleet under Epicrates, son of Polystratus, also operated among the islands, probably in the earlier part of the war; see F&B 160, n. 1. This fleet included light vessels from the islands and some Athenian *naves apertae*, an indication that the operation must have followed the arrival of Cento's fleet at Athens (Briscoe 117). A Cean decree (*BCH* 78 [1954] 340) also reveals Rhodian activity in the Aegean at this time, but provides no details. General references to Rhodes' part in the war: Cass. Dio 18.58.4; Zon. 9.15–16; Flor. 2.7.8; Strabo 13.4.2 (624). Thiel 202–49 gives the best account of the naval war.

three quadriremes to Athens to join the recently arrived Roman squadron under C. Claudius Cento. Cento had arrived in the fall with twenty ships in response to Athenian appeals for help against Macedonian raids from Chalcis and the Acrocorinth, and together with the Rhodians and three Athenian vessels he was able not only to stop the raids but also to seize Chalcis, where the Rhodians freed a number of prisoners.[24]

Shortly after the fall of Abydus an Achaean embassy appeared at Rhodes seeking a separate peace between Philip and the island, but the Rhodians refused, much to the relief of the Roman envoys, who then moved on to Syria and Egypt.[25] Despite their rejection of this peace feeler, however, the Rhodians did not contribute any aid to the allied cause at the beginning of the campaigning season of the following year, and only in answer to a specific Roman request that Rhodes take a part in the war were twenty ships sent west under the nauarch Acesimbrotus in the late spring. This squadron joined the Roman-Pergamene flotilla under L. Apustius, having just missed the capture of Andros, which had been turned over to Attalus. Now at a strength of some ninety sail, the united fleet unsuccessfully assaulted Cythnos and then sailed to the Chalcidice, where it failed against the naval base at Cassandrea, but sacked Acanthus. Returning south to Euboea, the allies scored the most important naval victory of the year by taking Oreus. During this operation the Rhodians, as the best sailors, were detached to blockade the Macedonian fleet in Demetrias. In September Attalus and the Rhodians sailed home and Apustius returned to Corcyra, leaving thirty Roman vessels on winter station at the Piraeus.[26]

In the spring of 198 Acesimbrotus' squadron met Attalus' twenty-

24. Polyb. 16.30.7, 31.3, 34.1; Livy 31.15.10–11, 16.6–8, 17.3, 17.6, 22.5–23.9; Zon 9.15. Both Polybius (16.28.1–9) and Livy (31.15.10–11) criticize Attalus and the Rhodians for their inactivity, which may be partly explained by the mutual distrust and differing aims of the two states (see Thiel 226–27; Starr 67–68); but allied failure at Abydus is most easily explained by the military situation (Niese II, 595; Walbank, *Philip* 133; esp. Hansen 126–27). Despite Livy's language, it is possible that the Rhodian vessels were already present when Cento arrived; see Briscoe 116–17.

25. Polyb. 16.35.1–2.

26. Livy 31.28.4, 45.1–16, 46.6–47.3. The *naves tectae* of the Rhodians were quadriremes and quinqueremes. Oreus was given to Attalus.

four ships off Andros, and after first plundering about Carystus, they joined the Roman fleet, now commanded by L. Quinctius Flamininus, for an assault on Eretria. This city was taken with little difficulty, and when the fleet moved back down the channel, Carystus surrendered immediately, allowing the allied force to move on to Corinthian Cenchreae. The port was easily captured, and while preparations were undertaken for the siege of Corinth, envoys representing Attalus, the Rhodians, the Athenians, and the Romans were sent to a meeting of the Achaeans at Sicyon to attempt to bring the league over to the allied side. Bowing to the realities of the military situation, the Achaeans deserted Philip, and while the other allies began the assault on Corinth, the Rhodians sailed for home because of the advanced season. The Corinthians meanwhile rallied to the support of the Macedonian garrison, and when Philocles was able to get reinforcements into the city, the allies abandoned the siege and departed, the Romans to Corcyra and Attalus to Aegina.[27]

This was the last Rhodian activity in Greek waters; in 197, with the Roman fleet operating in the west, the Pergamene squadron was sufficient to keep the Macedonian navy from emerging from its haven at Demetrias. At the end of 198, however, the nauarch Acesimbrotus is found representing Rhodes at the conference at Nicaea, where he demanded of Philip the return of the Peraea, the evacuation of Iasus, Bargylia, Euromus, Pedasa, Sestus, and Abydus, the return of Perinthus to Byzantium, and the freeing of all the markets and ports of Asia.[28] In making these demands Rhodes was pursuing its traditional policy of supporting the interests of the small Aegean states, but it may also be pointed out that all the towns specifically named were in Caria and the Hellespontine region, areas of particular interest to the island. As noted earlier, the Rhodians made specific mention of the markets and ports of Asia less to ensure their liberation, since a defeated Philip would probably have had to relinquish

27. Livy 32.16.6–17.3, 19.3–23.13; App. *Mac.* 7.1; Paus. 7.8.1–2; Plut. *Flam.* 5.3; Zon. 9.16.3. On the meeting at Sicyon, see esp. A. Aymard, *Les premiers rapports de Rome et de la confédération achaienne (198–189 avant J.-C)* (Paris 1938) 79–108; the premature departure of the Rhodians, probably because of the advanced season, is argued at 104, n. 5.

28. Polyb. 18.1.4, 2.3–4; Livy 32.32.11, 33.6–7; App. *Mac.* 8.1; Just. 30.3.

them in any case, than to guard against the possibility that these places might fall into the hands of Attalus. There was no need to name the islands, since they had for the most part already been liberated by the Rhodians and were under their influence, and Roman inclination to reward Attalus would probably not extend to giving him such a large number of now autonomous Greek states.

There is no mention of a Rhodian embassy at the subsequent conference in Rome early in the next year, but this must be an oversight, for Rhodes would surely have taken the simple step of sending a representative to a discussion of matters important to its interests. It may have felt that its demands were secure or that the talks would founder, but nevertheless, the smallest diplomatic risk would certainly justify the minimal effort of dispatching an envoy. Rhodes had played the diplomatic game too long to consider international matters settled until they actually were, and even if it felt entirely confident about the Roman attitude toward Rhodes, Attalus, who appeared to have the Roman ear, would represent a potential threat to Rhodian interests. It is reasonable to conclude, then, that a Rhodian embassy was present at Rome, but was for some unknown reason not mentioned by Polybius. It may be added that the Rhodians (as well as the Athenians and the Pergamene king) are missing also from the accounts of the later peace conferences at Tempe and in Rome, and they would unquestionably have sent envoys to those meetings.[29]

A record of Rhodian operations in the Peraea is lacking for the period before 197, but it is very probable that the strategos Nicagoras was active during those four years and captured the towns of Pisye, Idyma, and Cyllandus.[30] In the last year of the war his successor, Pausistratus, entered the Peraea with 2,600 mercenaries, 800 of them Achaeans, the remainder Gauls and Carians. He took the city of

---

29. Polyb. 18.10.1–2 says that all the allies consented to the truce and "it was decided . . . they should each send ambassadors"; 18.10.9–11 names the envoys of Aetolia, Achaea, Attalus, and Athens. Livy 32.36.8 says that all agreed and "they decided each to send a single ambassador," but 32.36.10 and 37.1 mention only *sociorum legati* and no names. It appears that the Rhodians were omitted by Polybius or his excerpter (Ullrich 46). That the Rhodians are not mentioned at the later peace conferences means nothing; neither are the Athenians or the Pergamene king.

30. *IG* xii.1 1036 (= *Syll.*³ 586); *Inscr. Lind.* 151; *SGDI* 4269; see Holleaux IV, 308, n. 3; F&B 99 and n. 1. Nicagoras was strategos of the Peraea; see above, chap. 4. For the location of these three towns, see F&B 71–73.

Tendeba, near Stratonicea, and was there reinforced by an allied contingent of 1,100 Achaeans under Theoxenus. The bulk of this force then met and defeated in a pitched battle a roughly equal number of Macedonians and other troops under Deinocrates, Philip's general for the Carian region. After the survivors had fled to Bargylia, Pausistratus, rather than immediately attacking Stratonicea, spent his time seizing the "forts and towns of the Peraea," and consequently allowed the city to be reinforced by Deinocrates and his troops. As a result, Pausistratus' subsequent siege ended in failure, and the Rhodians had to await Antiochus' help in recovering the city.[31]

Rhodes' actual participation in the war perhaps strikes one as a little less than glorious, but this limited engagement is understandable and stems partly from the nature of the conflict and partly from Rhodian aims. The Macedonian navy was hopelessly inferior to the allied fleets and after the campaign in Thrace spent the rest of the war at Demetrias, where it could be blockaded by a Rhodian squadron of only twenty sail. Aside from chasing the incidental pirate, the allied navy was thus limited to assaults on islands and coastal cities, chores that demanded fine marines rather than fine sailors. Its occasional failures notwithstanding, the allied fleet, with its large Roman contingent, was entirely adequate for the purposes of containing Philip's navy and detaching his allies; the final decision had to be gained on land.[32] Rhodes' contribution of twenty vessels, far below its potential naval capabilities, was sufficient in 199 and 198, while in 197 its presence was not required in western waters at all. It is unnecessary to search for other tasks with which to occupy Rhodian strength during the war years; there was simply no need for it to send more ships.[33]

Nor was it inclined to do so. Once the Romans were committed to

31. Livy 33.18.1–22. On the non-Greek mercenaries, see Briscoe 280–81. There is some confusion concerning the status of the Achaeans, but the 1,100 reinforcements under Theoxenus (see *Syll.*[3] 588 = *Inscr. Del.* 442) certainly appear to have been an allied contingent rather than a mercenary one (Aymard 163, n. 12; Launey I, 135). Later in the war against Antiochus, Pausistratus was nauarch; see below, chap. 7.

32. Thiel 209–15; the Romans had a total effective war fleet of around 75, of which 50 operated in the Aegean in 199 and 198, thus forming roughly half the allied fleet.

33. There may have been some unrecorded operations in Carian waters, but it is also unknown whether Philip had scored successes among the Sporades in 201. Nisyrus may have been captured by the Rhodians in 200, but no later (F&B 148–52).

war and once Rhodes had gathered most of the islands under its wing, it suited the Rhodians to let Rome and Attalus exert themselves to gain the victory that would bring satisfaction of their demands.[34] At the same time, however, they had to be careful that their interests would not be neglected. Rome was pledged only to exact certain general demands from Philip, and the final settlement could easily run contrary to Rhodian interests, particularly when Attalus remained the hard-working ally. When the war ended, Rome would clearly be the dispenser of the fruits of the victory, and it behooved the Rhodians to present at least the image of diligent allies, even if such a role might be suggestive of a client relationship with the Romans. Consequently, when Rome's request for aid in 199 made it apparent that the attempt to play the sleeping partner would not succeed, Rhodes promptly sent a squadron. In this instance the Rhodians paid for their maneuvering; had Rhodes been present at the capture of Andros, it very likely would have been left free, rather than handed over to the Pergamene king. The awarding of the island to Attalus followed the booty system of the previous war, whereby the Romans took whatever was not fastened down and the Greek allies got the real estate, but the action might also have been compensation to Attalus for Rhodes' extension of its influence over the other islands[35] and a pointed reminder to the Rhodians about participation.

Rhodes' absence from Greece in the last year of the war was in part due to the adequacy of the Pergamene squadron at Aegina, but there was also need of its presence in Asian waters. Antiochus had settled his affairs in Coele-Syria, and taking advantage of Attalid preoccupation in the west, he was now moving along the Cilician coast with a large army and navy, seizing town after town.[36] Whatever the Rhodians may have believed, the Romans certainly appear to have feared that the king might be coming to the aid of Philip, for without the

34. Van Gelder 126–27 recognizes Rhodes' desire to do no more than necessary, but he attributes it to antiwar feelings.

35. Thiel 235, n. 183.

36. Livy 33.19.8–11; Polyb. 18.41a.1–2; Hier. *in Dan.* 11.15–16 (= *FGH* 260 F 46). On Antiochus' campaign of 197–96 see esp. Schmitt, *Antiochos* 278–95 (with full sources); A. Mastrocinque, "Osservazioni sull' attività di Antioco III nel 197 e nel 196 A.C.," *Par. Pas.* 169 (1976) 307–22.

concurrence of their powerful western ally the Rhodians would hardly have taken their next step: they ordered Antiochus not to pass the promontory of Chelidoniae. With Rhodes' policy of fostering small independent states in the Aegean area, it was obviously in the interests of the island republic to keep Seleucid power out of Lycia, Caria, and the western seaboard of Asia Minor, but it would not challenge the overwhelming might of Antiochus without Roman backing. This presumption is borne out by the next move: while the king's ambassadors were in Rhodes protesting the order, the news of Cynoscephalae arrived, and the Rhodians promptly withdrew their demand. With Philip decisively defeated, Rhodes could no longer view Rome's military support as certain in a confrontation with Antiochus, and rather than risk what must be a ruinous war, it backed away from the challenge. Antiochus continued his advance, and by 196 the Seleucid house was once more dominant in western Anatolia and established in its hereditary Thracian lands.[37] The Rhodians, meanwhile, also profited, recovering with the king's aid the city of Stratonicea and bringing the Ptolemaic possessions of Caunus, Myndus, Halicarnassus, and Samos under their influence.[38] This maneuver was characteristic; when the desired policy could not be implemented, the Rhodians did not hesitate to accept the reality of the situation and instead worked wholeheartedly to reap every possible advantage from it. Such would be the case again during the war between Rome and Antiochus. At that time Rhodes fully realized that the Roman cause was threatening to its interests, but once it became clear that the Romans must win, Rhodes did not delay in joining their side in order to gain what it could from the victory.

37. Livy 33.20.1–13; Polyb. 18.41a.1 (this passage undoubtedly goes back to a Rhodian source, and the message was probably expressed more diplomatically than Polybius and Livy suggest); Ullrich 46–47. The Chelidoniae promontory was the limit set on the Persians by Athens in 449 (Plut. *Cimon* 13.4). There is no word of the whereabouts of the Rhodian fleet in 197, but it must have been in Asian waters; Rhodes would not have challenged Antiochus without some measure of immediate defense.

38. Livy 33.18.22, 20.11–12: "[Rhodii] causaque libertatis fuerunt Cauniis, Myndiis, Halicarnassensibus Samiisque." This passage must refer to a Rhodian protectorate, though the towns technically remained Ptolemaic, as the Rhodian purchase of Caunus about 191 demonstrates. On the acquisition of Stratonicea and Caunus, see above, chap. 4.

Rhodes emerged from the Second Macedonian War a stronger and more influential power than it had been at the outset. Territorially, it had not only recovered the Peraea but also incorporated into the state the island of Nisyrus and brought a number of Ptolemaic possessions under its control, forestalling their seizure by Antiochus.[39] More important, the Cyclades, which had hitherto informally recognized Rhodes' leadership, were now officially organized under Rhodian suzerainty in the form of the resurrected Nesiotic League. The islands were enrolled as Rhodian allies in 200, and it is probable, though not certain, that the actual league came into existence soon after, possibly at the end of the war.[40] The league apparently included almost all of the Cyclades, with the exception of Andros and Delos, but the scanty evidence does not allow the membership to be securely defined. Tenos and Siphnos were certainly members; Ceos almost certainly was; Amorgos, Cythnos, Ios, and Syros probably were. There is no evidence for the remaining islands, though it is likely that most also belonged.[41] Possibly to avoid trouble with the Romans, who were establishing increasingly close relations with Delos, the Rhodians chose Tenos, the second Aegean religious center, as the seat of the league government. Delos was left independent, but with close connections with the league, which desired the sanction of the sacred island.[42]

As might be expected, information concerning the league's organization is at a premium. Decrees were issued in the name of a federal synhedrion, about which virtually nothing is known, while ultimate authority was presumably in the hands of what appears to have been the chief Rhodian official, the "archon of the islands and of the nesiotic fleet." Beyond this title, however, information about this official is lacking; it is clear only that he was also commander in chief of the league navy, thus combining into one the Ptolemaic offices of

39. Nisyrus: *IG* xii.3 91 (= *Syll.*[3] 673); see F&B 147–52.
40. See above, n. 23; König 41–42; F&B 160.
41. Tenos: *IG* xii.5 817, 824, 918; Head 493; Siphnos: *IG* xii.5 817 (together with xi.4 760); Ceos: *BCH* 78 (1954) 340; Amorgos: *IG* xii.7 493B; Cythnos: *Ath. Mitt.* 23 (1898) 391; Ios: *IG* xii.5 1009; Syros: *IG* xii.5 652; see F&B 161–66. Amorgos and Ios were not actually Cycladic: Psd.-Scylax 59; Strabo 10.5.3 (485).
42. *IG* xii.5 817; F&B 165–66.

nesiarch and nauarch.[43] As for the federal navy, it is known only that there was an office of "nesiotic trierarch," which was held by an islander, and that the fleet was probably stationed at Tenos.[44] Finally, two honorific inscriptions from Cythnos and Tenos apparently reveal traces of the military organization. The Cythnian decree suggests the possibility that a Rhodian strategos held a general military command among the islands, probably under the "archon of the islands," while the Tenian decree indicates the presence of a Rhodian commander who seems to function as an epistatas. Whether this second official was in fact an epistatas and whether the office was confined to Tenos or found also on the other islands is impossible to say, however, and the inscription consequently reveals little about the mechanism of Rhodian control of the league.[45]

Despite the lack of details, it is nevertheless clear that the Rhodian league differed from its Ptolemaic predecessor in two very basic ways. First, the Rhodian organization, unlike the Ptolemaic, had a corporate existence, allowing it to grant federal honors and probably also federal citizenship, and second, it possessed its own navy.[46] Both of these measures were doubtless intended by Rhodes to give the koinon a greater sense of autonomous existence and thus, it was hoped, develop a more stable organization, which could ease Rhodes' burden in the Aegean. Certainly the federal navy could only benefit the Rhodians, augmenting their own fleet during emergencies and,

43. Synhedrion: *IG* xii.5 824 (= *Syll.*[3] 620). The synhedrion included a probouleutic body called *prostatai;* Rhodian suzerainty is indicated by mention of the Rhodian priest of Helios in the prescript. Archon: *IG* xi.4 752–53 (= *Syll.*[3] 582): ἄρχων ἐπὶ τε[τῶν νή]σων καὶ τῶν πλοίων τῶν νησιωτικῶν; see generally König 71–72; F&B 166–69.

44. *IG* xii.5 918 (the office was held by a Tenian). Dedications by the Rhodian navy suggest Tenos was the federal naval base: *IG* xii.5 913–14, xii. supp. 139, no. 317.

45. Cythnos: *Ath. Mitt.* 23 (1898) 391; Tenos: *IG* xii.5 830; see F&B 161, 168. It perhaps goes without saying that one mechanism of Rhodes' control was its tremendous economic influence among the islands. Whether there was a nesiotic coinage is unknown, but Tenos did mint bronze bearing the Rhodian rose (Head 493; see further F&B 170–71). It may also be assumed that Rhodes attempted to influence the islanders with its social institutions, as it clearly did in the subject Peraea (see above, chap. 4). An inscription of Tenian origin mentions a koinon of *eranistai* (*IG* xii.5 672).

46. The few surviving documents of the league make no mention of a *politeia* of the koinon, but *IG* xii.5 817 records a "proxenos of the koinon of the islanders."

more important, sharing the unending chore of policing the sea lanes during peacetime. The resurrection of the Nesiotic League thus not only formalized Rhodes' position of leadership in the Aegean but at the same time provided it with an apparently effective instrument for the mobilization of some of the resources of the communities under its protection. The Alexander-type tetradrachmas issued by Rhodes at about this time may have been in commemoration of the recreation of the league.[47]

Strategically, the defeat of Philip marked the end—for some time, it would seem—of any threat from Macedon, but more ironically, perhaps, the end of the war also saw the diminution of Pergamene power. Pergamum was still the friend of Rome and possessor of a strong navy, but the sole positive result of its efforts against Philip was the acquisition of Andros.[48] Much more was lost: hopes of a Pergamene thalassocracy were completely dashed, the old campaigner Attalus was dead of a stroke, and Eumenes II inherited a kingdom compressed by the advances of Antiochus and surrounded now on three sides by Seleucid territory.[49] Against these gains must be weighed the fact that Seleucid power was once again dominant in Asia Minor, and the Hellespont and towns of the coast, far from being free, were now under the control of the Syrian king. But though the situation in Anatolia was clearly not to Rhodes' liking, the Seleucid presence was not immediately threatening to the island republic. As leverage against Antiochus, Rhodes had its navy and its friendship with Rome, which was already in 196 challenging some of the king's conquests. That Antiochus was wary of Rhodes and cognizant of the benefits of its friendship is amply demonstrated by his calm reaction to the Chelidoniae injunction and his subsequent hon-

47. For examples see L. Muller, *Numismatique d'Alexandre le Grand* (Copenhagen 1855) 1154–67. The case is made by Sippel 92–119, who demonstrates that the Rhodian Alexanders were part of a large issue of relatively brief duration which may be dated to the beginning of the second century and whose odd nature is more easily understood in terms of public relations rather than hard economics.

48. Livy 31.45.7; see Hansen 71, nn. 7–8. Eumenes was allowed to keep Oreus, Eretria, and Carystus (Polyb. 18.47.10–11; Livy 33.34.10).

49. Attalus died in 197 after collapsing in Thebes from a stroke (Livy 33.2.1–3, 21.1). By 196 Pergamum had lost to Antiochus all but its hereditary lands; see Hansen 22–23, 70–71.

oring and advancement of Rhodes' interests in Caria. Moreover, although he had a stranglehold on the Hellespont and held most of the ports of Asia Minor, so long as he desired the neutralization or cooperation of the Rhodian navy, he was not about to make the slightest move antagonistic to the merchants of the island. Antiochus' demonstrations of Seleucid goodwill, such as the referral of the Lampsacus-Smyrna case to Rhodian arbitration,[50] also benefited Rhodes by strengthening its position with regard to the Romans, who in their fear of a war with the Syrians were surely loath to lose the Rhodian fleet to him. Rome, of course, had the capacity to launch its own large fleets, but the immediate naval strengths of the contending powers could be decisive in determining the character and location of the conflict. Were the Rhodian navy, and thus the Aegean, in his camp, at the outbreak of war Antiochus could sweep into Greece and use his navy to bar or hinder Roman operations across the Adriatic.

The century-old balance of power in the eastern Mediterranean was almost in ruins, shattered by the entrance of a new and overwhelmingly strong state into the Hellenistic circle. Though the balance seemed to be crumbling already in 201 with the decline of Egypt, had Rome not entered the arena, it was virtually inevitable that Philip and Antiochus, or their successors, would clash, thereby bringing Egypt at least the opportunity to regain its standing. With Egypt debilitated and Macedon exhausted, however, Rhodes now found itself in a precarious position, caught between the superpowers of the Roman republic and the Seleucid empire. But the position of a second-rank Hellenistic power had always been dangerous, and though Rhodes might now eye Rome and Antiochus with suspicion, its strategic situation was basically good. The field was narrowed, but there was an apparent power balance, and the island was friendly with both and tied to neither, the constant goal of its foreign policy. Antiochus was in fact cultivating Rhodes' favor, and the Romans were showing every sign of honoring their commitment to the freedom of Greece and evacuating their forces. If, however, Rhodes should suddenly be threatened by the Seleucid, it could appeal to the Romans, who, considerations of Greek liberty aside, would probably not suf-

50. See below, chap. 7.

fer all the naval power of the East to pass into the hands of the Syrian monarch. If it came to war between the two powers, the separation of the opponents by the Aegean should ensure that Rhodes and its navy would be courted by both sides, thereby presenting the island with the strategic latitude it desired. The greatest danger for the Rhodian republic lay beyond a war between Rome and Syria. For the moment the equilibrium was between two powers, and if one should defeat the other too decisively, the eastern Mediterranean could once again come under the aegis of a single state. And Rhodian diplomacy might for once find itself with nowhere to turn.

CHAPTER 7

The War with Antiochus III

DURING the period between Rome's wars with Philip and Antiochus, Rhodes' activities are almost entirely undocumented; notice of the island in the sources is limited to brief mention of two instances of arbitration and its participation in the short war against Nabis in 195. Rhodes' motivation for sending eighteen ships under Sosilas and participating in the sieges of Gytheum and Sparta is easily understood in view of Nabis' piratical policies, and his defeat brought the island the results it desired. Deprived of his naval bases and fleet and his contacts with the Cretans, Nabis ceased to be a threat to the sea lanes and to political stability in Crete. This result satisfied the Rhodians, though the Achaeans were disgruntled by the fact that Sparta remained under the power of the bellicose tyrant.[1] With the exception of the arbitration, nothing more is heard of the Rhodians until a squadron of their warships joins the allied fleet in 191, but it may be assumed that in addition to attending to its commerce, Rhodes devoted this time to settling affairs in the Peraea and consolidating its position among the islands.

Meanwhile, events in the Aegean were spiraling toward another major conflict. In 197 the cities of Lampsacus and Smyrna, doubtless with the prompting of Eumenes, refused to admit Antiochus and sent

1. Livy 34.26.11, 29.4–5, 30.7, 35.2, 5, 9–10, 36.2–3, 38.1–3, 40.7, 41.4; Zon. 9.18; Just. 31.3.1.

embassies to the Romans seeking guarantees of their freedom.[2] In reply the *senatus consultum* on the peace included a general proclamation of the freedom and autonomy of the Greeks of Asia, and specific demands were made of the king by an embassy to Lysimacheia in 196. Antiochus countered that he was willing to recognize the freedom of the autonomous cities, but only as a gift from himself, and when the Romans introduced the envoys from Smyrna and Lampsacus, he readily agreed to arbitration—by the Rhodians. Given the tremendous reputation of Rhodes, the Romans could hardly raise any objection about the fairness of this offer, and the conference broke up, a sure triumph for the Seleucid.[3]

It appears that the offer of Rhodian arbitration was never accepted by Smyrna and Lampsacus,[4] but there are two instances during the interwar period when Rhodian arbitrators were at work. Immediately after the withdrawal of Macedonian troops from Caria, Miletus went to war with Magnesia-on-the-Maeander in order to recover territory taken from it by Philip, and the conflict rapidly spread to neighboring states. From Rhodes' point of view, this war was highly undesirable, not only because it was right on the frontier of Rhodes' sphere of influence and disrupted its commerce, but also because it could possibly provide the circumstances for a further extension of Seleucid power in the area. Consequently, in late 196 the island is found successfully mediating an end to the dispute, heading up a negotiating team of representatives from Athens, the Achaean League, and eight Anatolian cities, at least half of which were within the Rhodian orbit.[5] The second involved the centuries-old dispute between Samos and Priene over a strip of mainland territory. The Rhodians intervened in order to prevent a conflict potentially damaging to two of its trading partners and possibly to extend its influence

2. Livy 33.38.3–7; App. *Syr.* 2; *Syll.*[3] 591; Polyb. 18.49.1, 52.1–3.

3. Polyb. 18.44.2, 47.1–2, 49.2–52.5; Livy 33.20.2, 34.3–4, 38.8–10, 39.1–41.4; Diod. 28.12.1; App. *Syr.* 1–4; Zon. 9.18.

4. The Romans made no reply to Antiochus' offer and the two cities are found still resisting the king in 192 (Livy 35.42.2).

5. *Syll.*[3] 588. The cities were Cnidus, Myndus, Samos, Halicarnassus, Caunus (?[Καυν]ίων; see Schmitt, *Antiochos* 280, n. 2), Mylasa, Teos, and Cyzicus. Myndus, Samos, Halicarnassus, and Caunus had been taken under Rhodian "protection" in 197 (Livy 33.20.12); Cnidus was probably economically influenced by Rhodes.

in the area. The disputed territory was awarded to Priene, but even Rhodes' reputation for fairness could not overcome a disagreement that had become virtually a tradition for the two states, and a permanent solution was not found for another half century.[6]

Individual Rhodians, all of them seemingly in the employ of Antiochus, are also found engaged in diplomatic activity in this period. Menelaus, son of Menecrates, and Apollophanes, son of Anaxipolis, both described as friends of the king, are honored by Calymnus and Mylasa, respectively, for unknown services or judgments, and in 196 or 195 a Rhodian named Eucles negotiated the betrothal of Antiochus' daughter Cleopatra to Ptolemy V.[7] It is not necessary to see in this employment of Rhodians any new or special policy on the part of Antiochus; Rhodians had a long tradition of service to foreign rulers and a strong reputation as negotiators, and who better to represent the Seleucid in Alexandria than a Rhodian? The Rhodian government of course had no control over individuals in foreign service, but the activities of these men could only enhance the reputation of the republic, and the island would not have been displeased by the marriage agreement, which at least temporarily protected Egypt from Seleucid invasion.

In 195 Roman apprehensions about Antiochus were multiplied by the arrival of Hannibal at the Seleucid court, but the Balkan peninsula was nevertheless evacuated by most Roman troops the following year. Negotiations between Rome and the king in 194 and 193 led only to a hardening of attitudes on both sides, and fearing war, Antiochus established contact with the disgruntled Aetolians, making a general promise to free Greece. Never the ones to act with excessive caution, the leaders of the league decided to force the issue, and in 192 they captured the key city of Demetrias and invited Antiochus to liberate the Greeks from Rome. Apparently convinced of the imminence of war and determined not to let this opportunity

6. *Syll.*³ 599 (= *Inscr. Priene* 37); see Magie II, 892–93, n. 99. Rhodes' decision in favor of Priene was confirmed when Rome finally settled the dispute in 135 (*Syll.*³ 688 [= *Inscr. Priene* 41]).

7. Menelaus: *OGIS* 243, dated to the 190s; see Hiller 791; Apollophanes: *BCH* 22 (1898) 382, no. 23. The dating is not secure, but the 190s seem likely; see Magie II, 1028, n. 74. Eucles: Hier. *in Dan.* 3.11.17; see Olshausen no. 134.

pass, the king moved with unusual boldness and crossed to Greece in the autumn with an army of 10,000. A short time later a Roman detachment was wiped out by Seleucid troops at Delium, and Rome declared war.[8]

Neither Rome nor Antiochus really wanted a war, but the combination of the king's justifiable stubbornness and Rome's imperious attitude and fears of a Seleucid threat produced an international powder keg, and the rash action of the Aetolians was the match that set it off. Spurred on continually by Eumenes, who wished to recoup his kingdom's losses and deal a blow to his traditional enemy, Rome sought to employ the traditional Hellenistic device of "Greek liberty" as a lever with which to pry the Syrian out of Europe.[9] But for Antiochus it was outrageous that he should be expected to do the bidding of a foreign power he considered at best his equal, and whose demands were illegal according to Greek international law.[10] Unqualified compliance with Rome's demands would only open the door to further intervention and undermine his imperial authority, especially in Anatolia. So far as can be discerned, Antiochus had no designs on Greece, but the atmosphere of growing mutual suspicion, played upon by Eumenes, and the presence of Hannibal at Antioch convinced both sides that armed conflict was almost inevitable, and Antiochus determined to seize the initiative in the struggle by responding to the Aetolian appeal and occupying Greece.

Rhodes' attitude toward the cold war between Rome and Syria is undocumented, but it is almost certain that Rhodes did not want to see the diplomatic struggle come to a contest of arms. Beyond the simple fact that a war in the Aegean world could only be injurious to the Rhodian economy, a conflict between Antiochus and the Romans would very likely upset the present satisfactory strategic position of the island. The aftermath of a war might just possibly see some

---

8. On these events see esp. E. Badian, *Studies in Greek and Roman History* (Oxford 1964) 122–35; A. Mastrocinque, "Roma e Antioco III. Guerra di propaganda e propaganda per la querra," *Atti Ist. Veneto* 136 (1977–78) 1–17.

9. See Hansen 74–77; M. L. Heidemann, *Die Freiheitsparole in der griechisch-romischen Auseinandersetzung (200–188 v. Chr.),* diss. (Bonn 1966) 54–61.

10. For a treatment of the legal questions involved, see E. Bickermann, "Bellum Antiochicum," *Hermes* 67 (1932) 48–66.

improvement in Rhodes' situation, but any major engagement of the two dominant powers involved the very high risk of a narrowing of its strategic alternatives through a dislocation of the balance of power. That Rhodes did not take its usual role of arbitrator must be due to a fear of compromising its position with regard to either of the powers, especially when there was a more or less constant if unsuccessful dialogue between Rome and Antiochus during these years anyway. This hesitation to become involved extended even beyond the outbreak of hostilities in 192. Sought as an ally by both sides because of its naval strength, Rhodes resisted deciding immediately for Rome, as it would have been military folly to declare against Antiochus before the Romans had fully committed themselves in the Aegean. Although Rhodes certainly did not relish the idea of an extension of Antiochus' control over Greece, the wisest course of action was to wait until events in the Balkan peninsula had played themselves out. Should the war end with Antiochus being merely booted out of Greece, or indeed being established there. Rhodes would naturally find its postwar position in Asia more comfortable if it had maintained a strict neutrality.

By the late summer of 191 the situation had changed: Antiochus had been driven from Greece, and the praetor C. Livius Salinator was at Delos with a Roman fleet of more than a hundred warships. Rome was going to carry the war to Asia, and the Rhodians now committed themselves and sent out a squadron of twenty-five vessels to join Livius' fleet.[11] It must now have seemed to Rhodes inevitable that the Romans would ultimately win, and rather than cling to a profitless neutrality, it determined to reap the various rewards available to a victorious participant.[12] The island certainly did not want war and the disruptions it brought, but war was now a fact, and the sensible policy was to gain what one could from the situation. Rome was, after all, ostensibly fighting for the freedom of the Asian Greeks, a traditional Rhodian goal, and if the Rhodians perhaps suspected Ro-

---

11. Livy, 36.42.8, 43.12–13, 45.5; App. *Syr.* 22. Livius had 81 *tectae* and about 25 *apertae;* Appian gives the Rhodians 27 ships.

12. G. De Sanctis, *Storia dei Romani* (Turin 1907–23) IV.1, 176, followed by Thiel 298: glory and spoils; M. Holleaux *CAH* VIII (1930) 218: spoils.

man motives, they nevertheless had the example of 194 before them. If the legions were evacuated from Greece, was it likely they would be maintained in distant Asia? Moreover, as it was almost a certainty that Rome would not keep a fleet in the east, the defeat of Antiochus would leave Rhodes and Pergamum as the only naval powers in the Aegean.[13] Such developments were not dependent on Rhodian participation in the struggle, but in general if there were going to be a rearrangement of Asian affairs, it behooved Rhodes to have some influence in the process, especially since faithful Eumenes certainly would. Finally, war in the Aegean and Asia Minor would be particularly disruptive to Rhodian commerce, and Rhodes' entry on the Roman side would aid in bringing the crucial naval war to a quicker conclusion.

The entire situation was of course fraught with strategic danger; the defeat of Antiochus would also be the defeat of whatever remained of the old balance of power. But not much remained of the balance anyway, and the Seleucid monarch would go down whether or not Rhodes remained neutral; better that the process be quick and of some profit to the republic. The Rhodians were aware of the danger and cannot be accused of climbing aboard the Roman bandwagon with only a shortsighted eye to the immediate spoils of victory.[14] When in the summer of 190 Antiochus attempted to open peace negotiations, the Rhodians responded favorably, demonstrating their willingness to forgo the benefits of a decisive victory in favor of ending the war and maintaining Seleucid power unbroken.

Neutrality was pointless once it was apparent that one side would gain a decisive victory; but did Rhodes commit a strategic blunder in not coming to the aid of Antiochus in an effort to maintain the only power that could act as a counterpoise to Rome? The events of the naval war demonstrated that the adherence of the Rhodian fleet to the Syrian monarchy rather than the allies would almost certainly have resulted in Seleucid control of the Aegean and the crucial Hellespont, a factor that *might* have won Antiochus a stalemate, but Rhodes was not provided with such hindsight. In 191 it saw Antiochus, who for

13. So De Sanctis IV.1, 176, followed by Thiel 298.
14. As do De Sanctis IV.1, 177; Thiel 298; Schmitt 132–33.

all the extent of his empire had struggled four years to wrest Coele-Syria from a weak Egypt, pitted against a state that had sent army after army against the Carthaginians, had defeated Macedon in three years, and now, with the exception of Aetolia, had the support of the major powers of the Aegean world. Rome had a habit of ending its wars only with victories, and the winner of the First Punic War would not easily be balked by a strong enemy fleet. To the Rhodians alliance with Antiochus appeared a ticket to eventual defeat, as well as being a struggle against two of the things the republic was definitely for: the autonomy of the small states of the Aegean and the suppression of the piratical Aetolians. Rome's cause was not Rhodes', destructive as it was to one of the key elements of the island's policy, the balance of power, but it nevertheless was the more reasonable choice. As in Rhodes' war with Philip, the pressure of events forced it to a decision ultimately inimical to its traditional strategy, and the wheel of events begun in that last war ground onward.

Rhodes' relationship with Rome during this war must have been the same as that during the previous one, a nonfederate *amicitia et societas,* providing it once again with the greatest possible freedom of action.[15] Its objectives were basically to bring the conflict to an end as quickly as possible and to attain a position of strong influence on the peace settlement and prior negotiations. Such influence would naturally be directed toward securing and possibly expanding Rhodian interests and hindering the development of Pergamene power. Rhodes would best serve these basic aims by vigorously exerting itself in the combat, and since it could take no part in a final decision on land, as Eumenes undoubtedly would, it must firmly establish its stock during the war at sea. That the island republic was successful in this effort is readily apparent from an examination of its maritime achievements.

The squadron of twenty-five ships sent out under Pausistratus in late summer of 191 missed the battle of Cissus, in which Livius and Eumenes defeated the Seleucid fleet, commanded ironically by the Rhodian exile Polyxenidas, but the simple presence of the Rhodian detachment had helped to force the Seleucid admiral to give battle

15. See above, chap. 6.

before the linkup of the three allied fleets.[16] With Polyxenidas shut up
in Ephesus and the command of the sea gained with a single blow, the
Roman and Pergamene fleets took up winter quarters at Canae, in
Pergamene territory, and the Rhodians returned home. In the early
spring of the following year Pausistratus sailed north to Samos with
thirty-six ships to wait there for Livius and Eumenes, not daring to
pass by Ephesus unaided.[17] The Rhodians undoubtedly realized that
the basic object of allied naval strategy ought to be the containment of
the Seleucid fleet in Ephesus, in order to force Polyxenidas eventually
to give battle against odds or see the Hellespont fall without a fight.
Livius apparently failed to understand this, however, and was con-
ducting operations in the northeast, despite the fact that the Roman
army could not reach the crossing for another half year. Pausistratus
was consequently forced to wait and moved his squadron to the
narrow Samian harbor of Panhormus, having received a letter from
Polyxenidas, who offered to surrender the entire Syrian fleet in return
for a cancellation of his exile from Rhodes. Thus lulled into careless-
ness, the nauarch sent nine ships off to Samos and Halicarnassus to
collect stores, and having ignored the warning information obtained
from a captive, he was subsequently completely surprised by the
Seleucid assault. His first thought was to defend the harbor entrance
against the enemy fleet, but quickly discovering that he was also
being attacked by land, the nauarch realized his only hope was to
make the desperate attempt to get his ships to open sea. With the
Seleucid fleet sitting right outside the harbor, however, the attempted breakout was virtually doomed beforehand, and those vessels that made it to the harbor entrance were easily picked off by
Polyxenidas. Pausistratus was killed, and of the remainder of the fleet
only five Rhodian and two Coan vessels escaped capture, being
equipped with the Rhodian fire basket.[18]

16. Livy 36.43.1–45.5; App. *Syr.* 22. For by far the best account of the naval war,
see Thiel 253–361. Polyxenidas continues the tradition of Rhodian condottieri in
foreign service and is found earlier with Antiochus on his expedition against Arsaces
(Polyb. 10.29.6); see T. Lenschau, "Polyxenidas," *RE* XXI.2 (1952) 1850–51.
17. Livy 36.45.6–8, 37.9.5. The Rhodians sailed unusually early—at the vernal
equinox, according to Livy, though perhaps actually in April.
18. Livy 37.9.6–11.14; App. *Syr.* 23–24. On the ship numbers, see appendix II.
The fire basket hung from poles projecting over the bows and was arranged so that the

Rising to the occasion of this disaster, the Rhodians sent another twenty ships north under a new nauarch, Eudamus, and these vessels joined the Roman and Pergamene fleets at Samos.[19] Livius then sent two Italian and Rhodian triremes west under the Rhodian Epicrates to deal with the piracy off Cephallenia, but at the Piraeus this squadron met the new naval commander, L. Aemilius Regillus, and accompanied him back to Samos.[20] At the ensuing war council Epicrates suggested that part of the fleet be sent south to seize the Lycian city of Patara. This proposal was clearly in the interests of the Rhodians, who were apparently bothered by hostile activity originating in that region. But the operation was also reasonable from the point of view of allied strategy, since, as Epicrates argued, capture of the town would free additional Rhodian resources for the war and would provide a base from which the allies could operate against the fleet being assembled in Cilicia by Hannibal. Regillus accepted the proposal, but not the inevitable consequence of decisively dividing his forces, and virtually doomed the expedition from the start by sending Livius south with only eight ships, while the rest of the fleet was moved to Ephesus. At Rhodes Livius had two more quadriremes added to the four Rhodian vessels in his command, but his force was still too small, and after some desultory fighting near Patara he sent the Rhodians home and sailed west to Greece. Hearing of Livius' failure, Regillus foolishly sailed south with the entire fleet, thus freeing Polyxenidas, but following an unsuccessful siege of Iasus, grum-

---

burning material could be spilled upon the deck of the enemy vessel. See Polyb. 21.7.1–4; Livy 37.11.13; App. *Syr.* 24; Walbank III, 97, for a late Ptolemaic grafitto of a similar but not identical device. According to Appian, the fire basket was invented by Pausistratus, and this claim is supported by a koinon of *technitai* at Rhodes named Pausistrateioi (*Annuario* 2 [1916] 139, no. 10; *Inscr. Lind.* 264); he is also associated with another war device by Polyaean. 5.27.

19. Livy 37.12.3–13.7; App. *Syr.* 25. Polyb. 21.7.5, a Suidas extract, wrongly named Pamphilidas as nauarch. Eudamus is named as nauarch in *IG* xii.3 103 (= *Syll.*[3] 673).

20. Livy 37.13.11–14.3; Epicrates is named in an earlier command in *IG* xi.4 751 (= *Syll.*[3] 582). The prominence of Epicrates and Pamphilidas in Livy's narrative suggests that the two were Eudamus' chief subordinates. Regillus stopped first at Chios, where he was visited by the Rhodian Timasicrates, who had been sent with two quadriremes to guard against pirates in the area; on these movements see Thiel 326–28.

bling among his officers persuaded him to put about and return to Samos.[21]

In the meantime Antiochus' son Seleucus had taken advantage of Eumenes' absence in the south to attack the port of Elea and lay siege to Pergamum. When Eumenes received this news, he promptly hurried home to his capital, leaving his ships at Elea, where they were joined a few days later by the Rhodian and Roman fleets. These developments attracted the attention of Antiochus, who moved his army to the vicinity of Elea and attempted to open negotiations with the allies. His precise motivations are impossible to know, but it is clear that his defeat in Greece, the Aetolian truce, and the approaching Roman expeditionary force had given the king second thoughts about the war. Given Regillus' demonstrated ineptitude in military affairs, it is not surprising that he did not immediately answer Antiochus, but instead called upon his allies for advice. Eumenes, with his lands occupied and his capital besieged by Seleucid forces, was understandably against any negotiations and argued that since any armistice must be approved by the consul L. Scipio and finally by the Senate, in the event that the negotiations failed, the tremendous delay involved would have lost the allies all opportunity of ending the war quickly. The Rhodians did not oppose Antiochus' idea, but the sources suggest their support of his request was something less than enthusiastic. Rhodian trade was undoubtedly suffering from the war and the island certainly did not wish to see Seleucid power broken, but the natural Rhodian inclination toward negotiation must have been tempered by the realization that any truce would greatly favor the Seleucid cause by providing time to gather forces and thus possibly prolong the conflict. In any case, Regillus heeded the arguments of Eumenes, and Antiochus was told he would have to await the arrival of the consul.[22]

The siege of Pergamum was soon broken, and the allied fleet then engaged in minor operations, sailing north to the defense of Adramytteum, then back again to Mitylene and Elea, and finally south to

21. Livy 37.14.4–17.10; App. *Syr.* 26.
22. Livy 37.18.1–19.6; Polyb. 21.10.1–11; App. *Syr.* 26. The language of Polybius and Livy suggests Rhodian lukewarmness: οἱ μὲν οὖν περὶ τὸν Εὔδαμον καὶ Παμφιλίδαν οὐκ ἀλλότριοι τῆς διαλύσεως ἦσαν; Rhodii haud aspernari pacem.

attack Phocaea. The city was promptly reinforced by Antiochus, however, and failing in their siege, the Romans and Rhodians returned to their station at Samos, while Eumenes was sent to Elea to begin preparations for the Roman crossing of the Hellespont, surely a foolish move. There was no pressing need to send any of the fleet to the Hellespont yet, and Regillus had excellent reason for keeping the Pergamene squadron with him at Samos; sooner or later he would have to split his forces in order to deal with the naval reinforcements expected from Syria.[23]

Word of those reinforcements was in fact not long in coming, and Regillus dispatched Eudamus with one Coan, one Cnidian, and thirteen Rhodian ships to bar the approach of the fleet being brought north by Hannibal. This was hardly a huge squadron, but the nauarch was probably expected to pick up more vessels at Rhodes, and in any case his sailors were the best in the Mediterranean. Further, the lopsided division left Regillus and his inferior Roman mariners with one hundred heavy ships against Polyxenidas' eighty-nine, and of those nineteen were manned by Rhodians, who could be expected to try at least to prevent the Romans from doing anything completely foolish. Eudamus arrived at Rhodes to find that Pamphilidas had already been sent east with thirteen ships, but departing immediately with six additional *apertae,* the nauarch was able to overtake his lieutenant at Megiste. The latter had meanwhile relieved the blockade of Daedala and other fortresses in the Peraea and had picked up four more ships, and the combined fleet consequently numbered thirty-two quadriremes, four triremes, and two Coan and Cnidian quinqueremes.[24]

The fleet took up station first at Phaselis, but unhealthy midsummer conditions and spreading disease forced them on to the Eurymedon, where it was learned that Hannibal was approaching Side. On the following day Eudamus sailed around the promontory and found the enemy fleet waiting in formation, ten triremes, thirty quadriremes and quinqueremes, and seven heavier ships in line per-

23. Livy 37.19.7–22.2; App. *Syr.* 26.

24. Livy 37.8.3, 22.2–5, 23.4. Pamphilidas was possibly the brother of Nicagoras, son of Pamphilidas, strategos in the Peraea in the previous war (*IG* xii.1 1036 = *Syll.*³ 586). It is not clear if the Coan and Cnidian quinqueremes were still with the fleet; Livy does not mention them when he describes the fleets at Side.

pendicular to the shore.[25] Eudamus, at the head of the Rhodian column, wheeled his leading vessels toward the right, forming a line to the left, but he failed to turn sharply enough and insufficient room was left for the rear ships, which were to form the left wing of his line. As a result, confusion and congestion prevented the rapid deployment of the left half of the Rhodian line, and the nauarch found himself engaging the enemy left, commanded by Hannibal, with only five ships. The Rhodians quickly sorted themselves out, however, as captains sped their ships toward the action on the sea flank, and superior seamanship began to tell as the *diekplous* punched hole after hole in the Syrian line. The enemy right and center were soon in serious trouble, and when the hard-pressed Eudamus finally signaled for help, ships from the victorious Rhodian left were able to speed to his rescue. With the battle now clearly lost, Hannibal began to retire and was followed by the rest of the Seleucid fleet. Because of sickness among the rowers, the Rhodians were prevented from mounting an effective pursuit and captured only one vessel, a seven, but Hannibal had been forced to retreat with more than half his ships disabled.[26]

Side can be considered something of a turning point in the war, and it was Rhodian naval skill that once again captured the victory, retrieving the situation after Eudamus had initially blundered by deploying too late and attacking too soon. That superior seamanship was further enhanced by the fact that the Seleucid naval command, mindful after Cissus of Roman boarding tactics, had concentrated on the construction of heavier warships, and with Phoenician crews unused to this style of fighting, these ships were easy prey for the nimble Rhodian quadriremes. Side was a relatively small-scale affair and not a single ship was sunk, but it prevented the linkup of the Seleucid fleets. Polyxenidas' hopes for numerical superiority over the Romans in heavy vessels were now limping eastward, and given the

25. Livy 37.22.5–23.6. Hannibal apparently had also a number of light vessels, as after the battle his crippled ships were towed by *apertae* (Livy 37.24.6). Livy 37.23.4 shows the battle took place in July–August; De Sanctis IV.1, 394; Myonnesus would thus have taken place in September.

26. Livy 37.23.7–24.9; App. *Syr.* 22; Zon. 9.20. Nepos *Han.* 8.4 wrongly makes the Rhodian numbers superior. Why the Rhodians did not employ the firebasket is unclear.

disabled and demoralized state of Hannibal's squadron, it was unlikely that they would soon return.

When the victorious Rhodians arrived home, it was decided to
send Chariclitus with twenty ships back to Megiste to watch for
Hannibal, while Eudamus sailed with seven vessels to Samos with
orders from the government to press Regillus to send an expedition
against Patara. It is probable that the nauarch, who must certainly
have realized that Polyxenidas should be the center of attention, did
little more than pass on the request, and the Roman admiral correctly
refused, dispatching only four ships under Pamphilidas. He was, on
the other hand, just barely persuaded by Eudamus not to commit the
mad act of conveying the entire fleet to the Hellespont. As it was,
twenty-three valuable Roman ships were sent off as a concession to
the admiral's honor, as he felt it unseemly that Eumenes alone should
ferry the Roman troops to Asia. Consequently, in the subsequent
battle of Myonnesus, the allies once more fought against numerical
odds.[27]

This final naval engagement was forced by Antiochus, who rightly
saw that it was now or never as far as the war at sea was concerned. If
his fleet did not act soon, the Roman troops would be across the
Hellespont unopposed, and the king would be forced once again to
face the dreaded legions. The time was also right in terms of numbers, as the Pergamene ships were still in the Hellespont and half the
Rhodian fleet was now off in the south. It was unlikely that Polyxenidas was ever going to get better odds, though he in fact did, when
Regillus soon obligingly sent north his "honor" detachment. Accordingly, Antiochus sent the fleet to nearby Notium, while he himself laid siege to the city with the army, hoping thus to draw Regillus
into battle. As expected, the Notians sent to Samos for aid, and
Regillus decided to move the fleet out, planning to sail first to Chios
for provisions. Before the departure, however, it was learned that the
latest wine shipment from Italy had not reached Chios, and that wine
and other stores had been offered to the king's fleet by Teos. Regillus
consequently took the fleet to Geraesticus harbor north of Teos in-

27. Livy 37.24.10–25.3, 26.11–13; App. *Syr.* 22. Chariclitus had commanded the
left at Side.

stead, and by plundering the fields around the city he was able to persuade the Teans to provide the necessary supplies. Meanwhile Polyxenidas had moved his fleet to an island off Myonnesus, and observing that the allies were anchored in a harbor with a narrow entrance, he began to hope that he might repeat the victory of Panhormus. That hope was soon dashed, however, when a chance collision alerted Eudamus to the dangers of the anchorage and the fleet was moved to the port of Teos, which was in any case more convenient for the loading of the stores.[28]

The naval showdown was finally initiated when word was brought to the allies that a large fleet had been anchored off Myonnesus for two days and was now preparing to depart. Completely surprised by this news, Regillus hurried to collect his scattered crews and get his fleet under way and in order before the enemy appeared. His own flagship led the still assembling column out to sea, while the Rhodians, having the fastest vessels, remained until last to bring up the rear, which would become the left wing of the line once all the ships had left the harbor. In his haste, however, Regillus began to move ahead before the line abreast had been completed, and as a consequence the fleet advanced in an echelon formation, with the landward portion of the line trailing behind the seaward. As it happened, Polyxenidas, unaware that the Romans had been alerted, still had his fleet in a column when the enemy was sighted, and when he led the van left in order to form a line abreast, he also managed to get his seaward wing ahead of his landward. Thus, as the two fleets closed and the sea flanks were on the point of making contact, the vessels nearer the shore were still at some distance from one another.[29]

The allied fleet was composed of fifty-eight Roman quinqueremes and twenty-two Rhodian vessels, probably mostly quadriremes, while the Seleucid was made up of forty-seven triremes, thirty-seven quadriremes and quinqueremes, and five heavier craft. Because of this nine-ship advantage, Polyxenidas was able to outflank the Ro-

28. Livy 37.26.1–28.11; Polyb. 21.11.13, 12.1. On the way to Teos, Regillus wasted a day chasing some 15 pirate craft, which he mistook for a detachment from the Seleucid fleet.

29. Livy 37.29.1–8. The echelon formation is surmised from Livy's description of the approach and battle; see esp. Thiel 353–55.

mans, and Regillus and the allied right wing were quickly threatened with envelopment and disaster. But the disaster never came. Perceiving immediately what was developing on the right flank, Eudamus abandoned his position on the unengaged left and led his squadron at top speed to Regillus' rescue. The tables were thus quickly turned on Polyxenidas, who now found himself on the defensive, hard pressed by the darting Rhodian ships, many of which were equipped with the feared fire baskets. Freed from the threat of envelopment, the Romans meanwhile were able to press ahead with their boarding tactics and soon broke through the Syrian center and turned on Polyxenidas' rear. With his left wing crushed and his center heavily damaged, the Seleucid admiral raised the signal for flight, and a favorable wind carried the crippled fleet back to Ephesus. Eudamus' dangerous but necessary tactic had worked, forcing Polyxenidas to give up the contest before his untouched right could close and take deadly advantage of the absence of the Rhodian squadron from the allied left. Polyxenidas had lost half his fleet—thirteen ships captured, probably by the Romans, and twenty-nine burned or sunk, the certain mark of Rhodian activity—while of the allied fleet two Roman vessels were destroyed and a Rhodian ship was captured in a freak accident.[30]

This was Rhodes' finest hour. The battles of Side and Myonnesus had broken the Seleucid navy, and both were undeniably Rhodian victories. The Roman Senate had not only failed to supply the allied fleets with sufficient ships, but had also appointed as admiral for the crucial year 190 a man who at every turn demonstrated his complete incompetence. Had it not been for Eudamus and his Rhodians, Regillus would clearly have been crushed at Myonnesus, and the Roman invasion of Asia Minor would have had to be postponed for at least a year, allowing Antiochus time to gather his forces and enlarge his navy. It is too much to say that Rhodes won the war for the Romans, but it is clearly because of Rhodes that it was won now, and not two or more years later.

With control of the sea irretrievably lost, Antiochus had little choice but to evacuate Europe, as he could neither defend his posses-

---

30. Livy 37.29.8–30.10; App. *Syr.* 27; Flor. 2.18.12; Just. 31.6.9. Appian has 25 Rhodian ships and total Seleucid losses of 29.

sions there nor prevent a crossing of the Hellespont.[31] The Rhodians meanwhile were dismissed by Regillus after an allied demonstration before Ephesus, but they sailed north to take part in the crossing operation anyway, both to share in the glory of what they had made possible and, more important, to advertise their achievement and presence to the influential Scipios. It appears that the Rhodians had already departed when Heracleides arrived with Antiochus' offer to negotiate, but if they were still present, Eudamus would surely have avoided compromising his country by supporting negotiations in which the Romans were obviously not interested.[32] The war was in any case in its final stage, and in the winter of 190/89 it ended with the king's defeat at Magnesia, but Rhodes had one final part to play. Motivated undoubtedly by a desire to end the conflict in Greece, in the summer of 189 the Rhodians joined the Athenians in sending an embassy to the consul M. Fulvius Nobilior at Ambracia to seek mitigation of the terms demanded of the Aetolians. Acting in concert with King Amynander of Athamania and Nobilior's half brother, C. Valerius Laevinus, the envoys were successful in obtaining milder conditions, and the Rhodians accompanied the Aetolian embassy to Rome, where they were instrumental in persuading the Senate to give final ratification.[33]

The summer of 189 saw Eumenes and envoys of Antiochus, Rhodes, and the communities of Asia Minor present in Rome for the final peace settlement and the disposition of the conquered territories. According to the terms of the peace, the Seleucid monarch was to withdraw from all of Cistauric Asia,[34] and the Senate, assuming, as in the wars with Philip and Nabis, the position of sole arbiter, was thus left with vast tracts of land to dispose of. Quite naturally wishing to grab as much as possible for himself, Eumenes argued that if the Romans did not retain possession of Anatolia—knowing full well

31. Livy 37.31.1–4; App. *Syr.* 28; Diod. 29.5.1.

32. Livy 37.31.6–7, 33.4–5, 34.1–36.9; App. *Syr.* 29; Diod. 29.7.1–8.2, 10.1; Zon. 9.20; van Gelder 139.

33. Polyb. 21.25.10, 29.1–32.15; Livy 38.3.7, 9.3–11.9; Flor. 2.9.3; Zon. 9.21. If the Büttner-Wobst emendation is correct, the Rhodian who spoke was Damon.

34. For the terms of the peace, see Polyb. 21.17.3–7, 43.1–27; Livy 37.45.14–17, 38.38.1–18; App. *Syr.* 39; Diod. 29.10.1; Zon. 9.21; Eutrop. 4.2; Walbank III, 156–62.

that they would not—then the next most deserving recipient of the spoils was himself, as his family's services to Rome clearly indicated. Anticipating that the Rhodians would request autonomy for the Asian Greeks, he contended that such cities as were given their freedom would in reality only become subservient to Rhodes, and the example of liberty would detach from Pergamum those cities previously subject to it.[35] When their turn to speak came, the Rhodians argued that freedom for the Asian Greeks was the only honorable course for the Romans and that Eumenes could be more amply rewarded for his services by the grant of such an area as Pisidia or Hellespontine Phrygia.[36] The reasons behind the arguments of both sides are clear enough: it was the Greek coastal cities and emporia that were important to both Rhodes and Pergamum. Eumenes was in fact correct in perceiving that their autonomy would not only be a loss to himself but a definite asset to the Rhodians, who could bring the free cities under their moral and economic leadership. This latter consideration was of course one of the basic reasons why Rhodes had traditionally supported the independence of the smaller Aegean states. In this instance the freedom of the Greek cities would serve two ends of Rhodian policy, not only potentially augmenting the influence of the island republic but also undermining the power of Pergamum, which now threatened to become Rhodes' most uncomfortable neighbor.

The Senate's reply to these arguments was a compromise of sorts. Those cities free on the day of the battle of Magnesia were to remain free; all other cities (except those in Rhodian territory) were to be subject to Eumenes. Rhodes was to receive Caria south of the Maeander and Lycia, with the exception of Telmessus, which went to Eumenes, while the Pergamene king gained the Thracian Chersonese and the remainder of Cistauric Asia—Lycaonia, the two Phrygias, Caria north of the Maeander, Milyas, Lydia, and Mysia. These territorial arrangements were presented as general guidelines to a sen-

35. Polyb. 21.18.1–21.11; Livy 37.52.1–53.28. On the historicity of the Pergamene and Rhodian speeches, see M. Gelzer, *Kleine Schriften* (Wiesbaden 1962–63) III, 186–89, who also demonstrates the likelihood that Polybius drew from Zeno.

36. Polyb. 21.22.5–23.13; Livy 37.54.3–28. Parts of the Livian version of the speech are probably added rhetoric (H. Nissen, *Kritische Untersuchungen über die Quellen der vierten und fünften Dekade des Livius* [Berlin 1893] 27).

atorial commission of ten, which traveled to Asia Minor the following year in order to attend to the details of the settlement. In the
autumn the commissioners were met at Apamea in Phrygia by the
proconsul Cn. Manlius Vulso, recently returned from his Galatian
campaign, and together they heard the claims of a variety of individual cities and peoples and drafted the final form of the peace treaty
and the new map of Anatolia.[37]

In making these arrangements the Senate was of course looking
first after the interests of Rome, which demanded the creation of a
strong state that could both maintain order in Anatolia and act as a
buffer against the Galatians and the Seleucid kingdom. Although at
heart the Romans probably cared little about the status of the Asian
Greeks, under the circumstances their treatment of the cities was
basically fair. They could hardly be expected to deprive faithful Eumenes of his subject towns, and it must have seemed just to the Senate
that those cities that had fought against Rome and the cause of liberty
should not gain their freedom. The settlement certainly does not
reflect any Roman hostility toward Rhodes.[38] The island was
awarded as much mainland territory as it might reasonably be expected to digest, and the Senate paid about as much attention to Greek
autonomy as it could, given the goals of Roman policy and the con-
flicting claims of Eumenes. That the Rhodians were in fact in high
favor with the *patres* is demonstrated by their influence on the negotiations with the Aetolians and by the Senate's reaction to the case of
Soli. At the meeting in Rome in 189 the Rhodians asked that this
Cilician town be declared free, and although this was a clear violation
of the peace treaty, the Senate gave its full support. When the Seleucid
envoys quite understandably resisted this demand, the Senate expressed its willingness to go to all lengths, and the Rhodians wisely
withdrew their requests.[39]

37. Polyb. 21.24.4–9, 45.1–11; Livy 37.55.4–56.6, 38.39.5–17; App. *Syr.* 44,
Mith. 62; Diod. 29.11.1; Eutrop. 4.2; J. Briscoe, *A Commentary on Livy, Books
XXXIV–XXXVII* (Oxford 1981) 384–88. For further details of the settlement perti-
nent to Rhodian affairs, see below, chap. 8.

38. As Schmitt 82 believes.

39. Polyb. 21.24.10–15; Livy 37.56.7–10. It should be noted also that the peace
treaty contained specific provisions concerning Rhodian properties and reparations

Rhodes now stood at the peak of its power.[40] The destruction of the Seleucid fleet and the withdrawal of the Romans left Pergamum as its only naval competitor in the east, and with a great land empire now in his possession Eumenes could be expected to turn most of his attention away from the sea. It is true that the Hellespont was now Pergamene, but most of the western seabord of Anatolia was either free or under Rhodian control,[41] and Rhodes remained mistress of the Aegean through its commerce and its leadership of the Nesiotic League. On the mainland Seleucid power had been pushed back beyond the Taurus Mountains, and Rhodian possessions had been quadrupled in extent by the acquisition of Lycia and southern Caria. The Syrian presence had of course been replaced by the more hostile Pergamene, but although Eumenes could be expected to work against Rhodian interests, it was not likely that he would venture to disturb the Roman settlement with outright aggression, especially against a friend of the Senate.

The real danger was not the Attalid kingdom but Rome, whose shadow now covered the Mediterranean world; should Rome determine to build an empire in the east or in some way become angry with the island republic, Rhodes must inevitably go under. But twice the Romans had withdrawn from the Aegean, forgoing any domination, and the two states were now on the best of terms, with no reasonable expectation that their interests would clash. Yet the fact remained that what the Rhodians had feared at the outset of the war had come to

---

and confirmed an exemption from Seleucid customs duties granted the Rhodians by Seleucus II (Polyb. 5.89.8, 21.42.16–17; Livy 38.38.11–12). Such attention to Rhodian concerns is hardly indicative of a hostile Rome.

40. A reflection of Rhodes' increased power and resources is found in the issue of a new series of drachmas, probably in the decade after Apamea. These new coins were slightly heavier than the older (which apparently continued to be minted), displayed Helios in profile rather than full face, and were marked with an incuse square, which earned them the name *plinthophoroi*. It has been thought (e.g., Head 640–41) that these coins appeared in 166, but *Syll.*[3] 633 demonstrates that they began to circulate before 173. It also makes sense that Rhodes should move to a heavier issue during the prosperity of the 180s and 170s, rather than in the wake of the disasters of the 160s. See L. Robert, *Etudes de numismatique grecque* (Paris 1951) 166–67.

41. For Pergamene possessions, see Schmitt, *Antiochos* 280–85; Walbank III, 166–69.

pass: Seleucid power had taken a heavy if not decisive blow, and there was now no counterpoise to the overwhelming power of Rome. The Greek monarchies might in the future recover and close ranks, but for the moment Rhodes was independent and powerful in the east only through a kind of Roman dispensation. If the attitude of the Senate were to change, the Rhodians would be without a strong ally to turn to.

CHAPTER 8

The Lycian Revolt
and a Bride for Perseus

A S a result of the settlement at Apamea, Rhodes' continental dominion now included the whole of Lycia, excluding Telmessus, and all of Caria south of the Maeander River, with the exception of the free cities of Miletus, Heraclea-by-Latmus, Myndus, Halicarnassus, Mylasa, and perhaps Alabanda and others.[1] Miletus and Heraclea, however, soon came under the de facto suzerainty of the island by means of an alliance,[2] and it is possible that by such means Rhodes also extended its influence over the other free Carian cities. The new acquisitions were easily brought into the governmental structure of the old subject Peraea, whose administrative apparatus was simply expanded to cover the enlarged territory. The Carian properties were naturally placed under the jurisdiction of the hegem-

---

1. Mylasa, Miletus: Polyb. 31.46.4–5; Livy 38.39.8–9; Heraclea-by-Latmus: *Syll.*[3] 618; Myndus, Halicarnassus: Livy 33.20.12; Alabanda: Schmitt 87, n. 1, against Magie II, 994, n. 32. It is not correct to assume that Iasus, Bargylia, and Pedasa remained free, since Euromus, which had the same prewar status, apparently became Rhodian: Polyb. 30.5.11; Livy 45.25.11. As pointed out by F&B 108, owing to the incompleteness of the Polybian narrative, it is very possible that there were other free cities. Cnidus, which had long been under Rhodian influence, now apparently became subject. In the period from Apamea to 167 Cnidian coinage displays Helios on the obverse and a lion or Aphrodite with the Rhodian rose on the reverse, sure symbols of Rhodian ascendancy; see Head 616; F&B 93, n. 3.

2. A treaty between the two towns dated to 180 is bounded by a wider Rhodian alliance, the language of which indicates the unequal nature of the relationship (*Syll.*[3] 633): μηθὲν ὑπεναντίον πρασσόντων τῶν δήμων τῆι πρὸς Ῥοδίους συμμαχίαι.

on for Caria, while for Lycia the Rhodians created a separate hegemon, who, like his Carian counterpart, was immediately subordinate to the strategos of the mainland.[3] To all appearances the administration of Lycia was to be identical to that of the older subject territory, and the Rhodians probably expected to establish in the area the same working relationship that had been so successful in Caria.

This was not to be, however. Unlike the situation in Caria, Rhodian rule in Lycia was from the start quite definitely unpopular. The territory had been granted to the republic by the Senate in its general directive of 189, but while the proconsul and ten commissioners were settling affairs at Apamea, they were approached by Hipparchus and Satyrus, envoys from Ilium, who pleaded that the Lycians not be punished.[4] According to Polybius, the commission, in an attempt to satisfy both sides, undertook nothing "ruinous" against the Lycians, but nevertheless gave the territory to Rhodes "as a gift." The Ilian envoys then toured Lycia proclamining their success in gaining the country's freedom, while the Rhodian representatives at Apamea, Theaedetus and Philophron, returned home and reported that Lycia was theirs as a gift from Rome. Then, as the Rhodians were selecting officials to organize their new provinces, ambassadors from Lycia arrived and proposed an alliance, only to be informed by Pothion, one of the prytanes, that they were not to be allies, but rather subjects of Rhodes. Astounded by this reply, the Lycians immediately declared their intention to resist any subjugation.[5] Not only did they believe their position to be correct, but they also feared that the bad blood that traditionally existed between them and the Rhodians, accentuated now by their recent wartime activities and piracy, would

3. *IG* xii.1 49 (= *Syll.*[3] 619): ἀγεμὼν ἐπὶ Λυκίας.
4. Polyb. 22.5.3.
5. Polyb. 22.5.1–5. Theaedetus was possibly the father of Astymedes and is mentioned in *Inscr. Lind.* 216, 217 and *IG* xii.1 852, 856. Philophron was possibly the son of Philophron, son of Xenophanes, who was proxenos in Delphi in 225 (*SGDI* 2649). Pothion (or Puthion [van Gelder 143, n. 1]) is otherwise unknown. Ullrich 56–58, followed by Schmitt 97, believes that Polybius employed a Rhodian source for this passage; given the details of the Rhodian assembly and the pro-Rhodian interpretation of the grant, this supposition seems likely. As F&B 112 point out, however, the account is probably not a Rhodian distortion of the events, as in that case the commissioner's response to the Lycians would not have been included, suggesting as it does that the Lycians might have had a case.

guarantee them harsh treatment, especially in contrast to the lax suzerainty of Antiochus.[6] Rhodes thus found itself faced with the novel prospect of an armed revolt.

The Rhodians were clearly convinced that Lycia was now completely subject to them, while the Lycians considered themselves subject only to the extent that they must form an alliance with the island, something they immediately attempted to do. It appears, however, that this misunderstanding was soon cleared up, undoubtedly through an appeal by both parties to the Roman commissioners, and that the Lycians were apprised of their position as subjects of Rhodes. Rather than appeal to Rome, as would be expected if they still felt their Roman-granted status was being violated, the Lycians simply revolted, and when a protest was finally lodged at Rome in 178, it was couched in moral rather than juridical terms and made no reference to Apamea.[7]

Thus it would seem that Rhodes was unconditionally awarded the country; but in the Senate's reply to the Lycian protest the Rhodians were informed that a study of the *acta* of 188 revealed that the Lycians had not been given to them as a gift, but as "friends and allies," a direct contradiction of Polybius' earlier statement. Such facts as are known, however, point to the conclusion that Rhodes was indeed granted complete control. The Rhodians certainly believed so, for they are not likely to have taken up arms contrary to the Roman settlement, and their response to the note of 178 was to send an embassy of their own to clarify matters before the Senate, which they thought had been taken in by the Lycians.[8] That the Rhodians did not appeal to the Senate during this ten-year interval suggests strongly that they considered the legal aspect of the conflict settled, and the fact that the Lycians themselves waited a decade before protesting to Rome indicates that they also realized they did not have a legal leg to

6. That the Lycians had been causing trouble during the war is evidenced by Rhodes' continual desire to capture Patara; but the hostility went back much further: Hom. *Il.* 5.628–62; Schol. Hom. *Il.* 5.639; *Lind. Temp. Chron.* 23.

7. Polyb. 25.4.1–4; Livy 41.6.8–10; Schmitt 118–19. Livy's source is clearly annalistic, Polybius' probably Rhodian; see Ullrich 58. Polybius is of course fragmentary for this period, but Livy would surely have reported it if any Lycian embassy had visited Rome before 178.

8. Polyb. 25.4.5, 5.1–4; Livy 41.6.11–12; App. *Mith.* 62.

stand on.[9] Further, it would seem strange behavior for the Romans to single out for special treatment in 188 a country that had been firmly behind Antiochus and then ignore the illegal oppression of that country for the next ten years. Finally, Polybius clearly states that Lycia was given as a gift, and he is implicitly supported by Livy, who places no qualifications on the grant.[10] The statements of 178, on the other hand, are reports of what the Senate had to say about the status of Lycia a decade after the settlement, and by then times had certainly changed.

With only Polybius' meager report of the events, it is impossible to know exactly what it was the Roman commissioners at Apamea told the Ilian envoys which led to the initial misunderstanding. Most likely the commissioners, as diplomats are wont to do, placated the embassy with general words about freedom and security from harsh punishment and then granted Lycia to the Rhodians, as instructed by the Senate.[11] The Ilian ambassadors, wishing naturally to amplify their success in obtaining good treatment for the Lycians, would have tended to exaggerate or elaborate on the Roman promises and thus further complicate matters. This is of course conjecture, but it provides the most reasonable solution to the problem. The key consideration, once more, is that all the evidence indicates that the misunderstanding, whatever its origin, was soon set straight, and although the Lycians rose in revolt, they did so as rebellious subjects and not as wronged allies.

This interpretation of the Lycian affair also eliminates the question of whether the ambiguity on which the misunderstanding was based was deliberate and thus an attempt to provide troubles for Rhodes.[12]

9. The delay is also a fatal flaw in the *"fides"* theory of Schmitt 124–27.

10. Polyb. 22.5.4: προσένειμαν ἐν δωρεᾷ; 22.5.7: δεδόσθαι . . . ἐν δωρεᾷ; also Polyb. 21.24.7–8, 45.8; Livy 37.55.5, 38.39.13; Diod. 29.11.1; App. *Syr.* 44; Eutrop. 4.4.3. App. *Mith.* 62 need only represent the view current in Sulla's time. For a discussion of the term ἐν δωρεᾷ, see Schmitt 98–103.

11. A. Heuss, *Stadt und Herrscher des Hellenismus in ihren staats- und völkerrechtlichen Beziehungen* (Leipzig 1937) 185 believes the commissioners interpreted the Ilian request to mean freedom from a punitive expedition and reassured them on that score; this is probably partly true.

12. So F&B 113; T. Liebmann-Frankfort, *La frontière orientale dans la politique extérieure de la République romaine depuis le traité d'Apamée jusqu'à la fin des conquêtes asiatiques de Pompée (189/8–63)* (Brussels 1969) 96–98.

The difference of opinion was soon settled in favor of the island, and it is extremely difficult to believe that the Senate would deliberately foster a misunderstanding only to clear it up again. Further, to accuse the Senate of such Machiavellian behavior is to read back to 188 the Roman attitude of 167, and there is in this earlier period not the slightest indication of any Roman hostility toward Rhodes, or any reason for there to be. And if there were hostility or fear, would the Senate have chosen such devious means, rather than simply granting the territory to Eumenes and thereby strengthening a more subservient ally? This understanding of the events does not, however, make it necessary to think the Romans incapable of handling in a clear manner the situation that faced them at Apamea.[13] Rome had had enough contact with the Greeks to be able to manage complex diplomatic arrangements with them, and the ambiguity arose only from an attempt to satisfy the Ilian embassy by avoiding an exact definition of the status of Lycia with regard to Rhodes.

Rhodes' immediate response to the Lycian resistance was to attempt to stamp out the revolt with armed force. This reaction is understandable; convinced that the Lycians had been placed unconditionally under their control, the Rhodians saw no reason to allow these erstwhile pirates the greater freedom of an alliance, which status, moreover, would provide an example dangerous to their position in Caria. They doubtless also considered that Lycia would be far more lucrative to the state as a subject than as an ally, but this hardly proved to be the case, as the acceptance of the challenge marked the beginning of at least fourteen years of counterinsurrectionary war. It may be doubted that the struggle rendered Lycia an absolute financial drain, as the Rhodians would have held the towns and collected whatever revenues were possible, but the loss of the territory soon after final pacification would deprive the island of a real return on its long investment.[14]

---

13. As believes Schmitt 93, 121.

14. According to Polyb. 30.31.4, the Rhodians fought three wars against Caria and Lycia, and Ullrich was the first to point out that only two of these wars were against Lycia. The first revolt was over by 178 (Polyb. 25.4.2); the second was still going in 174 (Livy 41.25.8). Polyb. 27.7.6 might suggest that the second revolt was all over by 171; having been put down after a decade of war in the first revolt, the Lycians certainly could not have possessed the capacity to carry on the second for very long.

The suppression of the Lycian revolt was of course an adventure for the Rhodians in territorial imperialism on the mainland, but it would be mistaken to view this action and the acceptance of Caria as marking any significant shift in the direction of the island's policy. Since the beginning of the third century, when Rhodes had acquired that part of Caria which became the subject Peraea, it had maintained a small imperial presence on the mainland and had found such an establishment profitable, especially after the acquisition of Stratonicea and Caunus. 15 At Apamea the frontiers of its subject territory were expanded tremendously by the simple decree of Rome, and Rhodes judged itself capable of garrisoning and in the case of Lycia pacifying this greater area. Insofar as its continental possessions were quadrupled and it shouldered the typically imperial burden of pacification, Rhodes may be considered to have adopted a more annexationist policy, but there had been and would be no plan of conquest. The Rhodians naturally felt themselves to be a stronger power, capable of exerting their authority over Lycia and Caria, but the island's basic interests still lay on the sea and in the emporia of the Mediterranean.

The first word of Rhodian activity after Apamea in fact concerns the defense of its trading interests. In 183 the Pontic king Pharnaces I suddenly seized the free city of Sinope, and as in 219, when the city was threatened by Pharnaces' grandfather, Rhodes' immediate response was to come to the aid of this important emporium. Since the city was already captured and the Rhodians were in no position to liberate it themselves, the reaction in this case took the form of an embassy to Rome in 182, an express recognition of Rome's power in the east. The Senate's reply to the Rhodians, and to the Pergamene embassy that was also present to complain about Sinope and Pharnaces' subsequent attack on Ariathes IV of Cappadocia, was to send legates to investigate the affair. This commission achieved nothing, but rather than join the coalition composed of Eumenes and various Anatolian princes, the Rhodians took no further action and remained neutral throughout the war, which ended in 179 with the defeat of the

15. See above, chap. 4.

Pontic king.[16] Though Rhodes preferred the city independent, it was not ready to disrupt its Euxine trade by declaring war on the ruler of Pontus and new master of Sinope; on the contrary, when in the course of the war Eumenes attempted to strike at Pharnaces with a blockade of the Hellespont, the Rhodians promptly took measures to force him to lift it.[17] The commercial center of Sinope was important to Rhodes, but in the area of the Hellespont and the Black Sea the prime element of Rhodian policy was the security of its commerce, and it is this factor that makes Rhodes' abrupt reversal intelligible.

Partly as a result of the action against the blockade, relations between Rhodes and Pergamum, never very good, became openly sour around 180. The Rhodians were undoubtedly not pleased by Eumenes' alliance with thirty-one Cretan cities in 183, and they must certainly have been annoyed in 179 when, despite the heavy terms imposed on him, Pharnaces was allowed to retain Sinope.[18] It is true that in 181 Rhodes sought and obtained from the king some sort of aid against the Lycian rebels, but several years later Pergamene troops are found supporting the Lycians with raids across the frontier.[19] It appears also that trade between the two countries broke off at this time, as Rhodian handles from the period 220–180 are found in overwhelming numbers in Pergamum, while those dated after about 180 are completely absent from the deposits. The reasons behind this break were undoubtedly basically economic and probably represent an emancipation of Pergamene commerce from Rhodian domina-

---

16. Polyb. 23.9.1–3, 24.1.1–3; Livy 40.2.6–8. It is not clear when the war actually began, though 183 is customarily given as the date. The Romans' unwillingness to become involved in a war over Sinope is hardly evidence of hostility toward Rhodes, as Schmitt 134 believes.

17. Polyb. 27.7.5; 180 is the most likely date, as Eumenes aided the Rhodians in 181 and relations between the two states deteriorated after 180 (E. Meyer, *Geschichte des Königreichs Pontos* [Leipzig 1879] 78). What precisely the Rhodians did to force the lifting of the blockade is unknown, but it presumably involved a demonstration with the fleet; Eumenes was in no position to add Rhodes to his list of active enemies.

18. Alliance: *Syll.*³ 627 (= *IC* iv 179); Polyb. 28.15.1?. See Hansen 101, n. 100, for a list of the cities, which included many in the Rhodian sphere of influence. The treaty contained provisions for the hiring of mercenaries. Sinope: Polyb. 25.2.3–10.

19. Aid: Polyb. 24.15.13. Eumenes, in the midst of his war against Pharnaces, was probably courting Rhodian support. Raids: Polyb. 27.7.6.

tion, but the deterioration of economic and political relations between the two states is clearly more than coincidental.[20]

Rhodian relations with Rome, on the other hand, appear to have remained amicable during the first decade after Apamea; at least there is no word of any friction between the two states. Although the Senate was becoming more and more imperious toward the Greek states and was probably irritated by the proud independence of the Rhodians, Roman concern for Asian affairs had become somewhat listless, and the island gave the *patres* no real cause for annoyance. The situation changed in 178, however. In that year Perseus, the son of Philip and new ruler of Macedon, accepted as his wife the princess Laodice, daughter of Seleucus IV; and as the Syrian navy was prevented by the treaty of Apamea from sailing into the Aegean and there was no Macedonian navy, the bride was escorted to Macedon by a Rhodian squadron. Having delivered their charge, the Rhodians were rewarded with golden crowns and timber for shipbuilding and subsequently paraded their naval strength in a grand review.[21]

Since the Rhodians had commercial interests in both kingdoms,[22] their action is entirely understandable as a gesture of friendship toward the two monarchs; such was traditional Rhodian policy. Escorting Perseus' Seleucid bride was undoubtedly also a demonstration of Rhodes' approval of the rapprochement of the royal houses,

20. Handles: Bleckmann 24–26; V. Grace, "Stamped Amphorae Handles Found in 1931–1932," *Hesp.* 3 (1934) 207, 209, 215–17. Rostovtzeff III, 1479–80, n. 68, suggests that possibly Delos now served as the clearinghouse for Pergamene goods. The extent of Rhodian economic influence in the Attalid sphere is also demonstrated by the wide circulation in the period after about 200 of the pan-Asian *cistophoroi,* silver minted on the Rhodian standard by cities dependent in some way on Pergamum (Hansen 221–23).

21. Polyb. 25.4.8–10; App. *Mac.* 11.2; Livy 42.12.3–4. The exact date is unknown, but as Perseus became king in the summer of 179, early the following year is most reasonable for νεωστί and βράχει χρόνῳ πρότερον (context of late 178). Appian says ὅλῳ τῷ ʿΡοδίων στόλῳ, but it is very doubtful that the Rhodians would pull all their naval vessels off other duties for this parade. *Syll.*[3] 639, a Delian inscription honoring Laodice, suggests that the procession may have stopped at the island.

22. See above, chaps. 2 and 4, and Rostovtzeff III, 1372, n. 59, for dedications in honor of Rhodians at Delos when it was under Macedonian influence. Relations with Macedon picked up again after the Second Macedonian War; coin finds show commercial ties with Histiaea and Macedon. See Robert, *Etudes* 189–92, 213–14; Hackens *BCH* 93, 715–22; Oeconomides 13–15.

but it would be wrong to see much more in it. In the face of Roman power in the west, the closer together the Greek world could draw, the better it suited Rhodes, but Rhodes was not about to bring on a war with Rome or violate its century-old policy by allying itself with either of the kings.[23] The Rhodians must have realized that for the moment, at least, the Hellenistic east was in no shape to challenge Roman power, and that to take any serious step threatening to Rome would be a suicidal policy. They did not in any case want an actual war, which would injure their commercial interests, but it is likely that they favored the creation of an eastern bloc that might face Rome on more even terms. In time Macedon and Syria would probably regain their strength, but meanwhile Rhodes must content itself with such small manifestations of its old policy of equilibrium as this approval of the union of the Greek east. The republic certainly knew that this action, inasmuch as it was a gesture toward Perseus and Antigonid-Seleucid cooperation, would probably find a cool reception in Rome, but it believed that delivering the king's bride could hardly seriously endanger its relations with the western power.

In all likelihood the affair would in fact have had no real impact on Rhodian-Roman relations had it not been for the arrival in Rome of an embassy from Lycia. The last embers of revolt in that country had been finally stamped out in 178, but later in that year envoys from the city of Xanthus appeared before the Senate bewailing their harsh treatment at the hands of the Rhodians. Probably to the astonishment of the envoys, the response of the Senate was to inform Rhodes that according to the *acta* of 188, Lycia had been granted not as a subject to be maltreated, but as a "friend and ally."[24] The evidence is of course only circumstantial, but it is difficult to avoid seeing a causal relationship between Rhodes' actions earlier in the year and this inflammato-

---

23. So Schmitt 136.
24. Polyb. 25.4.1–5; Livy 41.6.8–12; App. *Mith.* 62. It is tempting to see the hand of Eumenes behind the very timely arrival of the embassy, but there is of course no evidence. The embassy has been traditionally dated to September 177, as Polybius names the consuls for that year, but this date creates difficulties, and it is easier to assume that Livy's dating is correct and that Polybius' excerpter inserted the wrong consuls; see P. Derow, "The Roman Calendar, 190–168 B.C.," *Phoenix* 27 (1973) 350–54.

ry declaration. Sentiment against Perseus already existed in Rome, and with the ostentatious maneuvers of the Rhodian fleet driving home the potential significance of the island to the Macedonian king, the Senate must have been to some degree displeased with the Rhodians. Moreover, the *patres* certainly realized that their pronouncement would create for Rhodes the possibility at least of further trouble in Lycia, and it is not clear why they would have issued it if they had not been in some way annoyed with the island. It appears, then, that the arrival of the Lycians offered the Roman government the perfect opportunity to deliver an easy warning and reprimand to the Rhodians by declaring Lycia to be their friend and ally rather than their subject.

This definition of the original arrangement was of course simply not true; the grant of Apamea had been an unconditional gift. By what right, then, did the Senate now take this action and, more important, later in 167 free Lycia and Caria entirely?[25] It has been suggested that the original grant was "precarious"—that is, the territory was given to Rhodes, but Rome retained the actual ownership and right of disposal.[26] This can hardly be the case, however, for neither Polybius nor Livy presents the barest suggestion that the grant was precarious, and if it were, Rhodes would not have accepted the territory, as such terms would cramp its freedom of action and allow for Roman intervention in its affairs.[27] Further, in the directive of 178 the Senate makes no mention of possessing any residual rights over Lycia, but rather bases its intervention on the original settlement through a reinterpretation of its terms. When the Rhodians in fact ignored the directive, Rome undertook no further action, not even a note of protest, for eleven years, an inactivity that seems unreasonable if Rome considered itself to be the actual owner of the rebellious country.[28]

It is much easier to see Rome's actions in 178 and 167 as the redefining of its own policy and its attitude toward Rhodes. In 188 Caria and

25. See below, chap. 9.
26. So E. Täubler, *Imperium Romanum* I (Leipzig 1913) 234; De Sanctis IV.1, 257; E. Bickermann, "Notes sur Polybe. I," *REG* 50, 217.
27. Schmitt, 105–6.
28. Schmitt, 106–7.

Lycia were unconditionally given to the island for its part in the war, and with other matters drawing its attention, Rome ignored the subsequent struggle in Lycia as the internal affair of a distant Greek power. Ten years later, however, an appeal from the now defeated Lycia arrived at a time when the Romans were recently annoyed with Rhodes, and the Senate took this opportunity to dispense an effortless reprimand by simply reinterpreting the grant of Apamea.[29] From the Rhodians' point of view, this move was entirely illegal and arbitrary; but although the act was quite definitely motivated by political considerations, the Romans may nevertheless have felt morally justified, as it was on their account that the Lycians were now ruled and allegedly oppressed by Rhodes.[30] If the Senate were seeking legal justification, reference might be made to the initial ambiguous judgment of the commissioners, but such was not done, and it is likely that Rome simply considered that it had the right to interpret as it pleased the grants that it dispensed. It was less what Rhodes had done than the changing attitudes of the Romans that brought about the adverse judgment. More and more Rome was tending to view the independent Greek states in terms of client relationships, and if the Rhodians would demonstrate their ingratitude to Rome by favoring Perseus, Rome would demonstrate its displeasure by redefining its grant to the disadvantage of Rhodes. This is not to say that Rome considered the island a *clientela* in the sense that it did, say, the *civitates liberae* of Sicily or the small states of Greece which owed their independence to Rome; but insofar as Rhodes owed its possession of Caria and Lycia to the favor of Rome, it had a moral obligation of gratitude, and this obligation was violated in 178.[31] This changing attitude of the Senate

29. J. Larsen, *Greek Federal States* (Oxford 1968) 247: "This was probably not so much a definition of what had been done in 188 as an adoption of a new policy, but, since Rome tended to retain a ruling once made, the new policy was worded as a mere definition of the old."

30. The letter, which, according to Livy 41.6.11–12, the Senate sent to the Rhodians, in fact speaks in these terms.

31. On *clientelae,* see Badian, *For. Clien.* 33–95; Dahlheim 260–74. Polyb. 25.4.7 says the Romans seemed to have the objective of exhausting Rhodian resources and finances, but this interpretation is wrong; the judgment was a sign of Roman displeasure and a warning, and as a single act supported by no subsequent moves, it does not have the appearance of a planned economic assault. The passage appears to be

would be even more apparent a decade later, when Lycia and Caria were freed from Rhodes and it became clear that what was not juridically precarious was considered morally revocable. By its actions in the Third Macedonian War the island had shown itself to be ungrateful, and what Rome gave Rome could take away.[32]

The effect of the Senate's judgment was immediately felt by Rhodes, as the Lycians, so recently pacified, began once more to stir in revolt. Rightfully indignant, the Rhodians sent an embassy under Lycophron to set the Senate straight on the matter, but after hearing the arguments of the envoys, the *patres* put off their answer, probably indefinitely.[33] With Lycia now in open revolt again, the Rhodians ignored the senatorial resolution and reapplied themselves to the task of suppressing the Lycians, whose cause was now actively supported by Eumenes. The Romans, however, made not the slightest move to enforce their decision, and, foredoomed, the revolt was probably extinguished before the outbreak of the Third Macedonian War in 171. More important was the suspicion and antagonism engendered by the whole affair. Rome was now apparently suspicious of the intentions and allegiances of the island republic, while anti-Roman feeling in Rhodes was inflamed by the pronouncement on Lycia, which clothed in reality the danger that Rome represented to the independence of the island. Though the Rhodians correctly decided to defy the Senate in Lycia, they knew well the extent of Roman power and would not have rashly challenged it with hostile acts, but the awful seeds were sown. The Senate's action established among the Rhodian people the basis of a sentiment that within a decade would support political decisions ultimately disastrous to the Rhodian republic.

---

from a Rhodian source and as such would understandably suggest such a motive; see Ullrich 58.

32. So Schmitt 108–11. In his speech before the Senate in 164, the Rhodian Astymedes in fact concedes the possible logic of this reasoning, without, of course, accepting that it is at all just (Polyb. 30.31.5).

33. Polyb. 25.5.1–6.1. It would seem from Polybius' brief report that the Lycians did not renew actual hostilities until after the Rhodian embassy to Rome, which is understandable.

CHAPTER 9

The Third Macedonian War

FOR the six years from the Lycian affair of 178 to the eve of the Third Macedonian War there is virtually no word of Rhodes in the sources, but it would appear that during this period relations with Rome did not improve, while those with Pergamum certainly deteriorated even further. Eumenes' support of the Lycian rebels directly assaulted the Rhodians, while his hostility toward Macedon was, in the opinion of Rhodes, contrary to the interests of Greece and threatened to bring on a war between Perseus and Rome, possibly the last thing Rhodes wanted to see. Besides disrupting Rhodian commerce, a new Macedonian struggle, which in the light of past events must in all probability end in Perseus' defeat, would result in a drastic increase in Rome's sway over Greece. Although Antigonid power in the mid-170s was far from offering the perfect counterpoise to Rome, it did provide Rhodian diplomacy with some of the strategic leeway to which it was accustomed. Although the weakening or elimination of Macedonian power might not result in an actual increase in Rome's physical presence in Greece, by eradicating the last vestiges of any balancing power it would certainly leave Rhodes more sensitive to the will of the Romans. A final blow to Macedon would produce what Rhodian policy had constantly endeavored to prevent, the emergence of a single dominating power; the great danger inherent in the appeal to Rome in 201 was drawing ever closer to realization.

Consequently, when in early 172 Eumenes himself traveled to

Rome, the Rhodians were quick to send their own embassy to counter his expected denunciations of Perseus and perhaps themselves.
The king, however, addressed a closed session of the Senate, to which
the Rhodian envoys were unable to gain admission, and unopposed
he declaimed at length upon the war preparations and anti-Roman
deeds and intentions of the Macedonian monarch, possibly leveling
charges also against Rhodes. When after a few days the Rhodian and
Macedonian embassies were able to gain an audience, their arguments apparently fell on deaf ears, and Rhodian criticism of Eumenes, especially coming hard on the heels of the Macedonian defense, may well have increased suspicion of the island and sympathy
for the Pergamene king. Soon afterward, on his return home, Eumenes narrowly escaped assassination at Delphi, and the attempt was
immediately blamed on Perseus and further accelerated the plunge
toward war.[1]

At Rhodes anger with Eumenes was demonstrated by a refusal to
allow the Pergamene delegation to take part in the great festival of
Helios;[2] yet despite Rhodian sympathy for the Macedonian cause,
political wisdom still prevailed on the island. When a Roman legation
sounding out opinion in Asia and the islands arrived in Rhodes late in
the year, they found the republic ready to support the Romans with a
fleet of forty ships, prepared under the leadership of the chief prytanis, Hagesilochus, son of Hegisias.[3] About the same time envoys

1. Livy 42.11.1–16.7, 19.1, 29.2, 59.8, 45.5.5,9–11; App. *Mac.* 11.1–4; Polyb.
22.18.5; Cass. Dio 20.66.3. According to Appian and Livy, the Rhodians delivered a
scathing attack on Eumenes which aroused yet more hostility toward themselves and
Perseus, and Livy speaks of a conspiracy against Eumenes; but it seems best to follow
Gruen 68 in rejecting these passages as later fabrications; see also Meloni, *Valore*
134–42.

2. App. *Mac.* 11.3. The festival occurred every four years in September, at the end
of the Rhodian year; see U. Kahrstedt, "Zum Ausbruche des dritten römisch-
makedonischen Krieges," *Klio* 11 (1911) 426–27. Shortly before 172, it seems (Livy
42.12.7), two Rhodian judges in Achaea, Sosigenes and Diopeithes, canceled all the
honors granted to the king (Polyb. 28.7.8–10). There is no reason to doubt that the
two were Rhodians; see Walbank III, 335–36.

3. Polyb. 27.3.1–5; Livy 42.45.1–7; on Hagesilochus see below, n. 8. The significance of the forty ships should not be exaggerated; the Rhodians always had a fleet in
being, and with the possibility of war and a consequent surge in piracy, it behoved
them to have such a fleet ready. At 42.19.7–8 and 26.7–8 Livy mentions another fact-
finding embassy sent to Asia and the islands, composed of Claudius Nero and M.

with a letter from Perseus also appeared and requested that in the event of war the Rhodians, in the best tradition of their diplomacy, attempt to bring about a reconciliation of the belligerents, and if this attempt failed, that they act to prevent the extension of Roman power over all lands. The envoys were given a friendly reception and apprised of Rhodes' desire for peace, but the Rhodians nevertheless required that Perseus ask of them nothing that would be contrary to their friendship with Rome.[4]

The Rhodian response to the Roman and Macedonian embassies was one of support for Rome, but the mood of the people definitely inclined toward Perseus, and for the first time since the fourth century there is direct evidence of party politics in Rhodes. Livy states that Hagesilochus "had with many speeches influenced the Rhodians to give up the hope, often found to be an empty one, of favoring kings," and in their treatment of the reception given the Macedonian embassy, both he and Polybius speak of the "better part" prevailing.[5] Even allowing for distortion in Polybius' Rhodian sources, there is implicit in these passages opposition to the policy of supporting Rome, and this opposition revealed itself quite plainly in the reaction to C. Lucretius Gallus' request for ships in the spring of 171. The expected war had become a virtual reality, undoubtedly increasing popular feeling against Rome; and when the praetor's message arrived, insultingly delivered by a gymnastics trainer, the Rhodian assembly was stirred to a debate over the proper course of action. The chief prytanis, Stratocles, and his supporters backed a resolution to send ships and take part in the war with no hesitation, but Deinon and Polyaratus, the apparent leaders of the opposition, argued against the proposal, playing on hostility toward Eumenes by accusing him of being the author of the message and the one who was actually trying

Decimius, and reports that "Rhodios fluctuantes et imbutos Persei consiliis invenisse," but this embassy may be discounted as an annualistic mistake; see Schmitt 212–14. The Rhodian embassy to Rome described at 42.26.9 is clearly a fabrication; see Schmitt 144, n. 1.

4. Polyb. 27.4.1–10; Livy 42.46.1–6.

5. Livy 42.45.4: "multis orationibus pervicerat Rhodios, ut omissa quam saepe vanam experti essent, regnum fovendorum spe"; 42.46.5: "potentior esse partis melioris auctoritas coeperat"; Polyb. 27.4.9: νικῶντος αὐτοῖς τοῦ βελτίονος. On Polybius' Rhodian sources, see Ullrich 58–62.

to drag Rhodes into a ruinous war. The resolution finally passed, but only six quadriremes were dispatched. In view of Rhodes' potential naval strength, this meager response appears to represent a compromise on the part of Stratocles and his people, though the Rhodians may simply have supposed the Roman fleet already to be adequate. The five vessels sent under Timagoras to join Lucretius at Chalcis were in fact promptly dismissed by the praetor, who explained to them and the other naval allies that their assistance was not required.[6] The sixth ship sailed to Tenedus, where it intercepted the vessel carrying Diophanes, Perseus' envoy to Antiochus IV. Diophanes escaped but the Macedonian crew was captured and transported to Rhodes.[7]

When the political situation in Rhodes is analyzed, it is misleading to speak of pro- and anti-Roman or pro- and anti-Macedonian parties, as it is a fair assumption that the sympathy of the Rhodian people on the whole was definitely with Macedon. The Lycian affair had demonstrated the real threat Rome might pose to Rhodian independence, and this threat was accentuated by the Senate's refusal to allow the unaggressive development of Macedonian power; Rome, it seemed, would not rest easy so long as there was any Aegean state that might present the slightest threat to Roman security. Moreover, the growing imperious and disdainful attitude of the Senate and its officials, recently exemplified by Lucretius' use of a Greek slave as a messenger, engendered a basic popular dislike of Rome. How different was the appealing personality of the Antigonid king, who treated the Rhodians with every consideration and supported the cause of Greece! The average Rhodian might suspect that it was Rhodes' navy that really interested Perseus, but the affable young monarch, in contrast to the Romans and also his less moderate father, nevertheless won great popularity.

6. Polyb. 27.7.1–16; Livy 42.56.6–7, 45.23.6. On Deinon and Polyaratus, see below, nn. 12–13. Timagoras is possibly the Timagoras, son of Polemocles, who was involved in the arbitration between Samos and Priene (*Syll.*[3] 599); Stratocles is otherwise unknown. Although the Romans would make a very poor showing against the tiny Macedonian navy, the strength of their fleet was in fact adequate; it was the command that was lacking. On the naval war see Thiel 372–415.

7. Polyb. 27.7.14–15. As commander of the Rhodian ship Polybius has Timagoras, which must be an error.

But popular sentiment notwithstanding, in the realm of *Realpolitik* would it be wise to ignore the Romans and perhaps even support Perseus? A large segment of the Rhodian leadership did not think so, and this segment, composed of Hagesilochus, Stratocles, Philophron, Rhodophon, Agathegetus, Theaedetus, Astymedes, and others, may, for convenience, be labeled the Roman group.[8] In the opinion of these men, an appreciation of the extent of Roman power and resources indicated that in all probability Perseus would be defeated, and therefore it was best for Rhodes to curry the favor of Rome by supporting its cause, even though further development of Roman power was in itself contrary to Rhodian interests. This is not to say that for a moment these men had any sympathy for Rome; rather, they felt that Rhodes had no realistic alternative and that even neutrality might compromise its position with the inevitable victor, considering that some anti-Rhodian sentiment already existed in the Senate. They very probably never thought of Rhodes as a Roman client, but the Senate's pronouncement on Lycia had clearly demonstrated that the *patres* were very touchy about the actions of Rome's friends, independent though they might be. Once again Rhodes had to abandon its old principle of supporting the balance of power, not because this policy was no longer important, but because to support Perseus and the only counterpoise to Rome was to join in his almost certain destruction. As in the war with Antiochus, the Rhodian leadership realized that with or without Rhodes, Rome would triumph, and that given this unhappy but inevitable outcome, it behooved the island to join the winning side and reap whatever profit it could;[9] even the alternative of complete neutrality was too risky.

This time, however, the unpopularity of the Roman cause proved too much for the Rhodian people, and the emotional stresses fractured the political unity of the island, producing an opposition to the

8. Hagesilochus: Polyb. 27.3.3–4, 28.2.1–2, 16.5; Livy 42.45.3–6; Stratocles: Polyb. 27.7.13; Philophron: Polyb. 27.14.2, 28.2.3, 16.3; Rhodophon: Polyb. 27.7.3, 28.2.3 (described by Hagesander of Delphi [Athen. 10.444d–e] as a drunk and gambler); Agathegetus: Polyb. 27.7.3, 28.2.3; Theaedetus: Polyb. 27.14.2, 28.2.3, 16.3, 29.11.2; Astymedes: Polyb. 27.7.3 (possibly the son of Theaedetus). Hagesander (Athen. 10.444d) links a certain Combon (or Comeon or Comon) with Rhodophon, but this does not prove Combon a leader or adherent of the Roman group.
9. On the question of the inevitability of Perseus' defeat, see below.

traditional leadership. This opposition, which may be styled the Macedonian group, was under the leadership of Deinon and Poly-aratus and reflected the popular hostility toward Rome.[10] Although initially, at least, these men apparently realized that supporting Per-seus would be a strategically foolish gamble, they saw no reason why Rhodes should be obliged actually to aid Rome and Eumenes in their dirty work. There was, after all, no *foedus* between Rhodes and Rome, and neutrality was the right of every sovereign state. Perseus' later successes in the war and the resultant increased influence of this group may have led to a development of its aims toward actual support of the monarch, but because of the paucity of evidence, aside from the basic proposition of not supporting Rome, the specific policies of this group are not at all clear.[11] Polybius, undoubtedly drawing on an understandably hostile Rhodian source, describes the leaders of the Macedonian group in the darkest terms, accusing them of being in Macedonian pay, but such a reaction is only to be expected toward men whose policy bore such bitter fruit.[12] Although these men apparently worked through the assembly while the Roman group controlled the Council and prytanes,[13] it is not necessary to see them as demagogic villains or mere tools of the Macedonian king. Corruption was a charge commonly leveled against politicians who supported a foreign power, and though it is possible that this group received financial support from Perseus, it need not be labeled as bribery.

Events, of course, proved the policy of the Roman group correct. Perseus' chances of success, even with the full support of the Rhodian navy, were simply too small to justify Rhodes in running the risk of

---

10. Polyb. 27.7.4, 8–12, 14.2, 28.2.3, 17.14, 29.11.2, 30.6.1, 7.9–10; Livy 44.23.10, 29.7, 45.22.9. Livy 44.23.10 and Polyb. 29.5.7 mention also a Metrodorus who was an agent of the Macedonian group. Polyb. 30.8.5–7 details the fate of a ship captain named Thoas, who was apparently an errand boy for the group.

11. Polyb. 30.7.9–10 (through suspect, as the passage is an unrestrained condem-nation of anti-Roman politicians), 29.11.2, and Livy 44.23.10 tend to support the conclusion that the group ultimately thought of joining Perseus, but the entire ques-tion must really remain unanswered.

12. Polyb. 27.7.12, 30.7.9–9.21. Ullrich 60, 69–70 traces the passages to Zeno, who stood close to the Roman group.

13. See below.

equivocating in the struggle, much less in joining the king. It did indeed have every legal right to remain neutral, a course that possessed the very small strategic advantage of preserving its relations with Perseus in the event of a Macedonian victory, but the Roman group correctly perceived that the days when Rhodes could remain uncommitted in a war between Rome and a Hellenistic power had already slipped away. The group around Deinon and Polyaratus was ostensibly supporting the traditional policy of the island, refusing to aid one of the great powers to attain a position of dominance that would destroy the foundation of the republic's independence; but the reality of the Mediterranean world of 172 clearly indicated that their course of action would be pointless, and worse, probably damaging to Rhodes. As the Roman group understood, the old Hellenistic world of the third century, with its balance of contending powers, had vanished, and with its disappearance had come the final exhaustion of Rhodes' traditional strategy and the essential end to any real independence of action.

As has been seen, in 172 the Roman group was still firmly in control and despite growing sympathy for Perseus remained so in 171, although the small number of ships sent to Lucretius may reflect the rising influence of the Macedonian group. This influence was further increased by Perseus' successful campaign of 171,[14] and when an embassy from Macedon arrived in Rhodes in the winter of 171/70 to ransom the crew captured at Tenedos, Deinon and Polyaratus were able to carry a positive decision against the opposition of the Roman group, which wished to remain uninvolved.[15] In accepting the ransom the Rhodians were actually well within their rights, as they were not treaty allies of Rome and therefore not required to consult it concerning their actions. Moreover, the ransoming of prisoners was a common practice, and the crew of one Macedonian warship could hardly be decisive in the struggle. It may in fact even be debated whether Rhodes was legally at war with Perseus at this time; the sources, so far as they go, make no mention of any declaration of war, and the only hostile acts had been the dispatch of ships to Lu-

---

14. See P. Meloni, *Perseo e la fine della monarchia macedone* (Cagliari 1953) 211–51.
15. Polyb. 27.7.15, 14.1–2.

cretius and the capture of the ship at Tenedus; a state of war certainly did not exist later when Rhodes attempted to mediate. But no matter how correct the ransom, insofar as it was a small gesture toward Perseus, it could have repercussions on Rhodes' standing with Rome and was thus opposed by the Roman group.

Although the information is scanty, the six ships sent out in 171 appear to have been Rhodes' only contribution to the Roman effort, and there is no word of any Rhodian vessels' being dispatched in 170 or the remaining years of the war. Open ships under the command of Eudamus are found at Tenedus in the spring of 168, but they were undoubtedly looking after Rhodian commerce in the Hellespontine region rather than operating against Perseus.[16] Once again, Rhodes was acting quite correctly, since as a simple *amicus* it was not bound to contribute aid even when asked. It was certainly not constrained to offer aid unbidden, especially considering that in 171 its warships had been sent back as unnecessary. Doubtless the Roman group would have liked to offer help, or even to take part in the war, as a demonstration of Rhodian fidelity, but they were seemingly no longer able to carry such a measure in the face of popular feeling against Rome.

It should be noted that while in both the question of aid to the Romans and that of the ransom the Macedonian group may be considered to have been successful, control of the powerful prytanes and Council seems to have remained throughout in the hands of the Roman group, with Deinon and Polyaratus and friends exerting their influence through the assembly. Because of the lack of adequate information on the internal politics of Rhodes, this conclusion must of course be somewhat conjectural, but there are two indications in its favor. First, there is no word of either Deinon or Polyaratus holding office, and apparently no one else in the group was prominent enough to be named;[17] second, the embassies, which were appointed by the

16. Livy 44.28.3; Thiel 402; Meloni *Perseo* 350. If this Eudamus is to be identified with the victor of Side, as is likely, he must certainly have been getting on in years. Tenedus was an excellent base from which to patrol the Hellespont and its approaches, and in 168 Perseus sent a squadron there for just that purpose; the encounter with Eudamus' ships was completely friendly (Livy 44.28.1–3).

17. Livy 44.23.10 describes them as "principibus civitatis eius," but this alone is no evidence.

prytanes, continually included known members of the Roman group, even in 168. This weakness in the Council and prytanes was presumably something of a check on the Macedonian group, as the Roman group was apparently successful in packing the important embassies with its people and thus gaining some measure of influence over the implementation of the policies voted by the assembly.[18] In any case, it certainly appears that although the Rhodian people were persuaded to modify the policy of the men who made up the Roman group, they were unwilling to abandon their experienced leadership.

The year 170 added to the successes of the Macedonian monarch. Two Roman attempts at penetrating into Macedon from Thessaly were repulsed, the Dardanians were smashed in a quick campaign, the Molossians revolted and joined the king, and at the beginning of the winter Perseus succeeded in breaking into Illyria and opening communications with King Genthius, who appeared to be on the verge of joining him. The Roman navy, meanwhile, continued the practices of the previous year by doing little more than maltreating Greek cities.[19] This string of Macedonian successes and the Romans' harsh treatment of their allies and pointless plundering were having their effect on Greek opinion,[20] and with the loyalty of central Greece wavering, the Senate made an attempt to prevent further erosion of the Roman position. Lucretius and the land commander for 171, the consul P. Licinius Crassus, were punished for their depredations, while Lucretius' successor, the equally unworthy L. Hortensius, was censured. So far as possible, reparations were made to the various injured cities, and the Senate decreed that all requisitions by Roman commanders had to be accompanied by special senatorial authorization.[21]

The Macedonian successes of 170 served to intensify in Rhodes the debate over proper policy, but news of the *senatus consultum* on war requisitions, with its demonstration of some concern for Greek wel-

---

18. Noted also by O'Neil 472–73.

19. On the campaign of 170, see Meloni, *Perseo*, 258–84; on the naval war of 171–70, Thiel 386–95.

20. See Polyb. 27.9.1–10.5; Livy 42.63.1–2, 43.11.9. There were pro-Macedonian factions in virtually every state.

21. Livy 43.4.11–13, 8.1–10, 17.2; Zon. 9.22; Polyb. 28.3.3, 16.2; *Syll.*[3] 646.

fare, produced such a good impression on the people that Philophron and Theaedetus were able to pass a resolution favorable to the Roman group. Envoys were to be sent to the Senate and the new commander in Greece in order to "renew friendly relations" and generally clear up Roman suspicion of Rhodes, the embassy to Rome having the additional assignment of seeking permission to export Sicilian grain. This was an auspicious time for such a move; at the moment the Senate could ill afford to snub the Rhodians, and the successful completion of this mission would strengthen the position of the Roman group.[22]

The request to trade in Sicilian grain provides the one specific indication during the war of the adverse effect of the struggle on the Rhodian economy. The Macedonian conflict, with its usual concomitant outbreak of piracy, was doubtless injuring Rhodian commerce, while the eruption of the Sixth Syrian War in the winter of 170/69 severely dislocated the important grain shipments from Egypt. Antiochus' siege of Alexandria in particular must have brought exports to a virtual standstill, and the Rhodians sent an embassy under Praxion to the king in the fall of 169 to attempt to arrange a peace. Despite Rhodes' excellent relations with the king, the embassy was unsuccessful, but Antiochus nevertheless departed from Egypt soon afterward, leaving a guard at Pelusium for a possible return. Ptolemy VI Philometor was left ruling in Memphis, but his brother Ptolemy VIII Euergetes II controlled Alexandria, a situation that could not have had a salutary effect on trade.[23] It is impossible to gauge exactly how heavily these disturbed conditions weighed on the economy of the island, but the situation, especially with Egypt, was serious enough to prompt Rhodes to seek western grain,

22. Polyb. 28.2.3–4, 16.1–8.
23. Polyb. 28.17.15, 23.1–5. On the Sixth Syrian War, see W. Otto, *Zur Geschichte der Zeit des 6. Ptolemäers* (Munich 1934) 23–81. The manuscript has Πρατίων, an otherwise unknown name, and van Gelder 149, n. 2, suggests Πράξωνα; but Walbank III, 359 points out that Πραξίων also occurs and is closer to the manuscript reading. On the question of Q. Marcius Philippus' involvement in the peace attempt, see appendix III. The Rhodians were preceded by peace embassies from Achaea, Athens, and Miletus (Polyb. 28.20.1–3). The good relations between Rhodes and Antiochus are demonstrated by Laodice's Rhodian escort in 178 and various gifts from the king, including naval supplies (Livy 41.20.7; *Syll.*³ 644/45).

at a time when no Rhodian politician would wish to do anything that could possibly be construed as putting the republic in Rome's debt.[24] These economic considerations would form a strong motivation behind the peace embassies of 168.

In the spring of 169 Hagesilochus, Nicagoras, and Nicander were sent to Rome, while Hagepolis, Ariston, and Pancrates journeyed to Greece to meet with the praetor C. Marcius Figulus and the consul Q. Marcius Philippus. The Senate was aware of the discord at Rhodes, and probably for that reason, rather than despite it, the *patres* concealed any annoyance engendered by Rhodes' lack of commitment to the Roman cause, fearing that any show of hostility might swing the island into the Macedonian camp. The envoys to Rome were consequently given a cordial reception, and Rhodes was granted license to export 100,000 medimni of grain from Sicily.[25] An even warmer reception was accorded the embassy that visited the consul at his encampment near Heracleum, in Macedon. Philippus informed the envoys that he would pay no attention to any accusations against the island, and he gave them a friendly letter addressed to the Rhodian people. According to Polybius, he also took Hagepolis aside and suggested that the Rhodians attempt to mediate an end to the present war, but this incident may be rejected as an invention.[26] Leaving the Roman camp, the embassy went on to meet the fleet commander, Figulus, who also gave them a very kind reception, and then returned immediately home with the news of their encounters.[27]

24. Casson 182 believes that because of "wars and disturbances" the Pontic trade was not so rich as it once was, but as evidence he cites Strabo 7.4.6 (311), which says nothing to this point. On the other hand, in 171 Athens contributed 100,000 modii of grain to the Roman army (Livy 43.6.2–3), and it is likely that this grain came from the Black Sea; see *IG* ii² 903 for Athenian import of Pontic grain in 176/5. The declining numbers of Rhodian handles found in Athens in this period suggest that Athens was undergoing a gradual withdrawal from the commercial influence of Rhodes, a process that would be greatly accelerated by the settlement after Pydna (Rostovtzeff II, 629, III, 1647, n. 10).

25. Polyb. 28.2.1–7, 16.5–6. Aside from Hagesilochus and Hagepolis, who is part of a later embassy, these men are otherwise unknown; the name Pancrates (or Pancrateus) is found in inscriptions from the Peraea (F&B 20, no. 11; 31, no. 17; 35, no. 23).

26. See appendix III.

27. Polyb. 28.17.1–4, 10; App. *Mac.* 17.1.

The reaction among the Rhodians upon the return of the two embassies was generally one of satisfaction, but for differing reasons. Those associated with the Roman group were pleased with the success of the grain deal and the overall friendliness shown by Rome, while the Macedonian group, more interested in the causes of this cordiality and ready to interpret events in accordance with their own policy, concluded that all was not well for the Romans in Greece, despite their recent penetration into Macedon.[28] For the moment there was no alteration in Rhodian policy, but the events of the next half year continually strengthened the position of the Macedonian group. Philippus' foothold in Macedon was effectively stoppered, and Roman activity on this front came to a standstill until late in the spring of 168. Meanwhile, in the autumn of 169, Perseus' negotiations with Genthius finally bore fruit, and in the spring of the following year the Illyrian king opened a second front. His fast *lembi* began to harass Roman supply vessels in the Adriatic and Aegean, while the Roman fleet had deteriorated to the point where it could no longer even deal with the tiny Macedonian navy, which virtually took command of Aegean waters in the early spring and captured or sank transports almost at will. Finally, an appeal sent across the Danube resulted in the arrival in the spring of 20,000 Celtic warriors, half of them mounted, and this army stood poised on Macedon's northern borders, awaiting only its contracted pay before joining Perseus.[29]

The effect of these Macedonian successes was felt in Rhodes, where the people began to realize that Perseus' defeat was perhaps not inevitable after all, and that in any case the war might now drag on for years more. It can hardly be doubted that almost everyone on the island, no matter what their momentary political leanings, desired peace, not only because of sympathy for Perseus and the strategic considerations, but also, and probably more important, because this

28. Polyb. 28.17.11–14.

29. On the campaign, see Meloni, *Perseo* 285–335, 359–63; on the naval war of 169–68, Thiel 395–410. It is likely that the Illyrians were not always careful to distinguish between enemy and neutral shipping, and Livy 44.29.3–4 suggests that the Macedonians were not: "praeterquam si quae Macedoniam peterent, omnes aut supprimebat aut spoliabat naves." Such practices could only further injure Rhodian interests.

war, together with the one raging in Egypt, was ruining Rhodian commerce. As Deinon and his friends doubtless argued, Rhodes had a traditional role as peacemaker, and the time now certainly appeared ripe for such a move. Perseus would be more than receptive to mediation, and circumstances, at least as the Macedonian group saw them, indicated that Rome might be ready for an end to the struggle. If Rhodian arbitration were accepted and successful, the republic would gain not only peace, but also the most desirable outcomes for the war, a Macedon left strong enough to serve as a counterpoise to Rome, but not totally victorious. The worst the Romans could do would be to refuse the mediation, and a neutral state could hardly be censured for attempting to bring about peace.

Knowing Rome's tenacity and unwillingness to compromise in its wars, the experienced leadership of the Roman group must have seriously doubted the chances of a peace embassy, and must have argued that simply refusing the mediation was not at all the worst the Senate could or would ultimately do. But the majority of the people were now defintely in favor of such a move, and it was voted to send embassies to Rome and to the consul and the king in Macedon. Shortly after this decision, or perhaps at the same time, a joint embassy from Perseus and Genthius arrived in Rhodes seeking to persuade the island to join their coalition and take up arms against Rome. Deinon and Polyaratus and the more extreme leaders of the Macedonian group may possibly have supported this idea, but the Rhodian people would not go this far. While warmly received, the envoys were informed simply that Rhodes would attempt to bring about peace and that the kings should prepare themselves accordingly.[30]

In the late spring of 168, Hagepolis, Diocles, and Clinombrotus were sent to Rome, and Damon, son of Nicostratus, Hagesilochus, and Telephus were sent to the camp of L. Aemilius Paullus, the new consul in Macedon.[31] The object was to press for peace negotiations,

30. Polyb. 29.3.9, 4.7, 10.1–4, 11.1–6; Livy 44.23.4–6, 23.9–10, 29.6–8. Ullrich 65 believes that Polyb. 29.10.1–3 is to be included in 29.11.1–6, with 29.10.4–7 following both, but see Walbank III, 28.

31. Polyb. 29.10.4. The passage reads Δάμωνα Νικόστρατον Ἀγησίλοχον Τήλεφον, but every other Rhodian embassy known was composed of three persons. Van Gelder 150, n. 2, suggests that Νικόστρατον should be read Νικοστράτου, a very

but how strongly did the Rhodians in fact intend to back this move? There can be no sure answer, but it appears unlikely that Rhodes would go so far as to threaten openly to join Perseus or actually to do so should Rome refuse to negotiate.[32] A declaration of war on Rome, regardless of Perseus' recent successes, would involve the island in an extremely risky gamble. It would immediately lose most or all of its Peraea to the land forces of Eumenes, and though its adherence to the Macedonian cause might well swing Aetolia, Achaea, and other Greek states into the war against Rome, this was only a possibility. Doubtless the combined Rhodian-Macedonian-Illyrian navies would sweep Rome and Pergamum from the seas, but Rhodian strategists must have understood Rome's tenacity and potential naval resources; and certainly they remembered that Perseus' father had lost a similar war in a single battle. Rhodes' actual entrance into the struggle,

---

likely copyist's mistake, considering the similarity of ν and υ; identifying the leader of the embassy with a patronymic is paralleled at 28.16.5. Walbank III, 371, objects that embassies of four are found from other states and that the emendation would produce hiatus; but the size of non-Rhodian embassies is irrelevant, and there are many other examples of hiatus in Polybius, one as close as 29.10.6; see G. Benseler, *De Hiatu in Scriptoribus Graecis* (Fribergae 1841) 264–314. My thanks to Lionel Pearson for some thoughts on hiatus in Polybius. Diocles and Clinombrotus are otherwise unknown; Damon may be the Rhodian envoy who spoke on behalf of the Aetolians in 189 (Polyb. 21.31.6); Telephus is possibly the fleet commander named in *Stoicorum index Herculanensis* 56. According to Livy 44.14.5–15.8 (see also Cass. Dio 20.66.2; Zon. 9.22; Gell. 6.3.2), the Rhodians also sent an arrogant peace embassy to Rome in 169, but this statement contradicts everything else Livy and Polybius say and must be an annalistic anticipation of the real embassy. Livy says further that according to Claudius (Quadrigarius), the Senate replied by freeing Lycia and Caria, which event certainly did not take place in 169; see Nissen 261–62.

32. Polyb. 29.4.7: (Περσεὺς) ἔπεισε δὲ καὶ τοὺς Ῥοδίους συ[νε]μβαίνειν εἰς τὸν πόλεμον, but in view of what Polybius says, this cannot be; either it is simply the mistake of the excerpter or ἔπεισε should be read as ἔπειθε, a connative imperfect; see Ullrich 64–65. Livy 44.23.10 reads: "Metrodorus . . . adfirmabat Rhodios paratos ad bellum esse," but this does not mean that Rhodes intended to fight; moreover, Metrodorus, who is reporting to Perseus, has this information "auctoribusque Dinone et Polyarato, principibus civitatis," which renders it all suspect. Livy 44.14.12 has the Rhodians considering force, but this entire passage is spurious; see n. 31 above. The *Periocha* of book 44 states: "Rhodii miserunt legatos Romam minantes ut Perseo auxilio essent, nisi populus Romanus cum illo pacem atque amicitiam iungeret," but this is of course untrustworthy. On the other hand, Gell. 6.3.3–4 says that although the Rhodian assembly considered giving aid to Perseus in the event that peace was not made, "nullum super ea re publicum decretum factum est."

moreover, would impose an added burden on the already suffering economy of the republic, something the widespread commercial interests on the island could hardly desire. The fact that at the time the peace embassies were dispatched Rhodes also sent envoys to establish alliances with the Cretan cities certainly is no indication that it actually considered threatening to take up arms. With Cretan mercenaries fighting on both sides, it behooved the Rhodians to attempt to influence the cities, and in any case alliances with individual Cretan states were a traditional Rhodian mechanism for suppressing the island's endemic piracy, which had broken out anew during the war.[33] The question cannot be finally settled, since the peace embassies were apparently the result of a popular movement rather than the planning of the traditional leadership, but it remains difficult to believe that a man such as Hagesilochus would accept any part in a policy foolish enough to threaten Rome with war.

In any event Rhodes never got the opportunity even to open discussions on peace, since in one of the more disastrous coincidences in antiquity, its embassies arrived within several days of the battle that brought an end to the Antigonid monarchy. Reaching the consul's camp in the last days of spring, Damon and his companions met with a hostile reception and were informed by Paullus that they would have his reply on the matter in fifteen days. Within a week, however, the Macedonian army was destroyed at Pydna, eliminating the need for a reply, and the embassy returned home with the news.[34] The embassy in Rome, meanwhile, had not yet had an audience when the news of Pydna arrived in the city. The envoys were summoned before the Senate, and knowing that the *patres* were well aware of the purpose of the embassy, Hagepolis attempted to cover an extremely embarrassing situation as well as he could. Explaining the hardship and injury caused both Greece and Rome by the war, he said that the Rhodians had determined to seek peace on behalf of all Greeks, but since the war had been ended by the Romans, they now offered

---

33. Polyb. 29.10.5–7. That Polybius judges the mission to Crete to have made the peace embassies an ἀναπολόγητος ἁμαρτία proves nothing, contrary to Schmitt 148–49, who feels that Polybius would not have made such a statement if the alliances had not been intended to help pressure Rome into negotiations.

34. Livy 44.35.4–5; Zon. 9.23.

instead their congratulations. But the Senate, relieved now of any worries about Rhodian neutrality, was not interested in such explanations. If the Rhodians had really been interested in peace on behalf of the Greeks, the envoys were informed, they would better have sent their mission while the king was in Thessaly, destroying Greek cities. Since the embassies were dispatched when Perseus was surrounded, it was clear that the Rhodians were not really seeking peace, but only the salvation of the king. On this note the audience was ended, and Hagepolis and his colleagues left for Rhodes with ominous tidings for the future of their country.[35]

35. Polyb. 29.19.1–11; Livy 45.3.3–8; Diod. 30.24.1.

The End of Rhodian Independence

BEFORE Hagepolis arrived in Rhodes with news of the Senate's anger, word of the Roman victory at Pydna had long since reached the island, and this alone was enough to send the republic into a state of fear. Anxious to determine the Roman attitude and dispel any rumors concerning themselves, the Rhodians met the Egypt-bound embassy of C. Popillius Laenas at Loryma and by repeated entreaties persuaded the envoys to visit the island. In a speech before the assembly Popillius demonstrated an extremely hostile attitude, but its impact was softened by the milder words of his colleague C. Decimius, who told the Rhodians that many of their actions against Rome had been the work of a few agitators, who ought accordingly to be punished. Seizing upon this suggestion, the people decreed that all those convicted of supporting Perseus in word or deed would be condemned to death and proceeded vigorously to carry out this harsh measure, hoping thus to mollify the Romans.[1] Some of the leaders of the Macedonian group committed suicide and some fled. Deinon's end is unknown, but Polyaratus escaped to Egypt, only to be sent back to Rhodes by Ptolemy. On the way he unsuccessfully sought refuge at Phaselis, Caunus, and Cibyra, and was ultimately taken to Rhodes and then on to Rome, where he was presumably executed. The fear of Rome illustrated by Polyaratus' failure to find

1. Livy 45.10.4–15; Cass. Dio 20.68.1.

refuge was meanwhile demonstrated on a grander scale when the Roman embassy continued on to Egypt; at Eleusis Popillius drew his circle in the sand about Antiochus, and the Seleucid monarch bowed to Roman bidding and withdrew to Syria.[2]

The return of Hagepolis only reinforced the apprehensions of the Rhodians concerning their fate, and they hastened to send envoys to Rome to plead their case before the Senate. An embassy under Philocrates was dispatched, followed immediately by one under Philophron and Astymedes. Arriving in the capital during the winter of 168/7, they were met with a cold reception both in public and in private. When they requested an audience with the Senate to offer their congratulations on Rome's victory and to clear charges made against them, they were refused, and the consul M. Iunius Pennus explained on behalf of the body that the Rhodians were not among those considered to be entitled to such rights of hospitality as public lodging and a hearing before the Senate.[3]

The *patres* apparently wished to keep the Rhodians dangling for a while, but consideration of the issue was forced by the radical action of the praetor M'. Iuventius Thalna. With no prior discussion in the Senate, he proposed to the people that war be declared on Rhodes and a magistrate chosen to command the fleet, a move that foreshadowed the tactics of the Gracchi in its unconventionality, though it was not strictly illegal.[4] Thalna was undoubtedly an opportunist looking toward a naval command and political advancement, but he may possibly have been acting in collaboration with anti-Rhodian elements in the Senate who realized that a war vote would probably not succeed in that body, as in fact it did not. Whatever the case, his bypassing of the Senate was a threat to the power of the body, and two tribunes,

2. Livy 45.10.14; Polyb. 30.8.1–9.19. Otto 89, n. 4, believes that Polyaratus was already in Egypt as an ambassador. The ship captain Thoas was imprisoned by the Cnidians, who returned him to Rhodes for interrogation under torture.

3. Polyb. 30.4.1–3; Livy 45.20.4–8; Diod. 31.5.1; Gell. 6.3.5. Philocrates is otherwise unknown. Why the Rhodians should send two embassies, one hard on the heels of the other, is not immediately apparent, though it is clear that they wished to have a large and thus flexible delegation in Rome. Philocrates, it may be noted, did not speak before the Senate and was the messenger sent back to Rhodes, leaving the more experienced diplomats to watch affairs in Rome.

4. See T. Mommsen, *Römisches Staatsrecht*[3] (Graz 1887–88) III.2, 1046–48.

M. Antonius and M. Pomponius, were found to veto the proposal, actually dragging the praetor from the Rostra in the process. Dismayed by these events, the Rhodian envoys put on mourning garb and went about imploring the leading men in Rome not to condemn the Rhodians unheard, but Thalna's action may actually have aided them. As Rhodes' friends among the *patres* must have argued, the praetor's move made it politically inexpedient for the Senate to put off consideration of the Rhodian question any longer, and several days after the incident Antonius introduced the envoys to a meeting.[5]

Nothing is recorded of the speech of Philophron, who spoke first. Although Livy preserves a long oration delivered by Astymedes, it must be an annalistic invention, as it does not at all fit the negative criticism of Polybius, who appears to have seen a transcript of the actual speech. On the basis of Polybius' remarks, it seems that Astymedes spent much of his oration magnifying the services of Rhodes and minimizing its offenses in comparison with those of other states, and though the historian criticizes this tactic, somewhat unfairly, he does admit that the speech helped.[6] Whatever the precise effect of the two speeches on the minds of the Senators, a roll call of opinion revealed in particular the hostility of a group composed of those "who had been consuls, praetors, or legates in the Macedonian war." This was the extreme plebeian leadership of the years during and immediately preceding the war with Perseus, and these men now, as Thalna had done previously, called for a war against Rhodes, undoubtedly motivated by the possibilities of political and material profit to be found in defeating the wealthy republic.[7]

The Rhodians, however, found a perhaps unlikely champion in the person of M. Porcius Cato. In addition to the expected references to the friendship and past services of the island, he argued that even if the

5. Livy 45.20.9–21.8 (who places the mourning dress and entreaties before the incident with Thalna); Polyb. 30.4.4–6; Diod. 31.5.1–3.

6. Polyb. 30.4.6–17; Livy 45.22.1–24.14; Diod. 31.5.1–2a; Gell. 6.3.6. On Livy's fabricated speech, see Nissen 275. Polybius' comparison of Astymedes to a conspirator betraying information out of fear reveals the historian in one of his weaker moments.

7. Livy 45.25.1–2: "Infestissimi Rhodiis erant, qui consules praetoresve aut legati gesserant in Macedonia bellum"; Gell. 6.3.6–7; H. H. Scullard, *Roman Politics*[2] (Oxford 1973) 217–18.

Rhodians had indeed wished to see Perseus succeed, they could nevertheless not justly be punished for what was only an attitude. Moreover, they had felt thus not out of any real hostility toward Rome, but because of fear for the security of their own state, and if they had conducted themselves in an arrogant manner, should the Romans be angry simply because someone was more arrogant than themselves?[8] In presenting this defense, Cato was hardly acting out of any great love for Greeks. So far as can be judged, his motivations seemed to revolve about the moral aspects of the issue and the *utilitas publica* he believed would result from treating the Rhodians properly. That a war against Rhodes could not possibly be construed as a *bellum iustum* must have been in his mind, and such would have been an important consideration to the tradition-oriented senator. In the realm of senatorial politics, the support of Rhodes must also have represented Cato's conservative reaction to the upstarts of the new plebeian group, who most strongly advocated the war and stood to profit from it.

How much influence Cato's defense exerted on the minds of the *patres* is impossible to know. The Senate in general must have realized that a war against Rhodes was not necessary to bring about its submission to Rome. In any event, much to the relief of the envoys, war was not voted, although the reply to the defense of Rhodes' conduct was vague; nothing was said of the island's future relations with Rome or of what action, if any, might be taken against it. Upon receipt of this answer, Philocrates returned to Rhodes, while the more experienced Philophron and Astymedes remained in Rome to keep a close watch on new developments. In Rhodes the arrival of the news regarding the Senate's decision brought about a general rejoicing among the people, who had feared the worst, and in the relief of the moment the senatorial reproaches for their actions during the war were easily swallowed. It was immediately voted to send to Rome a

8. Livy 45.25.2–4; Gell. 6.3.1–55 (= Malcovati *ORF*³ frgs. 163–71), which preserves the fragments of Cato's speech. On the speech see A. Astin, *Cato the Censor* (Oxford 1978) 273–83; G. Galboli, *Marci Porci Catonis Oratio pro Rhodiensibus* (Bologna 1978) esp. 128–49, 273–330.

crown of 20,000 gold pieces and an embassy that was to seek by all means to conclude a formal alliance with the Romans.[9]

Thus did Rhodes accept the end of its freedom. For over a century and a half one of the mainstays of its policy had been the scrupulous avoidance of permanent or long-term alliances, but the world in which such a neutrality was possible had finally expired on the field of Pydna. In seeking an alliance with Rome, however, Rhodes was relinquishing more than just a facet of its foreign policy; it was surrendering altogether the completely independent management of its foreign affairs. Had it remained throughout in the good graces of Rome, Rhodes would not have been punished with the loss of Caria and Lycia and the freeing of the Delian port, and the pursuit of an alliance would perhaps not have been necessary; but insofar as the island's real freedom in world affairs was concerned, the end result would have been essentially the same, for Rome's will was now unquestionably dominant in the eastern Mediterranean. During the Macedonian War the cautious wisdom of the island had for once lapsed, but with the cool objectivity that had for generations characterized their dealing with the world the Rhodians now accepted the inevitable and volunteered their submission. For the proud republic, which had successfully withstood the assault of Demetrius Poliorcetes, it was perhaps the ultimate humiliation to request humbly an alliance with the state that had brought about its ruin, but both Rhodes and its businessmen now needed the security of a Roman *foedus*. So long as the island was not formally bound to Rome, it was in danger of being plunged into a disastrous war, and the insecurity of its nebulous relationship with the superpower on the Tiber would have a ruinous effect on its credit and commerce.[10]

9. Polyb. 30.5.1–4; Livy 45.25.4–7; Diod. 31.5.1–2b. Livy adds the freeing of Lycia and Caria as part of the senatorial reply at this point, but this passage is misplaced from later. For the worth of the crown Polybius has 10,000 and Livy 20,000, but because of the fragmentary nature of the Polybian text, which Livy is here translating literally, it is perhaps better to read the Polybius as ⟨διό⟩ μυρίων, rather than fault Livy; see Walbank III, 421–22.

10. Polyb. 30.5.6–10 (followed by Livy 45.25.9–10; Cass. Dio 20.68.3; Zon. 9.24) states that the Rhodians acted out of fear of Rome and in order to alleviate suspicion. Dio hints, probably unconsciously, at the economic motivation when he adds

The aged and experienced Theaedetus, well known as a leader of the Roman group, was appointed nauarch and departed for Rome in the early summer of 167, accompanied by Rhodophon and the crown. Since the nauarch was constitutionally empowered to conclude treaties, Theaedetus was thus able to deal with any situation that might arise in Rome, and the Rhodians were at least spared the humiliation of passing a formal decree regarding the termination of their own independence.[11] The alliance was not so easily obtained, however. The embassy must have reached Rome by late summer, but Theaedetus, along with the numerous other envoys who had gathered in the city, was not granted an audience until the beginning of winter. When he was finally able to present his case before the Senate, the *patres* presumably accepted the crown, but in their desire to make an example of the island they preferred to let the Rhodians and their economy suffer a while longer and deferred a decision on the *foedus*.[12]

Rhodes meanwhile was beginning to feel the effect of its poor standing with Rome. Soon after Theaedetus had departed for Italy, the subject city of Caunus revolted, calling upon independent Cibyra for aid, while Mylasa and Alabanda attacked Rhodian territory in the north, seizing the cities in Euromus. The fact that Lycia did not also attempt to capitalize on its rulers' difficulties and rise again in revolt speaks convincingly of the thoroughness with which that country had been subdued during its last revolt. Troubled though they might be in their dealings with Rome, the Rhodians were prepared to deal with any threats to their position on the mainland. They promptly sent troops under Lycon, and in the course of the summer he suc-

---

('Ρόδιοι) καὶ τιμὴν ἐκ τούτου καὶ παρὰ τῶν ἄλλων θηρώμενοι. For the economic effects of Rhodes' insecure position, see below.

11. Polyb. 30.5.4–5; Livy 45.25.7–8. It is not clear exactly what Polybius is trying to say in 30.5.5, and Walbank III, 422 (following Büttner-Wobst), adds οὐ before βουλόμενοι, to produce the sense that they did not wish to fail because of the vote on the crown and the embassy, but wished to make their attempt through the nauarch. Without the emendation the sentence seems to say that if they failed, they wished to do so because of the vote and embassy and wished to make their attempt through the nauarch. In neither case is the Greek or the meaning really clear. Livy, on the other hand, clearly states that by employing the nauarch they could avoid passing any resolutions that would make the disgrace greater should they fail.

12. Polyb. 30.19.14–16, 21.1–2.

ceeded in defeating the Mylasians, Alabandians, and Cibyrites and restoring Caunus and the area of Euromus to Rhodian rule.[13]

But Rhodes' troubles were only beginning. With tranquillity restored to the Peraea, the island was shocked by the arrival of the news from Rome. A reply to the petition for an alliance was as yet unreceived, but the Senate had in fact taken action; by a *senatus consultum* the gift of Apamea was revoked, and Lycia and Caria were freed from Rhodian authority.[14] As discussed earlier,[15] the grant of 188 had in no way been juridically "precarious," but Rome now nevertheless considered it revocable. In the generation that separated Apamea from Pydna the Romans had grown more and more to view their dealings with the Greek states in terms of client relationships, and as Rhodes had violated Roman trust by its actions in the recent war, there was a moral justification in taking from it what had been given as a reward some twenty years before. Much more important than these considerations of the unfaithful client, however, was the essential fact that with Perseus defeated and Antiochus humbled, there existed no one to question Roman decisions. The moral reasoning of the Senate may have had little validity in the minds of the Rhodians,[16] but behind it lay the convincing reality of the Roman legions, and neither Rhodes nor any other power dared to challenge the judgment.

The Rhodians had no choice but to accept the decree and the resul-

13. Polyb. 30.5.11–15; Livy 45.25.11–13; Strabo 14.2.3 (625). Livy has the order of events confused, placing Theaedetus and the military activity after the Senate's decree on Caria and Lycia. Lycon is otherwise unknown; van Gelder 156 suggests that he might be a foreign mercenary, as the name is unparalleled at Rhodes. In view of Rhodes' own long tradition of condottieri, this seems unlikely. On the meaning of "the cities in Euromus," see Walbank III, 426–27. It is difficult to see why troops from Mylasa and Alabanda should be found at Orthosia, well to the northeast, unless they were fleeing from the Rhodian army.

14. Polyb. 30.5.16, 24.1–2, 31.4; Livy 44.15.1, 45.25.6, 12; App. *Syr.* 44, *Mith.* 62. When exactly the *senatus consultum* was issued is not clear. Quadrigarius (Livy 44.15.1) wrongly places it in 169; Livy puts it in the reply to the first Rhodian embassy of 167, while Polybius has it around the time of the revolt of Caunus. The Polybian dating is to be preferred, not only because of the general reliability of Polybius, but also because it would make no sense for the Rhodians to be defending Euromus if it had just been freed from them.

15. See chap. 8.

16. In his speech before the Senate in 164 Astymedes in fact concedes the possible logic of this reasoning, without conceding that it is at all just (Polyb. 30.31.5).

tant loss of most of their mainland possessions and the years of effort spent in subduing the Lycians. Theaedetus died of old age in Rome soon afterward, but though compelled to spend his final days witnessing the humiliation of his country, he was at least spared the experience of the blows that would follow. In the very early part of 166 exiles from Caunus and Stratonicea arrived in Rome, and in response to their pleadings the Senate augmented the *senatus consultum* on Lycia and Caria by ordering the Rhodians to withdraw their garrisons from the two cities.[17] The "right of the strongest" which stood behind the earlier decree now displayed itself openly. Stratonicea had been a gift of the Seleucids in the middle of the third century and Caunus had been purchased from Egypt at the beginning of the second, so Rome did not have even the flimsiest of legal or moral pretexts in freeing them from Rhodes. Pydna and Eleusis were the justification for this decree, and once again the Rhodians were compelled to swallow their resentment and acquiesce to Rome's bidding. The final blow against the island was not long in following. Among the embassies in Rome in 167 was one from Athens which petitioned the Senate for the possession of Delos, Lemnos, and Haliartus. After first deferring their answer, the *patres* finally in early 166 awarded the places to the Athenians, but in doing so they stipulated that Delos should be a duty-free port.[18] This could only be a strike at the Rhodians, who drew large revenues from their harbor dues, but as will be seen, the loss of Rhodian trade to Delos was not so great as has been generally supposed.

The actions taken by the Senate were certainly directed against Rhodes, but they do not represent any systematic economic or political assault; such was hardly necessary in the case of a state that was literally begging to be made an ally of Rome. Of the three measures, only the freeing of Lycia and Caria sprang solely and directly from the intention of injuring the Rhodians, and in view of its qualities as a solution, the idea must have readily suggested itself. Having given the territories to the island, Rome could thus justifiably, at least in its

17. Polyb. 30.21.2–3, 31.6; Strabo 14.2.3 (652).
18. Polyb. 30.19.17–20.9, 31.10. The exact dating of this measure is also unclear, but as the decision was postponed from the beginning of the winter, it was presumably made sometime in early 166.

own eyes, free them and at a stroke deprive Rhodes of considerable revenues and ruin its influence on the mainland, while demonstrating to the world the result of Roman displeasure. The liberation of Caunus and Stratonicea was only an appendage to this larger measure, and had it not been for the arrival in Rome of refugees from those two cities, the Senate would not have taken this blatantly illegal action. As it was, they left intact the remainder of Rhodes' pre-Apamea Peraea.

The question of Delos is more complicated. Had it not been requested by the Athenians, the island would presumably have been left independent, but nonetheless still declared duty-free, since whatever reasons Rome had for creating a free port, they did not depend on the political status of the sacred island. The real question is whether the act was a distinctly political measure aimed at damaging Rhodes' economy and prestige or whether it was in fact motivated by Italian business interests. Although the measure would inevitably be both to the disadvantage of the Rhodians and to the advantage of Italian businessmen and thus would serve both ends, it was the political reason that must have figured in the considerations of the Senate. Possibly the idea was the suggestion of Roman commercial interests with contacts in the Senate and in the east, and the *patres* seized on the measure as coincidentally damaging to Rhodes in the vital areas of commercial revenues and influence. On the level of personal profit, those senators who were indirectly connected with commerce through the activities of their clients must certainly have been interested also in the positive aspect of the free port, but had the measure not served the political end that it did, it is improbable that enough interest or support could have been mustered in the Senate for its consideration.[19]

19. Holleaux, *Rome* 88; Rostovtzeff, *CAH* VIII, 631, 643; Badian, *For. Clien.* 101; and E. Gruen, "Rome and Rhodes in the Second Century B.C.," *CQ* 69 (1975) 80 rightly see the measure as a political one directed against Rhodes. The Senate would at this time have been even less willing than usual to act on behalf of the businessmen, since as recently as 169 there had been a tremendous row between the Senate and Equites over a harsh census and a proclamation against a large body of tax farmers; see Livy 43.16.1–16. As it happened, Italian interests on Delos did not become really strong until after about 130; see the survey of J. Hatzfeld, "Les Italiens résident à Délos," *BCH* 36 (1912) 5–218.

While it is clear that the Roman actions regarding Delos and Lycia and Caria were political blows against Rhodes, it is less easy to see exactly why the island was subject to such treatment. Polybius states that the Senate wished "to make an example of the Rhodians," and while he does not say for what reason, circumstances naturally suggest Rhodes' conduct during the war.[20] As the island had committed no hostile acts and was guilty only of neutrality and attempted mediation, however, it must be as an erring client that Rhodes was being punished.[21] Yet Rhodes had done nothing more or less than Ptolemy or Perseus' brother-in-law, Prusias, both of whom had remained neutral and offered to mediate; and not only were they not admonished for their behavior, but Prusias was in fact received by the Senate with honor after the war.[22] On the other hand, Eumenes, the most faithful of clients and vigorous and enthusiastic participant in the struggle, fell into disfavor despite his unqualified support of Rome. On the pretext that he had had secret dealings with Perseus, the king was refused an audience with the Senate at the conclusion of the war and virtually booted out of Italy, and henceforth Roman policy in Asia Minor was directed against Pergamum.[23]

The record of Rome's dealings with its "friends" demonstrates, then, that proper conduct was at least not the primary factor in determining its attitude toward Rhodes and others after the war. Was it perhaps concern about Rhodian power that played on the minds of the Senate? Rome undoubtedly had a healthy respect for the Rhodian navy, especially after its own poor showing in the war, but it is unlikely that the *patres* were unduly concerned about Rhodes as a serious military threat. Without a great land power to join it, the island was relatively harmless to the Romans, and the last great land power, the Seleucid empire, had just bowed before the demands of

20. Polyb. 29.19.5.
21. Badian, *For. Clien.* 100–101 and R. Errington, *The Dawn of Empire: Rome's Rise to World Power* (London 1971) 250–52 accept this notion, and many others seem to imply it.
22. Ptolemy: Polyb. 28.1.7–8; Prusias: Livy 42.29.3, 44.14.5–7 (see Meloni, *Perseo* 347, on this passage), 45.44.4–20; Polyb. 30.18.1–7; Diod. 31.15.1–3. Like the Rhodians, Prusias contributed a few ships (Livy 44.10.12).
23. Polyb. 29.5.1–9.13, 30.1.1–3.9, 19.1–13; Livy 44.24.1–25.12, 27.13; Diod. 31.7.2; etc. For Roman policy against Eumenes after the war, see Hansen 122–27.

Popillius. But if Rhodes could not pose a serious threat to Rome, neither could any other state in the Mediterranean, and this fact was of cardinal importance in shaping Rome's policy toward the Greek world after Pydna. With Macedon defeated and dismembered and Syria humbled, Rome no longer needed the goodwill of such second-rank powers as Rhodes and Pergamum, and it could now view those states as possible threats not to the security of Italy but to the Roman order in the east. Eumenes and the Rhodians were consequently prime candidates for Roman displeasure, the former because of his powerful position in Asia Minor and the latter because of their navy and the potential for leadership which their reputation created.[24]

In the case of the Rhodians, the Senate must have been moved as well by what might be termed a "bad attitude." More important in the Senate's eyes than any equivocation during the war was Rhodes' tremendous reputation for pride and independence, which made it a beacon for freedom among the Greeks and a thorn in the Roman imperial heel. Humbled and seeking an alliance, however, the island was useful to Roman policy and provided an instructive example, presumably the same example of which Polybius speaks. And finally, questions of policy aside, it seems that many senators were hostile to the Rhodians simply because of the islanders' fierce pride, and Cato was probably not far from the truth when he asked his colleagues if they were annoyed with the Rhodians just because they were more arrogant than the Romans themselves.[25]

The sanctions imposed on the Rhodians by the Senate were a heavy but far from mortal blow to the economy of the island. The loss of the mainland possessions deprived the state of a large part of its income, although exactly how much is unknown. According to Astymedes' speech before the Senate in 164, Caunus and Stratonicea alone returned 120 talents (720,000 drachmas) yearly, but the yield of Caria

24. De Sanctis IV.1, 344 and Schmitt 166–67 speak only of eliminating a future danger. Gruen 79–81 more correctly sees a Roman policy of eliminating any "source of trouble." Rostovtzeff II, 738 recognizes as a factor Rhodian popularity among the Greeks.

25. Gell. 6.3.50 (= Malcovati ORF[3] frg. 169). Though it doubtless disgusted some people, the servility of Prusias must have provided a sharp contrast to Rhodian behavior.

and Lycia as a whole is mentioned, unfortunately, only as a "large revenue." Nevertheless, if the harbor dues, which in the last several decades were providing an annual return of roughly a million drachmas, are described as a "principal resource of the city," then the mainland revenues must have constituted a fairly large portion of the current income of the state. Large though it might be, however, the loss in this case would not be disastrous to the republic, since with the exception of Stratonicea, Rhodian revenue from the Peraea was simply reduced to its pre-Syrian War level, and the state economy had managed quite well during that period.[26]

Ostensibly more serious to Rhodes was the creation of a free port at Delos, as this move struck directly at the heart of the island's economy, its commerce. There can be no doubt that the new status of Delos was damaging to Rhodian trade, but there has been a tendency to overestimate this damage,[27] chiefly, it seems, because of Astymedes' statement that the annual receipts from the harbor dues had fallen from a million to 150,000 drachmas.[28] Undeniably, Rhodes must have lost most, if not all, of the slave and luxury trade to Delos, and for quite good reasons.[29] The sacred island offered not only a duty-free harbor but also a loose commercial atmosphere more conducive to speculative dealings than that of Rhodes, with its tradition of maritime and commercial laws and aversion to foreigners.[30] Pirate slavers could deal openly at Delos, while foreign businessmen with capital to invest could find great opportunities in the developing markets of the island, in contrast to Rhodes, where an abundance of

---

26. Polyb. 30.31.4–7: πόλλη πρόσοδος; 31.12: κύριοι πόροι τῆς πόλεως.

27. See, for example, Schmitt 159–60, 163: "eine fast tödliche Wunde für die rhodische Wirtschaft"; Gruen 77: "The foundations of the Rhodian economy collapsed."

28. Polyb. 30.31.12. ἐλλιμένιον must be a customs duty rather than some kind of harbor fee; the size of the revenues collected would otherwise be impossible. See Lehmann-Hartleben 45, n. 1; Schmitt 161, n. 1. The rate was very probably the common 2 percent. For the correctness of Astymedes' statement, see below, n. 35.

29. On the Delian traffic in slaves and eastern wares, see Strabo 14.5.2 (668); P. Roussel, *Délos, colonie athénienne* (Paris 1916) 19–20; Rostovtzeff II, 794–95.

30. Rostovtzeff, *CAH* VIII, 644; Casson 180. On Rhodian exclusiveness toward foreigners, see Rostovtzeff, *CAH* VIII, 639–41. Italians would certainly not be warmly welcomed in Rhodes.

private capital was already available.[31] Levantine traders, carrying
products of the Near and Far East, would now bypass Rhodes and its
harbor dues for the more lucrative markets of Delos, where they
could deal directly with Italian merchants forwarding goods to western consumers.

On the other hand, there is no indication that the Rhodians lost
their grip on the vital grain trade.[32] Delos' harbors, even after the
improvements of the decades following 166, were never really suitable for the big grain carriers, whereas the large harbor and attendant
facilities at Rhodes had for two centuries been accustomed to the
importation and transshipment of grain.[33] Moreover, the trade in
cereals was a staid and generally nonspeculative business and would
find a more congenial atmosphere in the well-organized and -policed
port of Rhodes. Most important, whatever happened so far as the
ports were concerned, the island republic still possessed perhaps the
largest merchant marine in the east, and whether or not these vessels
employed the island's harbors in the shipment of their cargoes, it was
still Rhodian merchants that were carrying the goods and taking the
profits. Finally, despite the sanctions of 167–66, Rhodes remained a
very wealthy state, whereas in a century the markets and prosperity
of Delos had virtually disappeared. As purveyors of grain to Greece
and the Aegean, the Rhodians retained control of a vital service that
remained an economic constant, while Delos was ruined when more
stable conditions brought both the evaporation of the slave trade and
the shipment of eastern wares direct to Italy.[34]

How, then, is the meteoric fall in Rhodes' harbor receipts to be
explained? Part of the loss may be attributed to the diversion of the
slave and luxury trade to Delos, but this cause can hardly account for
a sudden drop in the revenues to a bare 15 percent of their original

31. See Strabo 14.5.2 (668–69); Casson 180.
32. So Rostovtzeff II, 777; Casson 179, 181–82. The later gifts of grain from
Eumenes II (280,000 medimni [Polyb. 31.31.1–3]) and Demetrius I (300,000 medimni
[Diod. 31.36.1]) do not mean that the island was short on these foodstuffs; grain was a
convenient commodity for Pergamum and Syria to give and could be easily disposed
of by Rhodes.
33. Casson 181. See Lehmann-Hartleben 152, n. 2, for literature on the Delian
harbors. On Delos' negligible grain traffic, see above, chap. 2.
34. See Rostovtzeff, *CAH* VIII, 647; Casson 181–82.

value.[35] The key to the answer lies in Astymedes' speech of 164, in his explanation of the loss of income: "The revenue of the harbor has ceased because of your [the Senate's] having made Delos tax-free and having taken away the freedom of the demos, by which freedom both the affairs of the harbor and all the others of the city attained a suitable authority."[36] The first of the envoy's two reasons for the loss is very clear: because Delos had been made a free port. But owing to the rather vague quality of the terms "freedom" (παρρησία) and "authority" (προστασία), the second reason is not immediately plain. What must be meant is that the Senate had taken from Rhodes its freedom of action, not by imposing any actual restrictions on the state but by constantly deferring the decision on an alliance and thus keeping the island in a kind of limbo regarding its relationship with Rome. The effect of this nebulous position was the undermining of the authority and prestige of Rhodes and its port; simply put, the insecurity of the republic's standing with the world power on the Tiber was ruining its credit.[37] So long as Rome had not defined its attitude toward Rhodes by granting it a *foedus,* no one could be certain that the Rhodian economy would not be wrecked the next day by some new sanction by the Senate, perhaps even a declaration of war. Businessmen would thus naturally avoid involving themselves in any but the most immediate and temporary dealings with interests associated with the Rhodian state. More specifically, and in explanation of the

35. The manuscript reading of Polyb. 30.31.12 is: τοῦ γὰρ ἐλλιμενίου κατὰ τοὺς ἀνώτερον χρόνους εὑρίσκοντος ἑκατὸν μυριάδας δραχμῶν νῦν εὑρήκατε [or εὑρί- κατε] πεντεκαίδεκα μυριάδας. Hultsch, followed by Büttner-Wobst, emended εὑ- ρήκατε to ἀφηρήκατε, which makes the loss 15 percent rather than 85 percent, and this reading is accepted by van Gelder 156, n. 1; Niese III, 196; De Sanctis IV.1, 356, n. 317; et al. But Astymedes refers to this loss as the "greatest misfortune," and Stratonicea and Caunus alone represented a loss of 720,000 drachmas a year; this was first observed by W. Ferguson, *Hellenistic Athens* (London 1911) 333, n. 1. See Schmitt 162, n. 1, for the other emendations, all of which preserve the 85 percent loss in revenue. Hiller 797 suggests that εὑρήκατε indicates Roman control of the harbor, but there is absolutely no evidence for this interpretation and it is clear from the context that Astymedes' statement is directed toward the Senate.

36. Polyb. 30.31.10: καταλέλυται γὰρ ἡ τοῦ λιμένος πρόσοδος ὑμῶν Δῆλον μὲν ἀτελῆ πεποιηκότων ἀφηρημένων δὲ τὴν τοῦ δήμου παρρησίαν δι' ἧς καὶ ⟨τὰ⟩ κατὰ τὸν λιμένα καὶ τἆλλα πάντα τῆς πόλεως ἐτύγχανε τῆς ἁρμοζούσης προστασίας.

37. Ferguson 333, n. 1, hints at this explanation: "The political factor explains the sudden paralysis of Rhodian commerce."

drastic loss of harbor revenue, the men who farmed the harbor receipts were now willing to bid only a fraction of what they had previously, partly out of the knowledge and expectation of a decrease in the traffic through the port and partly because of the risk involved in taking contracts with the Rhodian state. It is more than likely that the actual decline in the volume of business through the harbor was less than the 85 percent reflected in the tax receipts, as the tax farmers naturally attempted to underbid the expected real income.[38]

It was this insecurity and resultant loss of credit that was really hurting the Rhodian state. The creation of the free port and the loss of the mainland possessions were undeniably damaging to the revenue of the island, but Rome's constant deferment of the question of the *foedus* was eroding the very foundations of Rhodes' commerce and would seriously damage its economy if it continued. The senators doubtless realized as much, and for this reason continued to postpone their decision, while the Rhodians for their part continued to press for the treaty, seeing salvation of their credit and their economy in the regularization of relations between the two states.

After receiving the Senate's declaration on Caunus and Stratonicea in early 166, Philophron and Astymedes immediately departed for Rhodes, fearing that in their outrage their countrymen might refuse to obey the order to evacuate the Rhodian garrisons in the cities.[39] The two envoys and their colleagues in the Rhodian government recognized that outrageous though the decree might be, it must be obeyed. Noncompliance would bring further sanctions and perhaps the ultimate disaster of war, while strict obedience might finally move the Senate to grant the all-important alliance. The Rhodians swallowed the insult and gave up the cities, and in the summer of 165 an embassy under Aristoteles was sent to Rome to attempt once more to obtain a *foedus*. And once again the Senate put off its answer, saying that the time was not yet right for concluding an alliance.[40] Instead the *patres* sent an embassy under Ti. Sempronius Gracchus, probably

38. On the farming of the harbor dues, see Cic. *Inv. Rhet.* 1.30.47.
39. Polyb. 30.21.4–5.
40. Polyb. 30.23.2–4. The manner of the Senate's refusal tends to support the conclusion that it was delaying its answers in order to damage the Rhodian economy. Aristoteles is otherwise unknown.

in the later part of the same year, to investigate the situation at Rhodes.[41]

In the following year another Rhodian embassy, this one under Astymedes, traveled to Italy to plead again for an alliance. Astymedes' speech before the Senate, which is preserved in Polybius, was much more moderate than his earlier oration; he generally confined himself to detailing the losses suffered by Rhodes and pointing out that those few who had caused the trouble had been punished.[42] Only one item in the speech requires specific attention, and that is his statement that the Rhodian demos had lost their revenue, freedom (παρρησία), and equality (ἰσολογία).[43] It has been suggested on the basis of Polybius' usage of the terms παρρησία and ἰσηγορία (assumed to be the equivalent of ἰσολογία) in other instances that they also in this case apply to internal affairs, and that some limitation on the operation of the Rhodian constitution is thus meant.[44] Several considerations show that this interpretation cannot be correct. Not only is there no sign, other than this passage, of any suspension of constitutional liberties at Rhodes, but there is also the positive fact that Astymedes and Philophron rushed back to the island after receiving the order to evacuate Caunus and Stratonicea. Their reason for doing so was the fear that the people would refuse to obey the Senate's decree, and such a fear hardly makes sense if democratic government had been temporarily suspended.[45] Further, it is true that Polybius' use of these two terms together invariably refers to internal matters, but equally invariably the terms are combined in the phrase ἰσηγορία καὶ παρρησία,[46] whereas in the passage in question the order is reversed and the words are not bound into a phrase with καί.

---

41. Polyb. 30.31.19–20; Cic. *Brut.* 20.79. Gracchus delivered an oration while he was there.

42. Polyb. 30.30.1, 31.1–18. On the authenticity of the speech, see Ullrich 70–71.

43. Polyb. 30.31.16: διόπερ ὦ ἄνδρες ἀπολωλεκὼς ὁ δῆμος τὰς προσόδους τὴν παρρησίαν τὴν ἰσολογίαν ὑπὲρ ὧν τὸν πρὸ τοῦ χρόνον πᾶν ἀναδεχόμενος διατετέλικεν, κτλ.

44. Van Gelder 157; Schmitt 163–65.

45. Polyb. 30.21.4–5. The democratic government clearly continued to function after 164; see below, chap. 11.

46. Polyb. 2.38.6, 42.3, 4.31.4, 6.9.4, 5, 27.4.7. ἰσηγορία is used alone in two instances: 5.27.6 and 7.10.1.

Finally, though it might have the same meaning as ἰσηγορία, the word used is ἰσολογία, and the other instance of this word is definitely in reference to foreign affairs.[47] Considered in the context of the speech, the terms must refer to external affairs, and the passage is a summation of the losses previously detailed. πρόσοδος is the revenue lost from the mainland and the harbors, and παρρησία (which is used earlier in the speech to refer to foreign affairs) and ἰσολογία are Rhodes' independence and equality among other states, both lost to the republic through Roman hostility.[48]

How much effect Astymedes' oration had on the *patres* is unknown, but the Senate, having heard the report of the fact-finding embassy under Gracchus, decided that the Rhodians and their economy had been sufficiently damaged and finally granted the island an alliance.[49] Although the sources are silent concerning the nature of this treaty, it was in all probability a *foedus aequum*. Rhodes' activities in the years immediately following the alliance certainly indicate a fair amount of freedom in foreign policy, particularly its support of Calynda against Caunus (163), which action was taken without the prior consent of Rome.[50] Since the island had not been defeated in any war and had itself requested the alliance, it would moreover have been unusual for the senators to make the treaty *iniquum,* despite their hostility toward the Rhodians. But the most telling argument, and the one that also makes the question moot, is the fact that with the growth of Roman power the differences among the various types of *foederati* had in practice ceased to exist, and Rome tended to see even its nonfoederate *amici* as clients. The simple reality was that Rhodes hardly dared to act contrary to Roman bidding, whatever the exact

47. Polyb. 24.10.9: ἐξῆν ('Αχαιόι) . . . ἰσολογίαν ἔχειν πρὸς 'Ρωμαίους. ἰσο-λογία also occurs in fragment 165 BW, which deals with internal matters, but is considered to be of uncertain authorship by Schweighaeuser frg. 77.

48. So also J. Toulomakos, *Der Einfluss Roms auf die Staatsform der griechischen Stadtstaaten des Festlandes und der Inseln im ersten und zweiten Jhdt. v. Chr.,* diss. (Göttingen 1967) 131–32; Walbank III, 459.

49. Polyb. 30.31.19–20; Livy *Per.* 46; Zon. 9.24; see also Cic. *ad Fam.* 12.15.2 (on which Täubler 208–9); App. *B.C.* 4.66, 68, 70. The exact date of the treaty is unknown, but the first half of 164 seems most likely.

50. Täubler 209–10; H. Horn, *Foederati,* diss. (Frankfurt am M. 1930) 62–65; Schmitt 168–71; Walbank III, 461. On Calynda, see below, chap. 11.

terms of the treaty, and knowing this, the Senate would have had little reason specifically to make the alliance *iniquum*.[51]

The conclusion of the alliance with Rome brought Rhodes relief from the anxieties and insecurity stemming from Roman disfavor, but it also marked the formal end of Rhodes' independence and the final exhaustion of the policy that had for over a century and a half maintained that independence in the face of powerful neighbors. By the beginning of the Third Macedonian War the Rhodian leadership recognized and was prepared to accept the extinction of the island's strategic freedom, but never before had the republic been driven to a course of action so repugnant to it, and the emotional stresses involved in supporting the cause of Rome and Eumenes proved too much for the Rhodian people. In seeking to mediate between Rome and Macedon, Rhodes was committing no hostile act and in fact pursuing its policy of fostering peace, but the reality of the circumstances made it clear that even this much was to cross the will of Rome. Perhaps, like Eumenes, Rhodes might have suffered Roman disfavor even if its wartime conduct had been letter-perfect, but the Rhodians did not at the time know that, and the neutrality and attempted mediation must thus be considered one of the very rare instances of an error in Rhodian decision making.

The moment Rhodes realized its mistake, however, it reverted to a policy of calculated reason. With its long history of independence at an end, Rhodes hastened to give up the freedom that no longer existed and to secure the alliance it had forever avoided. Putting aside its pride, it accepted the humiliation of the Roman sanctions with the barest of protests; Rhodian independence might be dead, but the state could continue to live and prosper in the changed world. Many a Greek city had shown defiance in the face of even more hopeless odds, and there would have been satisfaction in seeing the cocksure attitude of the senators met with the kind of resistance they would find fifteen years later before the walls of Carthage. But such a reaction, though noble, would have been one of emotion; ever rational, Rhodes chose submission.

51. See Badian, *For. Clien.* 33–115. It should be noted that *foedus iniquum* is technically a modern term and denotes a treaty distinguished by various limiting terms, such as a clause requiring the preservation of *imperium maiestatemque populi Romani;* see Täubler 62–66; Badian, *For. Clien.* 25–26.

The Long Twilight

THE real history of Rhodes ends in 164 with the alliance with Rome, but the island republic continued to exist as a theoretically independent state for another two centuries, slowly sinking, like many another small Greek state, into the limbo of a Mediterranean dominated but not always directly ruled by Rome.[1] Unlike many others, the Rhodians did manage to maintain their high prosperity and even some of their international influence, but the period was nevertheless one of steady progress toward extinction as a political entity, as Roman domination hardened into direct imperial rule. As the Rhodians of 164 could hardly have failed to perceive, the world had altered dramatically in the last half century, and the narrowing of Rhodian strategic latitude that had begun in the third century with the decline of the Ptolemies now culminated in the Roman alliance. The world had changed, and if Rhodes were to guard its wealth and what was now its illusion of independence, its policies would also have to change.

The cornerstones of traditional Rhodian policy, the avoidance of entangling alliances and the concern for the power balance among the great states, had become meaningless; there was now only one great power, and the Rhodians had been compelled to conclude a permanent alliance with it. But it must be remembered that these lines of

---

1. For surveys of Rhodian history after 164, see van Gelder 157–77; Hiller 797–81; Schmitt 173–92.

policy were not ends in themselves, only means to the basic goal of the security of Rhodes and its commerce, and the exhaustion of the old policy thus did not spell disaster for the island. While the emergence of the Roman superpower meant the end of true independence for the republic, it also meant the end of serious threats to its security from any but the Romans themselves, and, the recent punishments notwithstanding, Rome appeared to have no real cause to launch an assault. Further, with the exception of creating the free port at Delos, the Romans took no steps against Rhodian commerce and actually aided the island and its merchants by guaranteeing the security of Egypt against Seleucid advances. Roman policy did not extend to imposing absolute peace in the eastern Mediterranean and may in fact have encouraged disturbances in Asia Minor,[2] but the Roman presence in the Balkan peninsula helped create throughout most of the Greek world the peaceful conditions that had been the goal of Rhodian policy.

The Rhodian leadership of course realized all this, and in place of the now obsolete strategies of the third century there emerged a new "Roman" policy, which would provide a background for the foreign-affairs decisions of the island. The Rhodians were too proud and too accustomed to independence to bend a knee in the manner of a Prusias, but they had survived all those turbulent decades by squarely facing reality, and the paramount reality for Rhodes now was the immense power of the city on the Tiber. What freedom of action the Rhodians had was dependent on Roman favor or disinterest, and the leadership must henceforth attempt to ascertain or calculate Roman reaction to any action the island contemplated. The lesson of the frightening years after Pydna was not to be forgotten, and the republic could no longer afford to fail to support, let alone openly disapprove of, Roman policies or actions, no matter how distasteful they might be. Nor could the experience of the last forty years be ignored; for the foreseeable future, at least, Rome would inevitably win any war in which it was involved, and in the event of a major conflict Rhodes must declare for Rome, no matter how appealing the objectives or how propitious the initial position of the opposing side.

2. See, for example, Hansen 120–26.

Pursuing such a policy with regard to Rome was the only realistic course available to the Rhodians, a fact that in itself strongly suggests that this course was in fact adopted; and what little information is known concerning Rhodian affairs in the period from Pydna through the Roman civil wars supports this idea. When in 164 Calynda, revolting from Caunus, requested protection and a return of Rhodian suzerainty, the island was careful to obtain senatorial approval of its actions, a caution especially warranted by the fact that the Senate had only just liberated the area from its own control. There is no account of the preliminaries of the war against Crete in the 150s, but it is likely that the Rhodians ascertained beforehand the probable Roman reaction, and in any case the Senate could hardly have objected to Rhodes' dealing with the piracy problem that it was ignoring.[3] When Scipio called upon the allies for help against Carthage in 147, the Rhodians promptly sent a squadron of unknown size under Telephus, even though to do so meant participating in the destruction of a friend and important commercial partner.[4] And finally, in 88 Rhodes was one of the handful of eastern states that resisted the temptations and very serious threat of Mithridates, providing refuge for the Italians fleeing the "Anatolian Vespers"; the Rhodians knew full well that despite the Pontic successes, the legions would win in the end.[5]

This policy served Rhodes well in the century following its alliance with Rome. So far as is known, the island was left completely undisturbed by the Romans, and Sulla even rewarded it for its resistance to Mithridates with the grant of Caunus and several islands.[6] Problems arose, however, when the growing political strife in Rome evolved into military conflict; when there was more than one Rome, to which should the Rhodians give their support? In the first civil war they apparently had little trouble deciding: rather than attempt to remain neutral, they immediately declared for Pompey, sending war-

3. On Calynda and the Cretan war, see below.
4. App. *Pun.* 112; *Stoicorum index Herculanensis* 56. Telephus is possibly the member of the embassy to Aemilius Paullus in 168 (Polyb. 29.10.4); according to the *index*, Panaetius served in this fleet.
5. Relations before the war must have been good, since the Rhodians had erected a statue of the king (Cic. *II Ver.* 2.65.159). On the Rhodian resistance, see below.
6. See below.

ships and slingers to fight at Dyrrachium and Pharsalus. The reasons for this decision are easy to surmise: because of his action against the pirates and his years in the east, Pompey was far better known to the Rhodians than Caesar, and they were also probably as ready as everyone else to overestimate his military talents. Further, as Cato doubtless argued when he visited Rhodes in 49, Pompey would be more easily identified with the Senate and the legitimate government than could his *popularis* opponent, and this would be an important factor for the conservative Rhodian leadership.[7] Once Pompey had been defeated at Pharsalus, however, the Rhodians displayed once again their traditional pragmatic approach to foreign affairs by promptly deserting him for the winning side. This move was of course soon proved correct; Pompey was assassinated, and a lenient Caesar not only refrained from punishing the island but renewed its alliance with Rome and took a squadron of its warships with him to Alexandria.[8]

Despite having chosen the wrong side, the Rhodians thus weathered the first civil war with little difficulty, but they were not to be so fortunate in the next. When Caesar was murdered, the island refrained from declaring itself for or against the conspirators, hoping no doubt to remain aloof from the conflict or at least to postpone the difficult decision until it was more clear who the winners might be. It has been assumed that the aristocratic elements supported the conspirators and the Senate, while the general populace was for Antony and the Caesarians,[9] but there is no good evidence for this easy projection of *optimates* and *populares* upon the Rhodians. Caesar had in all probability made a great impression on the island, and his prestige

7. Cato: Plut. *Cato Min.* 54.2; Dyrrachium: Plut. *Cic.* 38.4; Caes. *B.C.* 3.5, 26–27; Cic. *de Div.* 1.32.68–69, *ad Att.* 9.9.2; Pharsalus: App. *B.C.* 2.83; these were probably mercenaries. The tradition of Rhodian condottieri in foreign employ continued into the first century; see Launey I, 243–46.

8. Rhodian ships escort Pompey from Mitylene to Cilicia: App. *B.C.* 2.83. Gates closed to Pompeians: Caes. *B.C.* 3.102.7; Cic. *ad Fam.* 12.14.3, *ad Att.* 11.13.1. Caesar: App. *B.C.* 2.89, 4.68, 70; Caes. *B.C.* 3.106.1. The embassies recorded in *IG* xii.1 51, 701 may have been concerned with negotiations for the renewal of the alliance. M. Rostovtzeff, "Caesar and the South of Russia," *JRS* 7 (1917) 29, n. 6, suggests that the negotiator and friend of Caesar Theopompus of Cnidus, honored by the Rhodians in *IG* xii.1 90, played a role in the negotiations.

9. So Schmitt 185.

may explain the granting of ships to Dolabella in 43; but it must be noted that the Syrian governor was forced to *hire* the vessels and was not permitted to enter Rhodes itself.[10] The refusal later in the same year to admit Lentulus Spinther and to send ships to Cassius seems clearly due to a desire to remain uninvolved rather than to support his opponents, and the Rhodians pointed out to the tyranicide that their treaty forbade them to take up arms against Romans and that they would be happy to hear from the Senate on the request for ships.[11] It is true that Cassius' subsequent assault on the city cracked the traditional political unity of the Rhodians and that the division was between the aristocratic leadership and the people, but the issue was not the choosing of sides in the civil war. Rather, it was the question of how best to deal with the threat presented by Cassius. The inclination of the leadership to preserve the republic by acquiescing to the enemy demands would in all likelihood not have changed had the siege been laid by Dolabella or Antony. Likewise, in deciding to resist, the people were moved not by enthusiasm for the Caesarian cause but by visions of past glories conjured up by the demagogues Alexander and Mnaseas.[12]

The traditional leadership was of course correct in their hardheaded appraisal of Rhodes' real situation, and when it was perfectly clear that the city was doomed, they sought to save what they could and opened secret negotiations with Cassius' generals. There is no hard evidence that it was they that actually opened the gate to the enemy troops, but the fact that the city was not subjected to indiscriminate slaughter and plunder suggests that the deed was the result of their dealings. After its surrender the city was punished for its resistance,

10. According to Cass. Dio 47.33.2, the Rhodians "were well affected by the former Caesar"; Schmitt 184 and n. 7 believes this may refer to the renewal of the alliance on better terms. Hired vessels: App. *B.C.* 4.60. The Rhodians allegedly later claimed that the ships had been intended only as an escort (App. *B.C.* 4.61) and that they had acted out of fear for the Peraea (Cic. *ad. Fam.* 12.15.4, letter of Lentulus Spinther). Closed gates: Cic. *ad Brut.* 2.4.3.

11. App. *B.C.* 4.61, 66, 68; Cass. Dio 47.33.1; Cic. *ad Fam.* 12.14.2, 15.2–3 (letters of Lentulus Spinther).

12. See App. *B.C.* 4.66; he refers to the leadership as Ῥοδίων δὲ οἱ μὲν ἐν λόγῳ μᾶλλον ὄντες, οἱ εὖ φρονοῦντες Ῥοδίων and Ῥοδίων οἱ συνετώτεροι. Alexander was elected chief prytanis, Mnaseas nauarch; the two are otherwise unknown.

but in an orderly fashion and without the widespread destruction and loss of life that typically followed the capture of an enemy city. About fifty individuals, presumably leaders of the resistance, were executed and another twenty-five banished by Cassius, while the temples, treasuries, and private homes of the Rhodians were systematically stripped of their precious metals, providing the Romans with some 8,500 talents. To complete the humiliation, when he departed Cassius left behind 3,000 men under L. Varus, the first foreign garrison in Rhodes since the days of Alexander.[13]

If Cassius' sack had not stripped away all lingering delusions the Rhodians had about their place in the political structure of the Mediterranean, that task was completed after Philippi by the fleeing Cassius Parmensis, who burned part of the Rhodian fleet and sailed off west with the remaining vessels. Soon afterward Varus and his men quit the island, and while the Rhodians were again free, they were also completely helpless. For Rhodes the game was clearly played out, and with its defenses and fleet shattered, its foreign policy, insofar as it could be said that it had a foreign policy, was limited to cooperating with whichever Roman faction controlled the Aegean. It is true that when Q. Labienus and the Parthians overran southern Anatolia in early 40 the island remained loyal to Rome, but it was Labienus' lack of a fleet that allowed the Rhodians the luxury of such a decision. Later in the same year Antony finally visited the island, and in recognition of the resistance shown to Cassius he rewarded the republic with the grant of Andros, Naxos, Tenos, and Myndus.[14] Rhodes is not heard of again until 31, but with no alternative it certainly remained friendly to Antony, and after Actium was punished by Octavian with the cancellation of Antony's gifts. The new ruler of the Roman world left the Rhodians with their independence,

13. App. *B.C.* 4.72–74; Cass. Dio 47.33.4; van Gelder 170 for other, minor sources. Cassius left untouched, possibly because it was too big to be moved easily (van Gelder 382), the famous quadriga of Helios by Lysippus (Pliny *HN* 34.19.63).

14. Cassius and Varus: App. *B.C.* 5.2; Labienus: Strabo 14.2.24 (660); Antony: App. *B.C.* 5.7; Sen. *de Ben.* 5.16.6. On the basis of *IG* xii.5 38, Schmitt 186, n. 2, believes that Amorgos was "probably" also part of Antony's gift, but see F&B 163. The island also received aid for rebuilding and for its fleet from King Herod, who visited the island in 40 (Jos. *Jud.* 1.424, *Ant.* 14.377–78, 16.147).

but any notion of an independent foreign policy had clearly become meaningless, and when in A.D. 44 Claudius officially ended Rhodian autonomy and attached the island to the province of Asia, it could hardly have made any difference so far as Rhodes' external affairs were concerned.[15]

The primary reason for the steady deterioration of Rhodes' freedom of action in foreign policy was of course the continued growth of Roman power and influence and the concomitant decline in Rhodian strength. It should be noted, however, that Rhodes' position did not collapse overnight in the 160s, but rather weakened bit by bit in the course of the following decades as the world around the island changed. The development of Roman involvement in the east and the continued, if fitful, drive toward imperial rule undermined Rhodian influence in the area, while the resurgence of piracy and an apparent decline in state revenues put an increasing strain on the island's naval resources. Slowly but inexorably the Roman world simply closed in on the Rhodians, although as the resistance to Cassius illustrates, it took some time for the Rhodian spirit to bow to the reality of the republic's shrinking arena of effectiveness.

Rhodes' position on the Anatolian mainland was obviously weakened by the Roman liberation of Lycia and Caria, but its influence in the area remained nonetheless very strong for some time thereafter. Rhodes still possessed its old Peraea, as well as private property in free Caria and Lycia, and while its presence in Lycia had been too brief and brutal to produce lasting effects, its long history of economic and diplomatic penetration into Caria left it with a fair measure of influence in the region.[16] When the Calyndians revolted from Caunus in

---

15. Augustus: App. *B.C.* 5.7. Claudius acted because the Rhodians had executed some Romans (Cass. Dio 60.24.4). Nero restored Rhodian "freedom" in 53 (Tac. *Ann.* 12.58; Suet. *Nero* 7, *Claud.* 25; *IG* xii.1 2), Vespasian removed it in the early years of his reign (Suet. *Vesp.* 8), Domitian restored it again (*Syll.*[3] 819; see A. Momigliano, review of C. Wirszubski, *Libertas as a Political Idea etc.*, *JRS* 41 [1951] 150–51), and sometime in the first part of the second century it was lost for the last time (Psd.-Arist. 43).

16. Continued possession of the old Peraea is confirmed by Polyb. 30.5.12 and many inscriptions, such as *SGDI* 4275–76. *SEG* iv.247 suggests that Rhodes still possessed territory on the mainland in the second century of the Christian era. In their embassy to Rome regarding Calynda (Polyb. 31.4.1–5.5) the Rhodians also requested

164 and had already obtained immediate military aid from Cnidus, they appealed to the Rhodians for long-term protection, offering "to place themselves and their city in their hands." The Rhodians responded by sending a force to raise the siege of Calynda and sent to Rome to have the Senate confirm their repossession of the city, probably as an ally.[17] In this same period Ceramus, which had also been freed in 167, entered into a protective alliance with Rhodes after suffering some internal problems, and it appears that Euromus sought a Rhodian alliance for protection against its neighbor Mylasa.[18] In 155/4 Priene, hard pressed by Pergamum and Ariarathes V of Cappadocia, appealed to Rhodes for aid, and while it seems that the Rhodians did not respond, the request nevertheless further demonstrates the status the republic retained among the small states of the area.[19]

If Rhodes in fact refrained from going to the aid of Priene, it probably did so out of a desire to avoid crossing Pergamum, with which relations had been revived in the years following Pydna. For all their services to Rome, both states had been roughly handled by the Senate after the defeat of Perseus, and they now had a mutual interest in promoting political and economic stability in the Anatolian region, a goal that the Romans had little apparent interest in and sometimes seemed to work against.[20] The sources of the earlier antagonism

---

permission to reoccupy private holdings in the freed areas, and it seems reasonable that the Senate granted this request along with the repossession of Calynda. See Robert *Carie* II, 311–12 for Rhodian coinage at Cidrama after 167. Cos, which might be considered part of Caria, still had a cult of the nymph Rhodos in the first century (*Syll.*[3] 1000). Polyb. 30.24.1–2 does not mean that the Rhodians had treated the Carians as slaves; see F&B 122.

17. Polyb. 31.4.1–5.5. The Senate confirmed for the Rhodians "possession of the Calyndans." The Rhodian embassy was headed by Cleagoras, who is otherwise unknown.

18. Ceramus: E. Hicks, "Ceramus and Its Inscriptions," *JHS* 11 (1890) 113–19, no. 1 = Michel 458. ἐν δυσχερεῖ καταστάσει γενομένου τοῦ πο[λ]ιτεύματος suggests internal conflict, but mention is made of a sympolity, perhaps with Stratonicea, which may have been the source of the trouble; see L. Robert, *Villes d'Asie Mineure*[2] (Paris 1962) 60–61; F&B 110–11. Euromus: Hula-Szanto, *SB Wien. Akad.* 132 (1894) 9, no. 1.

19. Polyb. 33.6.7.

20. See, for example, the Roman commission to the Gauls in 167 (Polyb. 30.3.7–8; Livy 45.34.13–14).

between the countries had in part been made irrelevant by the growth
of Roman power and in any case had been overshadowed by the
problem of national survival amid the ruins of the Hellenistic system.
It was certainly in Rhodes' interest that the Pergamene kings should
undertake to check the unruly and non-Greek states to the east, which
were constantly threatening the peace and commerce of the area, and
resistance to Bithynian aggression and naval depredations was
important enough to the island, with its extensive Pontic trade, that
in 155/4 it contributed five quadriremes to the Attalid fleet, though
already hard pressed by the Cretan problem.[21] Further, though Pergamum had apparently emancipated itself from Rhodian commercial
domination, as one of the primary economic centers of the east the
island remained valuable to the Attalids as a clearinghouse for Pergamene wares, and Eumenes' gift to Rhodes of 280,000 medimni of
grain shortly before his death in 159/8 may be seen as a kind of
diplomatic expression of that fact.[22] What the Rhodians felt about the
extinction of the Attalid kingdom in 129 is unknown, but it is likely
that while many people despaired at the passing of yet another Greek
state into Roman hands, the realists understood that the extension of
direct Roman rule into Anatolia could be expected to increase the
security and thus also the prosperity of the region.

In the Aegean as well it appears that Rhodes' position began to slip
rapidly after Pydna, though information here is even scantier than in
the case of the mainland. There is no evidence for the existence of the
Nesiotic League after 167, but it is extremely unlikely that in punishing Rhodes the Senate had taken any action with regard to the islands.
In all the accounts of Roman actions and Rhodian responses there is
no mention of the league, and any interference by the Senate in this
area of the affairs of Rhodes and the independent nesiotic states would
have been blatantly illegal. It is true of course that the Senate's deci-

---

21. Polyb. 33.13.2. For the Bithynian war, see J. Hopp, *Untersuchungen zur
Geschichte der letzten Attaliden* (Munich 1977) 74–79.

22. Polyb. 31.31.1–3; Rostovtzeff II, 777; the proceeds from the sale of the grain
were to be invested in order to provide a trust for the support of education in Rhodes;
see Walbank III, 515, for further examples of this type of benefaction. According to
Diod. 31.36.1, Eumenes still owed 30,000 medimni at his death. On the date of the
king's death, see Hopp 3–13.

sion on the Anatolian possessions was also illegal, but there the *patres* could at least point to Apamea and attempt to cover their action with high-sounding legal and moral arguments. With the blows to Rhodes' prestige and the steady decline of its naval strength, the league probably came apart of its own accord in the decades following 167, but it is impossible to say anything definite beyond the fact that by 84 it certainly no longer existed.[23] Whenever the league broke up, however, it is clear that Rhodes retained a great deal of influence among the islands, partly because of its long economic association with the area and partly because even in its declining years the Rhodian navy remained the strongest maritime force in the Aegean and continued to pursue an antipirate policy.

With the disappearance of the Nesiotic League and the gradual evaporation of its power, Rhodes' attitudes toward the islanders apparently, and perhaps inevitably, changed. After the defeat of Mithridates, Sulla granted the republic a number of islands and the city of Caunus as a reward for its resistance, but within two decades all of these states had appealed to the Senate to be placed under Roman authority, preferring to be taxed by Rome rather than Rhodes. Shortly after Philippi the Rhodians were awarded Andros, Naxos, Tenos, and Myndus by Antony, but were soon deprived of these possessions, probably by Augustus, because of their harsh administration.[24] It appears that in an era of shrinking resources the old Aegean policy of alliance and direction was no longer possible or desirable, and instead Rhodes treated these chance possessions as completely subject, seemingly outdoing many another imperial power in its exploitation of their wealth. The world had changed and so had the onetime defender of the small states of the Aegean.

The most obvious manifestation of Rhodes' power was of course its navy; if Rhodes economic resources had been the backbone and

23. F&B 172.

24. Sulla: Cic. *ad Q. Fr.* 1.1.33, dated to 60. Molon's speech *Against the Caunians* (Strabo 14.2.3 [652]) should probably be associated with the appeal mentioned by Cicero. The Rhodian embassy to Sulla recorded in *Syll.*³ 745 may be connected with the donation, the date of which cannot be precisely fixed. Amorgos may have been one of the islands, but the evidence is ambiguous; see F&B 163–64. Antony: App. *B.C.* 5.7.29; Sen. *de Benef.* 5.16.6.

sinews of its policy, the navy had supplied the muscle, bringing more leverage to its diplomacy and a fine cutting edge to its military strength. It has sometimes been assumed that Rhodian naval capability plummeted after 167, but this notion is not at all borne out by the scanty evidence. It is true that the Rhodian navy now entered a period of decline, as a result of shrinking state revenues and the general decline of the island's influence and political activity in an increasingly Roman Mediterranean, but the fall was not so precipitous as some have thought.[25] The naval traditions of more than a century were not to be lost overnight simply because Rhodes had lost continental possessions that for the most part it had controlled only since Apamea, and in any case a healthy navy remained vital to Rhodian commerce, since the Romans showed little or no interest in dealing with piracy. What little is known of Rhodian naval activities in the century after Pydna in fact demonstrates that while the size and overall strength of the navy declined, the traditional high level of seamanship was generally maintained down to the civil war period.

The first test for the post-Pydna navy came in 155/4 when an apparent resurgence of Cretan piracy led Rhodes into a full-scale war (the Second Cretan) with that island.[26] The few surviving scraps of information clearly indicate that Rhodes had a rough time, but they reveal almost nothing about the quality of the navy, and to conclude that Rhodes' difficulties were solely or even partly due to a decline in its navy is unwarranted.[27] It appears that the Rhodians, disconcerted by the more nimble pirate vessels, were in fact defeated in a naval engagement, but no details of this battle survive, so that no judgment on the quality of the Rhodian fleet is possible. There is, on the other hand, a strong tradition that the Rhodian admiral, Aristocrates, was a dismal failure, and it is easier to believe that the Rhodians suffered from being badly led than that their naval skill had slipped so dramatically in little more than a decade.[28] With regard to the war in general, it must be remembered that for the first time Rhodes was fighting

25. E.g., Schmitt 178: "Mit der rhodischen Seegeltung war es zu Ende."
26. On the war in general, see van Effenterre 267–69; Brulé 61–66.
27. So conclude Niese III, 324–25; van Gelder 160; Schmitt 178; et al.
28. Naval: Diod. 31.38.1. Aristocrates: Polyb. 33.4.1–4; Diod. 31.37.1. He is otherwise unknown and was probably nauarch rather than strategos.

against a united Crete, a fact that could only increase tremendously the magnitude of the republic's task. The Rhodians could no longer employ their traditional tactic of striking with their Cretan allies at those cities that served as bases for the pirates, and with their limited capabilities for a land campaign they were probably reduced to swatting at the fast pirate squadrons, a job that would have been even tougher if the Nesiotic League had already come apart. The fact that the Rhodians appealed to the Achaeans for help suggests strongly that the problem lay in land operations, and only when the military aid was not forthcoming was Astymedes sent in 153 to request that the Senate put an end to the conflict.[29] These circumstances may betray a certain decline in the general power and spirit of the Rhodians, who seem in addition to have suffered some internal problems in the course of the war, but they say little or nothing about the quality of their fleet.[30]

Nothing is known about the squadron sent to the Romans in the Third Punic War, but the events of the First Mithridatic War clearly demonstrate that the Rhodian navy was as skilled and effective as ever. When the Pontic fleet approached the island in 88, the Rhodian fleet, under the nauarch Damagoras, son of Euphranor, sailed out to meet it. Being seriously outnumbered, however, the Rhodians feared envelopment, and retired in good order to the security of the harbor, from which they were able to skirmish successfully with the enemy squadrons. Two incidents recorded by Appian illustrate the truth of Diodorus' claim that the Rhodians were superior in every respect except numbers. In a general engagement brought about when a Rhodian bireme attacked a Pontic merchantman, the Rhodians, though outnumbered, were able to sink a number of enemy vessels and return to the harbor with a captured trireme and its crew. In a second instance Damagoras, retiring with six ships before an enemy

29. Achaeans: Polyb. 33.16.1–8. The Rhodian ambassador was Theuphanes (see Ullrich 78), who is otherwise unknown. Senate: Polyb. 33.15.3–4. Astymedes, who was nauarch on this occasion, had served in several earlier embassies. That the Cretans in Diod. 31.45.1 put to sea at night in order to avoid the enemy ships suggests that the Rhodian navy was doing a credible job, even if it was unable to control the sea lanes completely.

30. Polyb. 33.17.1–5; Diod. 31.43.1.

squadron of twenty-five, turned suddenly on his pursuers and dispersed them, sinking two ships in the process. Appian also relates that the Rhodians spread havoc among a convoy of troop transports and triremes, but these ships had already been scattered and damaged by a storm and were consequently easy prey.[31] Because of numbers Mithridates still controlled the sea and the island was unable to send ships to Sulla in Greece, but a Rhodian squadron was part of the allied fleet that finally defeated the Pontic navy at Tenedus in 85. It is noteworthy that the Roman commander, Lucullus, chose Damagoras' vessel as his flagship for the conflict.[32]

In the Third Mithridatic War twenty Rhodian warships made up half of the squadron with which C. Valerius Triarius blockaded Heraclea, and it was primarily through the skill of the Rhodians that the Heracleot fleet was defeated. In 67 Rhodes was apparently the only allied state to supply ships for Pompey's operations, and while there is no word of their performance, it cannot be doubted that they excelled in the strong suit of the Rhodian navy, pirate chasing. A squadron of twenty vessels joined the Pompeian fleet in the first civil war, but the detachment was put under the command of a Roman, C. Coponius, who in pursuit of the enemy in the Adriatic led the Rhodians into a storm, which destroyed sixteen of their ships.[33] This disaster was hardly the fault of the Rhodians and is in clear contrast to their subsequent performance at Alexandria.

Among the thirty-five warships hastily collected by Caesar on his way to Egypt were ten Rhodian vessels under the command of Euphranor, and in the critical naval battles of the Alexandrian war this little squadron played probably the most important role. In the first naval skirmish with the Egyptians, along the coast west of the harbors, the Rhodians bore the brunt of the successful fighting, while at

31. App. *Mith*. 24–26, 46–47; Diod. 37.28.1; Cic. *II Ver*. 2.65.159. It is difficult to reconcile Appian's mention in *B.C.* 4.71 of an important Rhodian victory at Myndus with the account presented in *Mith*. 24–26, since those engagements all took place near Rhodes. Damagoras is mentioned in *IG* xii.1 41, 46; Maiuri no. 18.

32. App. *Mith*. 33, 56; Plut. *Luc*. 2.2–3, 3.3, 8–10.

33. Triarius: Memnon 50 = *FGH* 434 F 34; Pompey: Flor. 3.6.8; Coponius: Caes. *B.C.* 3.5, 26–27; App. *B.C.* 2.59; Cic. *de Div*. 1.32.68, *ad Att*. 9.2; Plut. *Cic*. 38.4. Appian gives Coponius 20 ships and does not record the losses; Caesar mentions 16 vessels, all of which were sunk.

the crucial battle in the harbor of Eunostus, Euphranor and his sailors were clearly the architects of the victory. When Caesar hesitated to pass through the narrow channel in the shoals that covered the harbor and the enemy fleet, Euphranor volunteered his Rhodians, and as expected, the four vessels that were able to pass the channel together were immediately attacked by the Alexandrian front line of twenty-two heavy warcraft. There followed a demonstration of the skill that had built the Rhodian reputation; the ships, hampered by lack of sea room and outnumbered 5 to 1, not only covered the successful deployment of the remainder of the fleet but also managed to avoid taking any damage.[34] In the ensuing engagements around the mole the Rhodians probably played a minimal part because of the nature of the fighting, but it was their naval prowess that brought Caesar that far.

This was to be the last great exploit of the Rhodian navy, and Euphranor himself was not fated to survive his victories. In an encounter off Canopus, his ship, as usual, led the charge against the enemy, and having sunk one quadrireme, he pursued a second too far and was surrounded. Unfortunately his bold move was apparently not adequately supported by the Roman fleet commander, Ti. Claudius Nero, and Euphranor went down with his ship. His death brought to an end the long line of great Rhodian admirals. The just praise heaped on him and his sailors by the author of the *Bellum Alexandrinum* is accentuated by the events of the following year, when the Rhodian fleet went into battles under the inexperienced command of the demagogues Alexander and Mnaseas.[35] With thirty-three ships they attacked the heavier and numerically superior fleet of Cassius at Myndus and were quickly surrounded and forced to flee with the loss of five vessels, only to repeat the performance and lose another two ships as Cassius closed in on the island.[36] These were the

34. Caes. *B.C.* 3.106, *Alex.* 1, 11, 13–16; App. *B.C.* 2.89. Euphranor is mentioned in *IG* xii.1 1132 and is possibly the son of the Damagoras who fought against Mithridates. There were nine Rhodian ships in the harbor battle, one having already been lost, possibly in the coastal skirmish.

35. Caes. *Alex.* 25; see 11 and 15 for praise of Rhodian skill. Sailors and marines from the Rhodian squadron later fought at the battle of Ruspina (Caes. *Afr.* 20).

36. App. *B.C.* 4.66, 71–72; Cass. Dio 47.33.3. Cassius had 80 ships at the second battle, an unknown number at the first.

last engagements of the Rhodian navy, and though defeats, they are in a way fitting; even here, at the end of their history, the Rhodian sailors, confident in their superior skills, were ready once more to sail into the face of adverse odds.

Yet while the quality of the post-Pydna navy remained high, it nevertheless had increasing difficulty in dealing with its primary task of suppressing piracy. In part this failure was due to the gradually weakening position of Rhodes, which no longer commanded the economic and diplomatic resources it once did. It was not so much a case of a decline in state revenues limiting shipbuilding and naval operations as it was a decline of Rhodian influence in an increasingly Roman-dependent Aegean shutting off traditional antipirate mechanisms. The Second Cretan War provides a good example of Rhodes' problem: not only was it unable to employ its traditional tactic of setting the Cretan cities against one another, but it also failed to gain the help of the Achaeans, who, though inclined to aid the republic, decided to wait for Rome's opinion. Further, with the dissolution of the Nesiotic League the unending job of policing the sea lanes and eliminating pirates fell completely to the Rhodians, and while their navy was excellent, it was not large enough to be everywhere at once.

Complicating matters was the fact that at the same time that Rhodes' ability to deal with the piracy problem was diminishing, the problem itself was growing. Directly responsible for this growth was Rome, which through its political arrangements in the east and its neglect of maritime affairs had created an environment perfect for an explosion of piracy. With Italy providing a growing demand for slaves and the free port of Delos with its lax laws providing a convenient marketplace for those slaves, the problem would have been bad enough,[37] but the development of the Cilician pirate nests created a seaborne menace far more threatening than any Rhodes had faced before. The wild regions of Cilicia Tracheia provided the ideal base for pirates, but until Apamea the predatory inclincations of the area had been for the most part kept in check by the Seleucids and Ptolemies, who traded control of the territory. The settlement of Apamea, because it deprived Antiochus of a navy, effectively placed

37. See Strabo 14.5.2–3 (668–69).

Cilicia beyond Seleucid control, however, and soon robber chieftains were establishing themselves throughout the region and even cooperating with the occasional Syrian usurper, such as Diototus Tryphon, who established Coracesium as the most important Cilician pirate nest. With their bases secure and with only the Rhodians to hinder them, the Cilician pirates multiplied rapidly, and by the end of the second century no part of the eastern Mediterranean was safe. Entire communities made alliances with them in order to protect themselves.[38] Even in its heyday the Rhodian navy could not have dealt adequately with a menace of this magnitude, since the problem called for land forces and a large rather than an especially skilled navy. Only Rome could organize the necessary resources, and after a number of unsuccessful attempts interrupted by Mithridates it finally did so in 67. By that time the pirate fleets controlled the entire Mediterranean and were raiding even Italy at will. Pompey's rapid sweep of the seas was a triumph more of organization than of skill and daring, but it was nevertheless fitting that the Rhodian navy should have taken part in the largest and most effective antipirate operation the Mediterranean world had seen.[39]

Behind Rhodes' navy and all its policies was of course its economy, and although information in this all-important area is so scarce as to be almost nonexistent for the period after Pydna, it is clear that by the middle of the second century the best years of the republic's economy were already behind it. State revenues were certainly down after 167, even if it is assumed that the tremendous drop in harbor dues reported by Astymedes was a momentary dislocation brought on by the temporary collapse of Rhodian credit.[40] The harbor receipts must have

---

38. See Strabo 14.5.1–2 (668–69); Cass. Dio 36.20.1–21.3; App. *Mith.* 92; Ormerod 190–208. The extent of the threat and the importance of Rhodes are indicated by a Roman law passed about 100 (*SEG* iii.378; see M. Hassall, M. Crawford, J. Reynolds, "Rome and the Eastern Provinces at the End of the Second Century B.C.," *JRS* 64 [1974] 195–220); it attempted to organize joint action against the pirates among the eastern states, and specifically named Rhodes to carry out the diplomatic contacts.

39. Rhodian participation: Flor. 1.41.8; Strabo 11.1.6 (492).

40. See above, chap. 10.

declined to some extent because of the competition from Delos, and the loss of Caunus and Stratonicea and post-Apamea Peraea could only be an absolute loss to the island. The apparent general decline of Rhodian trade in this period would also have meant a decrease in tax revenues, while the added naval burden resulting from weakening Rhodian influence, dissolution of the Nesiotic League, and the growth of piracy represented a loss in real income to the state. Although hard evidence is lacking, this assumed decline in revenues appears to be reflected in exactly those spheres more or less dependent on the fiscal condition of the government. The apparent sorry condition of the city's defenses in 43/2 must have been due in large part to deficiencies in state resources, while in the area of coinage the middle of the first century saw the last issues of Rhodian silver and its replacement with bronze.[41] There is also an impression of generally smaller naval squadrons after 167, but it must be remembered that the Rhodian navy had always emphasized quality over numbers.

For all this, however, Rhodes remained even in its decline a wealthy society, and long after its absorbtion into the Roman empire it was still celebrated for its affluence and the magnificence of its capital city.[42] Despite the lack of information, the reasons for this continued if declining prosperity are not difficult to discern. Although the creation of a free port at Delos in all probability diverted the bulk of the Levantine trade away from Rhodes, there is no reason to believe that Rhodes' control of the eastern grain trade was affected in any serious way. This entrenched position in the distribution of so vital a commodity continued to provide a strong foundation for the island's economy, and while it must be assumed that in the latter part of the first century the Rhodian grip loosened as Egypt fell under increasing Roman influence and finally domination, the process could only have been a gradual one, allowing the island to adjust to the new economic realities of the empire. Moreover, though the long-range distribution of grain ultimately passed into Roman hands and Egyptian supplies were increasingly diverted to the west, pre-

41. Head 641–42, *Greek Coins* 260–70.
42. Strabo 14.2.5 (652–53); Dio Chrys. 33.55, 100–101, 146; Psd.-Arist. 43.

sumably in Italian bottoms, there is little reason to doubt that local distribution in the Aegean area remained under Rhodian control.[43]

A similar supposition may be made about the island's commerce in general; as Roman power grew in the second and first centuries, Rhodes' share of the long-distance trade shrank. Declining numbers of Rhodian handles reveal that in the course of the first half of the second century Rhodes was squeezed out of Italian and Sicilian markets, while the destruction of Carthage eliminated its most important business partner in the west. The simultaneous razing of Corinth must have benefited the Rhodians, who were in the best position to step into the commercial breach, but continued decline is revealed by the virtual disappearance of Rhodian handles by the end of the first century.[44] This does not mean, however, that the island lost its position in the local trading network. For three centuries its traders, businessmen, and merchant marine had played a primary role in the economy of the eastern Mediterranean, and it is only to be expected that despite the waning influence of their country, individual Rhodian merchants held their own against Italian competition in the Aegean and accommodated themselves to the new center of economic power on the Tiber.[45] Rhodian prosperity persisted, even after the terrible sack by Cassius, and its most obvious foundation was Rhodes' continued if diminished role in the commercial structure of the Mediterranean, now the Roman Empire. After the victory of Augustus, Rhodes, unlike the other states of the east, refused to

43. See chap. 10 above; Casson 181–87. It is also possible that Rhodian vessels carried some of the trade to the west. Rhodian relations with Egypt apparently and understandably remained friendly to the end; Ptolemy VIII Euergetes II was honored when he visited the Peraea in 162 (Polyb. 31.17.3). The republic's relations with the last Seleucids are obscure, though it is likely it followed the Roman lead; Demetrius I's gift of 300,000 medimni of grain in the 150s (Diod. 31.36.1) certainly indicates favorable relations, and for whatever it may suggest, Antiochus VII Sidetes was in Rhodes when his call to the throne came (App. *Syr.* 68). Strabo 14.5.2 (669) states that the Rhodians gave the Syrians no assistance against pirates because they were not friendly toward them, but the meaning of this statement is not clear, as it is inconceivable that the Rhodians would for any reason tolerate piracy.

44. See Bleckmann 24–27, 30; Rostovtzeff II, 775–78.

45. See, for example, the persistence of Rhodian handles even on Delos (Grace *BCH* 76, 525; Kent 128–34).

accept a remission of its debts,[46] and this refusal could only have sprung from the desire to preserve its credit and financial integrity. That the Rhodians should willingly suffer the hardships imposed by the pursuit of such a severe policy is evidence of the continued importance of their commercial activity.

Rhodes thus remained prosperous and economically active in the years following Pydna, but it was a changed society that entered the new age of the principate. The decline in economic and political importance was accompanied, inevitably, by a change in attitude, as the Rhodians were forced to come to terms with the shrinking significance of their state and its increasing dependence on Rome. To be sure, such things as the erection of a thirty-cubit statue of the Roman people and the institution of a cult and festival of Roma were merely window dressing, serving the needs of Rhodian foreign policy in the post-Pydna era.[47] The spirit and pride of the island republic was too strong to dwindle rapidly and vanish like that of some of its illustrious neighbors. Better evidence is provided by the stand against Mithridates and the desperate decision by the Rhodian people to resist Cassius. But the pressures of a "Roman" foreign policy and the ever more apparent reality of growing impotence in international affairs could not fail to take their toll of the Rhodian psyche. The focus of Rhodian pride was gradually shifted backward, to the days of past greatness, and inward, to the material and cultural achievements of the island.

Though its navy was now insignificant and its trade mostly local, Rhodes of the principate remained famous for the skill of its sailors and for its wealth, and its democratic government, a growing anachronism in the autocratic Roman Empire, continued to evoke praise. The island became a kind of museum of Hellenic achievement. No

---

46. Dio Chrys. 31.66–67.
47. The statue was erected immediately after the alliance was granted (Polyb. 31.4.4). Inscriptional evidence for the cult comes from the first century: M. Segré, *Par. Pas.* 4 (1949) 72–82, no. 2. For the festival from the second century and later: *IG* xii.1 46, 730 (= *Syll.*³ 724); Maiuri nos. 18, 34; *Inscr. Lind.* 229, 482; see Schmitt 175, n. 1. Rhodian cults of course persisted on Rhodes (*Inscr. Lind.* 438: Demos of the Rhodians, A.D. 50), but also outside the island; the cult of the nymph Rhodos is found in the first century on Cos (*Syll.*³ 1000) and Amorgos (*IG* xii.7 245).

longer the economic hub of past days, Rhodes emerged now as a
popular resort and center of cultural activity, drawing visitors from
throughout the Roman world. Among them were many Romans out
of favor with the current government, and it is fitting that in its last
years Rhodes should have become the most popular place of exile in
the early principate.[48] Gradually sinking into anonymity and absorbtion into the Roman cosmopolis, the most fiercely independent of the
Hellenistic states and the last important polis used the surviving
scraps of its freedom to harbor the political dissidents of the ruling
power.

48. Rhodes, along with Lesbos, Samos, and Cos, was granted exception to a law of
A.D. 12 which deprived islands closer than 400 stades to the mainland of their right to
harbor exiles (Cass. Dio 56.27.2). The future emperor Tiberius was of course the
most famous exile to live on Rhodes. For praise of *clara Rhodos* (Hor. *Carm.* 1.7.1) in
the early empire, see Dio Chrys. 31 and Psd.-Arist. 43.

APPENDIX I

The First Contact with Rome

The evidence for the formal contact between Rhodes and Rome in the fourth century is found in Polybius' comments on the Rhodian embassies to Rome in 167 (30.5.6–8):

> For so businesslike was the policy of the Rhodians that although they had for almost 140 years [σχεδὸν ἔτη τετταράκοντα πρὸς τοῖς ἑκατὸν] shared in most glorious and excellent deeds with the Romans, they had not made an alliance with them. The reason the Rhodians acted this way should not be passed over. Desiring that no ruler or prince should lose hope of aid and alliance from them, they did not wish to bind themselves with anyone or be engaged by oaths and treaties, but preferred by remaining unencumbered, to gain advantage from any and all.

The corresponding section of Livy (45.25.9) is clearly a translation of Polybius and provides no further information:

> For the Rhodians had for so many years maintained their friendship [*amicitia*] in such a way that they did not tie themselves to the Romans with a treaty of alliance, doing so for no other reason than to avoid cutting off from the kings the hope of their aid, should it be necessary, or from themselves the hope of gathering fruits from the goodwill and fortune of the kings.

Cassius Dio (20.68.3; cf. Zon. 9.24) reiterates the Rhodian foreign policy described by Polybius and Livy, but makes no mention of any association with Rome.

The apparent meaning of the Polybian and Livian texts is that in or about the year 306, formal diplomatic contact between the two governments was established, the result of this meeting being a treaty of friendship rather than any sort of military alliance. This is the interpretation accepted by writers before Holleaux, the treaty generally being understood to have something to do with commerce.[1] But there is a problem here: aside from Polybius' comment, there is no mention in the extant sources of any contact between the two states until the Pergamene-Rhodian embassy of 201.[2] What, then, is to be made of the "most glorious and excellent deeds" shared by Rhodes and Rome during the century before the outbreak of the Second Macedonian War?

Holleaux was the first to be bothered by this seeming lack of common deeds and voiced a strong protest against the historicity of the treaty, pointing out further arguments against it.[3] A formal *amicitia,* with its oaths and neutrality clause, would in fact have curtailed the freedom of the Rhodians, in direct opposition to their policy, as stated by Polybius and Livy. Moreover, Rhodian efforts in the First Macedonian War to bring peace between Philip and the Aetolian League reveal a distinctly nonneutral policy toward Rome, as Philip's interests against Rome would have been served by a cessation of hostilities on his Greek front. Finally, there is the statement of M. Valerius Laevinus to the Aetolians in 212 that they were the first *gens transmarina* to enter into an *amicitia,* a passage in Livy describing Attalus as the sole *amicus* in Asia in 205, and Astymedes' failure to make any mention of the long span of Rhodian-Roman relations in his speech before the Senate in 164.[4] In the face of this contrary

---

1. J. Droysen, *Geschichte des Hellenismus*[2] (Gotha 1877–78) II.2, 154 and n. 2; T. Mommsen, *Römische Geschichte*[8] (Berlin 1888–94) I, 384, 417, 776; Niese I, 325, n. 5; van Gelder 106.

2. Livy 31.2.1.

3. M. Holleaux, "Le Prétendu Traité de 306 entre les Rhodiens et les Romains," *Mélanges Perrot* (Paris 1902) 183–90, later in *Rome* 30–46, 335–36; followed by Täubler 204–6; Heuss, *Völk. Grund.* 31; Badian, *For. Clien.* 33; et al.

4. Livy 26.24.4, 29.11.1–2; Polyb. 30.31.3–18.

evidence, the treaty of 306 cannot stand, and with the air of a fetial priest declaring an *indictio belli,* Holleaux pronounces Polybius subject to an *emendatio.*

An emendation of Polybius, to the extent of eliminating the πρὸς τοῖς ἑκατόν, is ostensibly appealing, since "nearly forty years" would more or less cover a period when Rhodes and Rome undeniably performed great deeds together.[5] But tampering with the sources is bad policy, especially in a case such as this, when one is forced to account for words that have accidentally found their way into the text.[6] The recourse to emendation is particularly weak in this instance, for not only does the removal of "hundred" still leave one with problems,[7] but the alternative—accepting the text intact—is also historically possible, as Schmitt has demonstrated in an exhaustive treatment of the question.[8]

If one deals with the text of Polybius as it stands, what can be made of the passage? It seems unreasonable that Polybius is making a gross error, even if it is assumed that he is following Rhodian sources.[9] He states a particular if approximate period of time, which in itself is bare evidence for the veracity of the statement, and it is difficult to believe that he could expect his readers to swallow such a specific tradition if it had no basis in reality. The natural conclusion is that something in fact did happen about 306, that there was some sort of formal contact between Rhodes and Rome.[10] Livy indicates that the result of this

5. So Holleaux, *Rome* 44–46, and those who follow him.

6. Holleaux *Rome* 45, n. 1, suggests that a scribe, used to seeing the words πρὸς ταῖς ἑκατόν (ὁ) whenever Polybius marked an Olympiad, unconsciously added the masculine form to σχεδὸν ἔτη τετταράκοντα (μ́); For the problems with this suggestion, see Schmitt 8.

7. σχεδὸν ἔτη τετταράκοντα seems a very inexact way to describe a period lasting at most 34 years; better ὑπὲρ τριάκοντα; see T. Walek-Czernecki, "La Politique romaine en Grèce et dans l'Orient hellénistique au troisième siècle," *Rev. Phil.* 49 (1925) 138–39; Schmitt 9–13, who discusses also the emendation of De Sanctis.

8. Schmitt 1–49.

9. Ullrich 67–68. Polybius does in fact criticize his Rhodian sources earlier, in 16.14.1–20.9.

10. The year 306 or early 305 appears to be universally accepted as the most reasonable date, as 307 would be exactly 140 years earlier and 304 marks the end of Demetrius' siege of Rhodes, after which (according to Schmitt 30–31) the city had other concerns. This postsiege argument is not convincing, however, as it is hard to see how repairing the damages of the siege would have hindered a trade contact when it did not

meeting was an *amicitia,* and this statement is acceptable if *amicitia* is understood in its barest form, that of simple diplomatic recognition.[11] With this interpretation most of Holleaux's arguments, dependent on a stricter understanding of *amicitia,* may be ignored, but there remains the absence of any common great deeds for the century before the Second Macedonian War.[12] The explanation is not, however, difficult to find. It must be either that Polybius' Rhodian sources, ever ready to sharpen the prestige of Rhodes, vaguely projected the common undertakings of the second century throughout the entire period from about 306 on,[13] or that Polybius himself unwittingly does so through the inexactness of his phrasing.[14] Two historical truths—an isolated contact in the fourth century and deeds shared in the second—are thus combined to produce a historical exaggeration.

Concerning the circumstances and practical results of the meeting, nothing definite can be said, except that Rhodian commerce was almost certainly involved and that the initiative came from Rhodes. Rome was still embroiled with the Samnites and the subjugation of the Italian peninsula and would have had no reason to seek out a distant Hellenistic state, while Rhodes, with its commercial interests in southern Italy and Sicily, could have had good reason to contact the new power in the peninsula.[15] It is likely that the meeting involved

---

even hinder the building of the Colossus. Consequently, 303 and even 302 are possible dates.

11. See Matthaei 182–204, esp. 191; Heuss, *Völk. Grund.* 25–59, esp. 46, 54. It is also possible that Livy, faced with Polybius' passage and with no knowledge of any common deeds for the first century of the period, merely substituted *"in amicitia fuerant"* (Schmitt 11).

12. Holleaux's argument concerning supposed Rhodian hostility toward Rome during the First Macedonian War is based on a misunderstanding of Rhodian policy; see chap. 5 above. Schmitt 16–29 deals with Holleaux's other and even more minor objections.

13. So Schmitt 14.

14. Walek-Czernecki 139, followed by Schmitt 13.

15. For a convenient survey of Rhodian commerce and contacts with and in the west, see Schmitt 32–49; F. Walbank, "Polybius and Rome's Eastern Policy," *JRS* 53 (1963) 2–3. Schmitt suggests (43–46) that Rhodian involvement with "Tyrrhenian" pirates may have provided occasion for contact with Rome, a supposition that is just possible (see also Ormerod 127–30), but the postulation of joint Rhodian-Roman action against pirates as the basis for the glorious deeds is completely speculative. As

some discussion of trade, but this must remain a matter of speculation, because of the lack of knowledge both in this particular instance and concerning ancient trade in general.[16] In any case, the importance of the contact must not be overestimated. Although Rhodian intercourse with the Italian peninsula continued on a private level, the official meeting of the two republics was apparently a passing affair, and they did not meet again for another century.

---

later history demonstrates, the Romans were very slow to act concerning pirates, and if the Rhodians were there to do the job anyway, they had even less reason to bestir themselves.

16. So cautions Schmitt 46–47, who nevertheless gives the impression that he believes some sort of "*Handelsvertrag*" was concluded.

APPENDIX 2

Rhodian Fleet Strength in 190

The figures all balance if one assumes (1) that the 20 ships lost at Panhormus (Appian) include the one sunk (Livy) and (2) that Appian's figure for the number of Rhodian ships at Myonnesus is wrong. An exact accounting of Rhodian strength is nevertheless not possible, because the ships of Rhodes' close allies Cos and Cnidus are sometimes counted in a Rhodian squadron and sometimes not.

PANHORMUS

36 Pausistratus (L. 37.9.5)
−20 captured (A. *Syr.* 24), including −1 sunk? (L. 37.11.11)
16 = 7 escaped (includes 2 Coan [L. 37.11.13])
    + 9 detached (L. 37.10.11)
+20 Eudamus (L. 37.12.9; A. *Syr.* 25)
36 at Samos
− 4 to Patara (L. 37.16.11) ————————————————→ + 3 from Rhodes (L. 37.16.3)
32   7 to Patara → to Rhodes (L. 37.16.13)
−13 to Rhodes (+ 1 Coan + 1 Cnidian [L. 37.22.2]) → + 6 at Rhodes (L. 37.22.4)   13 Pamphilidas
19   19 (+ 1 Coan + 1 Cnidian) +4 in Caria (L. 37.22.3)
+ 7   ————
26   SIDE   17

                                                 +17
                                                 36 Eudamus (+ 1 Coan + 1 Cnidian [L. 37.23.4])
− 4 to Patara (L. 37.25.3)   to Rhodes (L. 37.24.10)
22 at Samos   −20 to Patara (L. 37.24.12) → 20
                                                 16
MYONNESUS   − 7 to Samos (L. 37.24.13)   + 4
22 Eudamus (L. 37.30.1)   9 at Rhodes   24 at Patara
− 1 captured (L. 37.30.9; A *Syr.* 27)
21

APPENDIX 3

Q. Marcius Philippus
and the Rhodians

When Philippus was visited by Rhodian envoys at Heracleum in 169, according to Polybius (28.17.4), he took Hagepolis aside and said that "he wondered why the Rhodians did not attempt to end the present war (τὸν ἐνεστῶτα πόλεμον), since such was particularly their business." This incident is repeated by Appian (*Mac.* 17.1): "Marcius instructed the envoys to persuade the Rhodians to send an embassy to Rome to end the war between the Romans and Perseus."

Some scholars believe that despite Appian, the war referred to by Philippus was the one between Antiochus and Ptolemy,[1] but the textual evidence certainly does not support this contention. The clear statement of Appian must indeed be set aside, since it is not independent evidence, but the Polybian message can nevertheless refer only to the Macedonian conflict. If the "present war" in 28.17.4 is the Syrian War, then "for the war about Coele-Syria had already broken out" at 17.6 is unnecessary, Polybius' second explanation of Philippus' motives (17.7–8) makes no sense, and there was small reason for the Macedonian group at Rhodes to see the request as a sign that the Romans were "in the greatest difficulty" (17.13–14). Further, 17.15 reads: ἀπέστειλαν δὲ καὶ πρεσβευτὰς εἰς τὴν Ἀλεξάνδρειον, and in

---

1. Scullard 287; J. Ooteghem, *Lucius Marcius Philippus et sa famille* (Brussels 1961) 90–93; Gruen 72–74; among others.

this same passage "the present war" is not specifically qualified with "between Antiochus and Ptolemy."[2]

It has been argued that although Polybius was referring to the Macedonian war, evidence external to this passage demonstrates that Philippus must actually have been referring to the Syrian conflict and that consequently Polybius himself distorted the incident.[3] The evidence for this view, however, is circumstantial and less than convincing. That the Rhodians ultimately did send an embassy to Egypt, that Philippus was instructed by the Senate to deal with the Syrian problem, and that he asked the Achaeans to mediate demonstrates nothing; Philippus was in fact only instructed to write to Ptolemy, and the request to the Achaeans served to head off an Egyptian request for aid.[4] Also, while it is true that the suspicious circumstances of Philippus' advice "left room for hypothesis and insinuation,"[5] this fact of course does not prove that Polybius actually insinuated anything. These suspicious circumstances in fact make it less likely that the consul was referring to the Syrian War, since Roman interest in a negotiated end to that conflict was a matter of record, and it is consequently difficult to understand why Philippus would communicate his suggestion in such a secretive manner.

While the circumstances surrounding Philippus' advice do not demonstrate that Polybius distorted the event, they do make the whole incident immediately suspect as a Rhodian invention, despite the general reliability of the historian. In the first place, the suggestion came in a private aside to Hagepolis and was not subsequently publicly announced in Rhodes, but instead was leaked to the Macedonian group through a private conversation, circumstances very convenient for the insertion of something that was never said. Second, when the Rhodians later defended themselves before the Senate, they made no word of Philippus' suggestion, though one would expect this to be among the first things they would mention in defense of their actions. Finally, if the story is accepted as true, Philippus had to

2. Ooteghem's rather weak arguments are dealt with by J. Briscoe, "Q. Marcius Philippus and *Nova Sapientia*," *JRS* 54 (1964) 69.

3. Gruen 72–74.

4. Polyb. 28.1.9, 29.23.1–25.7.

5. Gruen 73.

have been acting on his own; if the Senate had wanted the mediation, why this strange way of going about it? Certainly the *patres* had no reason to try to trick Rhodes, as they had no desire to stir up possible trouble with the island at this time.[6]

With Philippus acting on his own initiative, however, it is hard to see exactly what his motives could be. He could not have acted out of fear for his own position,[7] since once Perseus had evacuated Tempe, the Roman situation was secure; if the embassy arrived during the brief period before Tempe was cleared, fear will still not do, since the Roman army would have had to capitulate or starve long before the Rhodians could have taken any real action.[8] Polybius suggests that he had a real desire for peace because of fear of developments in Egypt, but there is no suggestion that any other Roman leader felt this way, and Philippus would hardly have expected the Senate to accept such a major change in policy.[9] Polybius also suggests that he wished to compromise the Rhodians, and it is perhaps just possible that he did.[10] The plebeian leadership of the war years was hostile to Rhodes, and such a devious motive would have been in keeping with Philippus' crafty character;[11] he could have been thinking of possible profit for himself or his political associates from a future imbroglio with Rhodes. This suggestion smells of hindsight, however, since the peace initiative *would* have compromised the Rhodians, and Polybius' stated ignorance of Philippus' actual motives only makes this notion even more suspect as a case of effect shaping cause.

These considerations are admittedly not conclusive, and it is possible in each case to devise a counterargument that supports the veracity of the story. Philippus' clandestine behavior, for example, could have been due to a desire to keep Perseus from knowing that the mediation was Roman-inspired; Hagepolis' silence at Rhodes could

6. App. *Mac.* 17.1 in fact states that Philippus acted ἀφ' ἑαυτοῦ.

7. T. Frank, "The Diplomacy of Q. Marcius in 169 B.C.," *CP* 5 (1910) 358–61.

8. See J. Kromayer, *Antike Schlachtfelder in Griechenland* (Berlin 1907) II, 285–94.

9. Polyb. 28.17.5–6.

10. Polyb. 28.17.7–9.

11. Hostility: Livy 45.25.2; Philippus: Livy 42.38.8–43.3; F. W. Walbank, "A Note on the Embassy of Q. Marcius Philippus, 172 B.C.," *JRS* 31 (1941) 86–93; Briscoe, *JRS* 54, 66–73.

have been due to a desire to keep from strengthening the position of the Macedonian group; and the later lack of any mention of the affair in the Rhodian defense could have been due to a belief that Philippus would simply have denied having suggested anything. Acceptance of the consul's words involves such contrived explanations, however, that Ockham's razor ought to cut in favor of rejection, especially since an obvious and simple reason can be found for the Rhodians to invent the incident: in justifying the later peace embassies, the story is an apology for Rhodian policy.[12] The whole issue is in any case not a crucial one, since sufficient reason for the Rhodian peace offensive can be found without accepting Philippus' clandestine suggestion.

12. Accepted by De Sanctis IV.1, 306; Meloni, *Perseo* 318.

Index

Names and toponyms mentioned on successive pages are indicated by inclusive numbers, and references to notes are indicated only by page. No references are made to the maps and chart. Rhodians are indicated by asterisks.

Library of Congress Cataloging in Publication Data

Berthold, Richard M.
    Rhodes in the Hellenistic Age.

    Includes index.
    1. Rhodes (Greece: Island)—History.   I. Title.
DF261.R47B47   1984   938'.08   83-23127
ISBN 0-8014-1640-X (alk. paper)